THE SAMUEL AND ALTHEA STROUM
LECTURES IN JEWISH STUDIES

SAMUEL STROUM, businessman, community leader, and philanthropist, by a major gift to the Jewish Federation of Greater Seattle, established the Samuel and Althea Stroum Philanthropic Fund.

In recognition of Mr. and Mrs. Stroum's deep interest in Jewish history and culture, the Board of Directors of the Jewish Federation of Greater Seattle, in cooperation with the Jewish Studies Program at the University of Washington, established an annual lectureship at the University of Washington known as the Samuel and Althea Stroum Lectureship in Jewish Studies. This lectureship makes it possible to bring to the area outstanding scholars and interpreters of Jewish thought, thus promoting a deeper understanding of Jewish history, religion, and culture. Such understanding can lead to an enhanced appreciation of the Jewish contributions to the historical and cultural traditions that have shaped the American nation.

The terms of the gift also provide for the publication from time to time of the lectures or other appropriate materials resulting from or related to the lectures.

THE SAMUEL & ALTHEA STROUM
LECTURES IN JEWISH STUDIES

The Yiddish Art Song
performed by Leon Lishner, basso,
and Lazar Weiner, piano
(stereophonic record album)

The Holocaust in Historical Perspective
Yehuda Bauer

Zakhor: Jewish History and Jewish Memory
Yosef Hayim Yerushalmi

Jewish Mysticism and Jewish Ethics
Joseph Dan

The Invention of Hebrew Prose: Modern Fiction and the Language of Realism
Robert Alter

Recent Archaeological Discoveries and Biblical Research
William G. Dever

Jewish Identity in the Modern World
Michael A. Meyer

I. L. Peretz and the Making of Modern Jewish Culture
Ruth R. Wisse

The Kiss of God: Spiritual and Mystical Death in Judaism
Michael Fishbane

Gender and Assimilation in Modern Jewish History: The Roles and Representation of Women
Paula E. Hyman

Portrait of American Jews: The Last Half of the 20th Century
Samuel C. Heilman

Judaism and Hellenism in Antiquity: Conflict or Confluence?
Lee I. Levine

Imagining Russian Jewry: Memory, History, Identity
Steven J. Zipperstein

Popular Culture and the Shaping of Holocaust Memory in America
Alan Mintz

Studying the Jewish Future
Calvin Goldscheider

Autobiographical Jews: Essays in Jewish Self-Fashioning
Michael Stanislawski

The Jewish Life Cycle: Rites of Passage from Biblical to Modern Times
Ivan Marcus

Make Yourself a Teacher: Rabbinic Tales of Mentors and Disciples
Susan Handelman

Writing in Tongues: Yiddish Translation in the Twentieth Century
Anita Norich

Agnon's Moonstruck Lovers: The Song of Songs in Israeli Culture
Ilana Pardes

Agnon's Moonstruck Lovers

THE SONG OF SONGS IN ISRAELI CULTURE

Ilana Pardes

UNIVERSITY OF WASHINGTON PRESS
Seattle and London

Printed and bound in the United States of America
Design by Thomas Eykemans
Composed in Minion, typeface designed by Robert Slimbach
18 17 16 15 14 13 5 4 3 2 1

UNIVERSITY OF WASHINGTON PRESS
PO Box 50096, Seattle, WA 98145, USA
www.washington.edu/uwpress

LIBRARY OF CONGRESS CATALOGING-IN-PUBLICATION DATA
Pardes, Ilana.
Agnon's moonstruck lovers : the Song of Songs in Israeli culture /
Ilana Pardes. — First edition.
pages cm. — (Samuel and Althea Stroum lectures in Jewish studies)
Includes bibliographical references and index.
ISBN 978-0-295-99302-7 (hard cover : alk. paper) —
ISBN 978-0-295-99303-4 (pbk. : alk. paper)
1. Agnon, Shmuel Yosef, 1888-1970—Criticism, interpretation, etc.
2. Bible. Old Testament—In literature.
I. Title.
PJ5053.A4Z85 2013 892.4'35—dc23 2013033577

The paper used in this publication is acid-free and meets the minimum requirements of American National Standard for Information Sciences—Permanence of Paper for Printed Library Materials, ANSI Z39.48–1984.∞

For Robert Alter with abiding gratitude and friendship
And in memory of my brother-in-law, Itamar Pitowsky

Contents

Acknowledgments

I HAD the honor and privilege of first presenting this book (in its primary form) as part of the Samuel and Althea Stroum Lectures series at the University of Washington in the spring of 2010. I am very grateful to the Jewish Studies Program at the University of Washington for inviting me. Special thanks to Gad Barzilai, Michael Rosenthal, and Naomi Sokoloff for their warm hospitality during my stay in Seattle.

I began to work on *Agnon's Moonstruck Lovers* as a fellow at Scholion Center for Interdisciplinary Jewish Studies at Hebrew University, where I took part in a research group on "The Exegetical Imagination" during three blissful years 2008–2011. It was an exceptionally stimulating and warm intellectual setting. I am grateful to all members of the group and to the director of Scholion, Israel Yuval. I have a special debt to my dear friends and fellow imaginative exegetes, Galit Hasan-Rokem, Ruth HaCohen, and Richard (Richie) I. Cohen, for their ongoing support and insightful suggestions—vital to broadening my understanding of the interrelations between the different artistic realms of the Song's reception. I also had the great benefit of being at the CAJS at the University of Pennsylvania in the fall of 2009 and am grateful to the fellows of the research group on "Secularism and its Discontents" and to David Ruderman, the director.

I've had the pleasure of having other readers along the road. Eitan Bar-Yosef generously read the entire manuscript and was helpful in every imaginable way—conceptual, structural, not to mention many other comments that enriched my book. I am also indebted to Ruth Ginsburg for illuminating conversations regarding the psychoanalytic nexus of Agnon's writings. Melila Hellner-Eshed and Rut Kaniel Kara-Ivanov were my guides to the Zohar's readings of the Song and I am grateful for the many hours we spent together.

I've also benefited from a much appreciated conversation with Yehuda Liebes on Agnon's use of the Zohar. Many thanks go to Maya Barzilai for her comments on the Introduction and to Ethan Katz for his vital feedback on the historical dimension of the book. Rafael Weiser was of great help at the Agnon Archive. Many other fellow-travelers contributed to this book at different junctures: Gannit Ankori, Leora Batnitzky, Alon Confino, Sidra Dekoven Ezrahi, Chana Kronfeld, Vivian Liska, Ruth Nevo, Michele Rosenthal.

Many thanks go to the editorial team at the University of Washington Press. I am indebted to Jane M. Lichty for her meticulous and thoughtful editing and to Mary C. Ribesky and Tim Zimmermann for their invaluable help.

I would like to express gratitude to my astute students at Hebrew University, especially the students of "The Song of Songs as Cultural Text" (2006 and 2008) and "Secularism and its Discontents" (2011). In the fall of 2012, while working on the final touches of this book, I had the great pleasure of teaching two seminars on related issues in the Department of Comparative Literature and Jewish Studies at Harvard University. I am indebted to my students in these seminars for their insightful comments. I am also grateful to David Damrosch, the chair of Comparative Literature, for his exceptionally gracious hospitality.

I owe much to my remarkable research assistants: Noa Koren Agostini and Yael Kenan. My greatest debt is to Batnadiv HaKarmi-Weinberg, a scholar and an artist at once, who edited the book with incredible sensibility, knowledge, and commitment.

I presented various chapters of the book at different universities over the past few years: The Hebrew University of Jerusalem, the University of California, Berkeley, Stanford University, Indiana University, University of Florida, University of Virginia, University of Chicago, University of Antwerp, University of Pennsylvania, Harvard University, and Brandeis University. I am grateful to the comments of the audiences on these occasions.

For financial support, I am indebted to the Israel Science Foundation for a generous research grant and to Scholion.

My family members—Itamar, Keren, and Eyal—were, as always, an unending source of inspiration. This time around our excursions were closer to home—Talpiyot and Jaffa (rather than whaling routes in New England), but home, with their help, turned out to be as adventurous as distant seas. To write this book meant, among other things, to travel with them in time to my childhood in Jerusalem, to the neighborhoods where the kind of Hebrew University scholars who gripped Agnon's imagination once roamed about.

Agnon's Moonstruck Lovers is dedicated to Robert (Uri) Alter, my dear mentor and friend. The beginnings of this book lie in many ways in a seminar he taught on Agnon's poetics in the spring of 1979 (my first seminar as an undergraduate). Uri's inspiring seminars and groundbreaking books have accompanied me in ever-changing ways in different realms—from the Bible as literature to the Bible in modern literature and modern contexts. I cherish our ongoing dialogue and am very grateful for his unstinting support and generosity over the past three decades.

This book is also dedicated to the memory of Itamar Pitowsky, my brother-in-law, whose presence is sorely missed. His academic specialty was in the realm of physics and quantum theory but he was also a fond and very knowledgeable reader of literature. His sense of irony was akin to that of Agnon and his sense of humor was unparalleled. I had the pleasure of sharing with him some of my discoveries while writing this book.

Jerusalem, October 2013

AGNON'S MOONSTRUCK LOVERS

1

Introduction

UPON THE HANDLES OF THE LOCK

In "Reflections on S. Y. Agnon," an essay published in *Commentary* in 1967, shortly after Agnon received the Nobel Prize, Gershom Scholem sets out to explore the literary genius of his close friend.[1] Scholem defines Agnon as a remarkable classicist who ventures to set limits to the "anarchic" processes of secularization in Israeli culture, above all, to the "lawlessness and roughness" of the revived Hebrew language and the concomitant treatment of the Bible as a "national saga" rather than a "holy book." "The reader of Agnon," he writes, "cannot help feeling that a good deal of the master's work was produced as a kind of desperate incantation, an appeal to those who would come after him. It is as though he were saying: 'Since you do not accept the continuity of tradition and its language in their true context, take them in the transformation which they have undergone in my work, take them from someone who stands at the crossroads and can see in both directions.'"[2]

Scholem returns in this essay to some of the observations he had made in his well-known 1926 letter to Franz Rosenzweig, where he expressed his deep concern over the dire consequences of the Zionist revival of Hebrew as a spoken language and the neglect of its sacred overtones. "The secularization of language is only a *façon de parler*, a phrase! It is impossible to empty out words which are filled to the breaking point with specific meanings. . . . Those who initiated the rejuvenation of the language believed blindly and almost obstinately in its miraculous power. . . . They walked and still walk above this abyss. . . . May it not come to pass that the imprudence which has led us on this apocalyptic road ends in ruin."[3] Forty years later, Scholem sounds less apocalyptic. The revival of Hebrew is no longer a new phenomenon and seems more vital in its "anarchic" disposition (even in the 1926 letter, his anxiety was mingled with a certain heretical fascination). More importantly, Scholem's approach is now different because this essay serves as a grand homage to the ways in which Agnon "immortalized" the forgotten "forms and cadences" of the Hebrew language in his prose.[4] Whereas his contemporaries emptied out the holy tongue and regarded the Bible as a founding national text, knowing virtually nothing about rabbinic and medieval language and literature, Agnon, claims Scholem, is the one modern Hebrew writer, the one "master," who is an "heir to the totality of Jewish tradition."[5] Better still, he is the one writer who is intimately familiar with both the traditional world and secular culture. As such, he holds the admirable power to stand at the "crossroads" and deliver a profound cultural plea on behalf of the textual treasure he had rescued in his work. It is, to be sure, a "desperate incantation" that cannot possibly undo the chasm, but it can at least serve as partial mediation between past and present, while spurring readers to look in "both directions."

Seeing in "both directions" is a capacity Agnon developed at an early stage of his life. Agnon was born in 1887 as Shmuel Yosef Czaczkes—"Agnon" is a pen name he adopted later on in life—in the town of Buczacz in Eastern Galicia. He was the firstborn son of an observant family of solid economic means and an extensive tradition of erudition in Jewish literature. His formal education followed traditional lines, at least in its early period: he studied Bible and Talmud at various *hadarim*. But he also had the benefit of reading with his father the writings of great Jewish philosophers, Hasidic tales, and Galician maskilic writing. Thanks to his mother, Agnon was exposed to German literature, and already as a boy he had read the great works of European tradition. From his early adolescence, he was immersed in rich cross-cultural readings in which Jewish and modern European literature mingled freely. After the Kishinev pogrom, he became involved in Zionist circles in Buczacz, and in the spring of 1908 he immigrated to Palestine. Like many other members of the Second Aliyah, he became nonobservant while taking part in the thriving new literary scene in Jaffa.[6] In 1912, Agnon moved to Berlin, where he met leading Jewish intellectuals, among them Scholem, Martin Buber, and Rosenzweig. During his stay in Germany, Agnon continued to be nonobservant, but on his return to Palestine in 1924 he chose to live in Jerusalem and to become observant yet again.[7] In another passage in "Reflections on S. Y. Agnon," Scholem comments on these oscillations in his friend's life: "He was not what could be called an observant Jew when I knew him first, but even then he gave the impression of being a bearer of spiritual tradition. Now, in his later years, when he has become an observant Jew, he still gives the impression of being a man of complete intellectual freedom and of utterly unorthodox mind."[8]

This book began with an urge to rethink the pivotal cultural role of the Bible in the Israeli context through Agnon. Literary hermeneutic giants can, I believe, offer us splendid opportunities of this sort. If Dante is the literary guide to Italian biblicism and Melville to the Bible of antebellum America, Agnon, I will be arguing, is indispensable to the understanding of Zionist biblical culture.[9] Indeed, it is Agnon's position at the crossroads—his unorthodox perception of both religion and secularism—that makes him such a remarkable observer of this exegetical enterprise. To be sure, Agnon shares Scholem's concerns vis-à-vis the secularization of the Bible and the neglect of precious layers of Jewish tradition, but he by no means remains solely in the realm of admonition. To him, the Zionist obsession ("interest" is too mild a word) with the Bible, the great passion with which a professedly secular culture seeks to define itself via none other than a sacred text, is primarily a cause for wonder and reflection. Even while laying bare the dangers entailed in Zionism's construction of a national epos upon a text whose underlying echoes and ghosts it barely knows, Agnon savors the charms, paradoxes, and absurdities of these interpretive endeavors. With his unparalleled sense of irony, he goes so far as to provide a view of Zionist biblical culture as a fascinating, if peculiar, chapter within the ever-surprising history of the reception of the biblical text.[10]

Though many of Agnon's books and tales revolve around Zionist exegetical scenes, the topic has received but little scholarly attention. Adi Zemach mentions David Ben-Gurion's obsession with the Bible briefly in his reading of "Forevermore," but in extensive studies of Agnon's hermeneutics there is no substantive discussion in this connection.[11] Early critics were primarily interested in the question of Agnon's debt to and departure from Jewish sources. Meshulam Tochner was the most eloquent spokesperson of those who regarded Agnon as a traditionalist; Baruch Kurzweil and Dov Sadan were the leading figures in spelling out the Agnonian break with tradition; and Gershon Shaked underscored the paradoxical qualities of Agnon's irreverent-reverent position.[12] Recent critics such as Anne Golomb Hoffman and Yaniv Hagbi have taken an altogether different route in their emphasis on the fascinating affinity between Agnon's approach to midrashic and mystical exegesis and poststructuralist perceptions of textuality and hermeneutics.[13]

The paucity of studies on Agnon's interest in Israeli biblicism is hardly surprising. "As a rule," writes Robert Alter, "Agnon chooses to give the impression that he is much more withdrawn from the modern world than he is in fact." His writer's persona was that of "an isolated artist, standing at his lectern—a relic of the talmudic academies which he prefers to a writing desk—inscribing Hebrew characters . . . with the painstaking care of an old-world craftsman, his ears closed to the stridencies of the contemporary reality around him."[14] Agnon's activities as an anthologist only augmented this notion. Throughout his career, he devoted much time to producing different anthologies of Jewish lore and learned commentaries, among them *Days of Awe* (*Yamim nora'im*), *The Stories of the Baal Shem Tov* (*Sipurey ha-Ba'al Shem Tov*), and *Book, Writer, and Story* (*Sefer, sofer ve-sippur*), bringing together an incredibly rich amalgamation of commentaries, from the Midrash, *Sefer Yetsirah* (Book of Creation), the Zohar, Hasidic tales, and other, lesser-known sources. These rather esoteric compilations (which never acquired the popularity of Bialik and Rawnitzky's *Sefer Ha-Aggadah* [The Book of Legends])—serve as a fascinating window into Agnon's exegetical laboratory, into an almost internal dialogue of unparalleled erudition through which he surveys the vast archives of Jewish literature and culls his building materials.[15]

But what makes Agnon's hermeneutic project all the more remarkable, I suggest, is his capacity to move beyond the traditional interpretive scope and to probe exegetical realms that appear in no compilation, not even his own. Much as Agnon's language entails a bold modernism despite its heavy reliance on Biblical, Rabbinic, and Medieval Hebrew, so too the profusion of traditional commentaries in his writings and anthologies does not preclude an avid interest in modern exegetical trends and endeavors. Commenting (rather playfully) on his peculiar style, Agnon once declared: "My language [is] a simple, easy language, the language of all the generations before us and of all of the generations to come."[16] The same principle holds for his aesthetic-hermeneutic project. Exegesis, for Agnon, comes copious and unbound, confined by no temporal or generational boundaries. Far from being "simple," his oeuvre strives to be all encompassing: to embrace all prior commentaries while plunging into contemporary contexts, and even anticipating future shifts.

In investigating Agnon's exegetical project and Israeli biblicism side by side, I combine lines of inquiry that do not usually appear together. This combination of literature and cultural history can complicate, I believe, the common perception of the Zionist Bible as a quintessentially secular phenomenon in studies such as Anita Shapira's "The Bible and Israeli Identity."[17] Shapira's essay, which has become the most influential historical account in this connection, opens with a consideration of the rise of the Bible as the Zionist epos during the Second Aliyah. Quoting Labor leader Yitzhak Tabenkin, Shapira notes that most of the pioneers had Bibles in their rooms. "It was their bridge between the land they had imagined and the land they found upon arrival," vital to their transformation of Palestine's strange geography into a new national home.[18]

The cultural centrality of the Bible, according to Shapira, was reinforced after the establishment of the State of Israel. Ben-Gurion, who prior to 1948 hardly ever referred to the biblical text, became its greatest advocate after the War of Independence was over. In "Uniqueness and Destiny" ("Yihud ve-yi'ud"), he hailed the Bible as the primary model for the young state. "In this homeland, the Hebrew nation was born, grew up and crystallized, and here it created its eternal testament . . . the book of books. In the future, the national enterprise and education will rest on these two [pillars]: the land and the book." In the 1950s, Ben-Gurion went so far as to host prominent Bible scholars in his home, offering a central scholarly forum for the consideration of biblical texts that seemed pertinent to current politics. The press "found it piquant that the Prime Minister and Minister of Defense devoted time to spiritual concerns, and it gave broad coverage to these 'fateful' questions."[19]

Ben-Gurion's "Bible-mania," in Shapira's terms, was accompanied by a growing emphasis on the values of a new literalism. In a famous letter from 1953, Ben-Gurion claimed that within the context of Zionism "the Bible shines in its own light" (*ha-tanakh zore'ah be-'or 'atsmo*) and need not be obscured by later rabbinic interpretations.[20] "The books of the Bible," he writes in this letter, "declare the glory of Israel. As to the glory of God—that is declared by the heavens. . . . The Holy One, blessed be He, does not need an identity card."[21] To Nathan Rotenstreich, who criticized him for endorsing a "historical leap" that overlooks the cultural achievements of the Jewish people since biblical times, he responds: "The books of the Bible tip the scales for Israeli youth . . . they are fresh, up to date, relevant, immediate in terms of geography and plot, [and] inspiring."[22] Nothing in the Oral Law seemed to bear such qualities for Ben-Gurion, which is why he did not hesitate to radically invert the traditional preference of studying the Talmud to the Bible. While Shapira sheds light on key moments in the reception of the Bible within the Israeli context, she does not consider the ambiguities at stake, nor does she pay sufficient attention to the ways in which secular and religious exegetical practices may be embedded in each other.

A book that is most relevant to the understanding of Agnon's approach to Israeli biblicism, even though it does not deal with Israeli culture, is Jonathan Sheehan's *The Enlightenment Bible: Translation, Scholarship, Culture.*

Sheehan's reassessment of the European Enlightenment Bible partakes in a new trend of rethinking the normative treatment of the Enlightenment as synonymous with the rise of secularism. His aim is not to lay bare the hidden religious patterns used within secular frameworks in order to reinforce authoritarian moves (à la Carl Schmitt) but rather to call attention to the role of religion in defining the project of modernity, whether negatively or positively. Even as religion seems to recede, it remains "essential to the self-image of modernity, which can no more dispense with religion than embrace it." The Bible is Sheehan's clearest witness. If indeed modernity were entirely secular, "this provincial and archaic artifact should long ago have been discarded." Instead, it is redefined as "one of the sturdiest pillars of Western 'culture,'" the vital base of its literary, historical, and ethical heritage.[23] Focusing on Protestant scholars and translators in eighteenth-century England and Germany, Sheehan traces how the Bible was transformed from a book justified by theology to one justified by culture. Against the predominant tendency to regard the Enlightenment as an anticlerical age, he underscores the ways in which the "Bible survived, even thrived, in this cradle of ostensible secularization."[24]

The Zionist Bible is, in many ways, the heir of the Enlightenment Bible. Israeli society in the twentieth century was more invested in secularism than eighteenth-century and nineteenth-century Germany and England were. Yet this greater commitment to secular paradigms did not prevent Zionist exegetes from defining their national project via the Bible and passionately seeking new ways to redefine the significance of the biblical text.

ONLY YESTERDAY AND THE QUESTION OF BIBLICAL RECEPTION

Balak, the enigmatic, mad dog of *Only Yesterday* (*Tmol shilshom*; 1945) is an irresistible point of departure for my consideration of Agnon's response to the Zionist reception of the Bible. Appearing in the midst of the novel and dismantling its realistic line, this dog approaches Isaac Kumer, the protagonist, as he paints on a marble tablet in one of the neighborhoods of Jerusalem. Isaac is amused by the dog clinging to him with such passion and mischievously writes *kelev meshuga*—"mad dog"—on Balak's back. The inscription, unknown to the dog, becomes the instrument by which Isaac's life and that of the dog are ruined. When Balak, at the very end, bites the "owner of the brush" (*ba'al ha-mikhol*) in a desperate quest for a truthful decoding of the inscription on his back, the perplexed Isaac, infected by rabies—or by the maddening, contagious words he had painted—becomes ill and eventually dies.

Figure 1.1: Avigdor Arikha (Romanian-born French-Israeli, 1929–2010). *Sixteen Illustrations for Stray Dog*, by S. Y. Agnon, published by Tarshish, Jerusalem, 1960. Ink on paper. Collection of the Israel Museum, Jerusalem. Bequest of Dr. Moshe Spitzer, Jerusalem. Photograph: Israel Museum, Jerusalem, by Avraham Hay. © Estate of the artist.

Upon the publication of the novel, Kurzweil wrote a letter to Agnon asking him to explain the symbolism of the dog Balak. Agnon replied with a characteristic pseudo-naive, ironic tone, refuting any allegorical intensions on his part ("ve-'af be-Balak lo nitkavanti le-shum alegoria she-ba'olam"). Agnon's denial of allegory by no means prevented Kurzweil from writing an essay titled "On Balak, the Demonic Dog," where he construes the dog as a symbol of "desire, sin, archaic powers, instinctual turmoil, insanity, and madness," serving as such only for those who, like Isaac Kumer, are torn between their deep emotional bond to past traditions and their equally forceful attraction to the new modes of Zionist life in Palestine of the Second Aliyah.[25]

In denying allegory, Agnon was not only taunting Kurzweil, I presume, but also urging his readers to resist the temptation of viewing Balak as a consistent allegory, *mashal*, with a definable message, a *nimshal*. In *Only Yester-*

day, as well as elsewhere, Agnon explodes the concept of allegory through an overwhelming proliferation of potential interpretive routes. His inconsistency is partially inspired by the midrashic tendency to compile diverse interpretations side by side, but there is a distinct modernist preoccupation in his excessive hermeneutics.[26] Not unlike Walter Benjamin, he insists that humanity is cut off from truth, "not by a lack but by an excess of signification."[27] He seems to agree with Benjamin that allegory underscores the complication of signification in modernity, in a world in which language has lost its Adamic, magical qualities and has become instrumental, in a world that can offer no perfect accord between words and things.[28] The inscription on the dog's skin defies the fissure between word and meaning: the dog and the writing are supposedly one. But it is a mock merging that only leads to the dog's death, without solving the haunting riddle of an inscription cut loose, open to unending commentaries.[29]

Kurzweil's reading was among the first in a long series of attempts to interpret the stray dog. To mention but a few other salient interpretive lines: the dog has been read as a comment on "the face of its generation" (Arnold Band), as a canine blend of Faust and Mephistopheles (Dan Miron), and as a Kafkaesque parable on modernity reminiscent of the "Penal Colony" (Hillel Barzel).[30] Most relevant to my interest in Israeli biblicism are readings of the dog's inscription in relation to secular Zionism and the battle over the Hebrew language during the Second Aliyah. Even within this constricted topic, critics have differed in their approach. Whereas Aharon Bar-Adon construes the association of Balak with this debate as representing Agnon's ultimately passionate endorsement of the Zionist linguistic revival, Todd Hasak-Lowy has argued that the dog is Agnon's response to Scholem's letter to Rosenzweig. Agnon, much like Scholem, he argues, criticizes the advocates of the revival of Hebrew for overlooking the hazardous outcomes of such secularization and the abyss above which they walk.[31]

If I may heap yet another reading on Balak, let me suggest that the question at stake is not merely the changing status of the Hebrew language but also—and perhaps even more so—the perplexing phenomenon of the Zionist revival of the Bible. That the dog is called "Balak" already intimates that the biblical text is part of the drama. Balak, as one recalls, was the wicked king of Moab who summoned the sorcerer Balaam to curse the Children of Israel as they approached the Promised Land (Numbers 22–24).[32] Behind the evocation of King Balak in *Only Yesterday*, as Sidra DeKoven Ezrahi points out, one can trace yet another character pertaining to this biblical episode: Balaam's ass.[33] This legendary ass destabilizes the realist line of the biblical text as she opens her mouth and rebukes her master for failing to notice the angel blocking the road. To the extent that the dog Balak stands for the Zionist Bible, his affinity with King Balak and Balaam's ass underscores the heretical, antithetical bent of this new exegetical enterprise while questioning its sense of literalism and realism. However enchanting Zionism's adoption of the biblical text may be, it seems to have revived the forbidden, heretical, cursed world of wicked kings and pagan sorcerers rather than reenact the world of the chosen.

But above all, it is Agnon's memorable metacommentary on the reception of Balak and his inscription in book 4 of *Only Yesterday* that calls to mind the biblical text. In keeping with Agnon's fondness for self-irony, the history of the ever-increasing commentaries on *kelev meshuga* surely anticipates the exegetical excess apparent in the plethora of critical essays on the dog Balak; but in its great proportions and variegated readership it serves as an incredibly amusing parody of the unexpected twists and turns in the exegetical history of the Book of Books.

Accounts of Balak first appear in print, the narrator recounts, in the ultra-Orthodox newspapers of Jerusalem, where the dog is condemned for being "a heathen and heretic," behaving insolently in going "bareheaded with the letters of the Holy Tongue on his skin."[34] When the Jerusalemite newspapers reach secular Jaffa, the people of Jaffa think that the dog must be a parable. Perplexed, they try to figure out its meaning. "This one says, There's something to this; and that one says, We have to derive the implicit from the explicit. But what is explicit here no one explained. Meanwhile opinions were divided, and there were as many opinions as there were inhabitants of the city" (485). As the havoc caused by the story of the dog increases, all the Zionists of Jaffa flock to an urgent meeting. "Thirty-six speeches were delivered that night and every speaker said something new. (A phenomenon that may not have happened since the day Jaffa became a metropolis for speakers)" (486).[35]

The circulation of the text reaches epic proportions as it begins to influence nothing less than "science and life and art both within the Land [of Israel] and Outside the Land" (489). Scholars who come to study the Holy Land—"its flora, or the manners of livestock, animals, and birds there, or the inhabitants of the Land and their customs, or other kinds of research whose name hasn't yet been researched by research" (489)—regard the incident of the dog as a typical Jerusalemite custom of writing inscriptions on dogs that serve as scapegoats. "Even Hasidism was enriched by the adventures of Balak" given that they too invented tales about the mad dog, despite the fact that he was an "unclean animal" (490–91).

Agnon is fascinated by every imaginable interpretive mode—be it ultra-Orthodox, scholarly, artistic, or Hasidic—but he has a special interest in the exegetical obsessions of secular Jaffa. Jaffa's Zionist exegetes may regard themselves as different and set themselves in opposition to the Jerusalemite ultra-Orthodox community, but in their fervent attempts to decipher the text and in turning this hermeneutic enigma into a central cultural event, they are far closer to Jerusalem than first appears. No one in *Only Yesterday* seems to be able to remain outside the exegetical whirl.

Beyond Balak and his inscription, Agnon provides an explicit consideration of Jaffa's biblical culture in his vivid description of Sonya's bluntly secular approach to the biblical text. "Sonya," we are told through a mélange of third-person narration and a paraphrase of Isaac's admiring perspective, "doesn't read newspapers."

> By the time the newspapers reach the Land, they have grown old and their words are history. And she doesn't like history, but she does like the Scriptures. And for that she has to thank Doctor Schimmelmann, who lectures to a group of young women on the Prophets. Before Dr. Schimmelmann came, she didn't realize that there was anything interesting in the Scriptures, but first we have to correct its text. You learn that the Prophets weren't idlers, but were people like you and me, who lived the life of their time and suffered the pain of their generation. If you like, they were the journalists and orators of their period. With Dr. Schimmelmann's emendations, there are prophecies that read like modern articles. The same is true of the narrative part of the Holy Scriptures. If you like, they're oral feuilletons, for we can't say that there were newspapers in their day. And even satire you find in the Bible. Open the Book of Jonah and you've got a biting satire on a nationalist prophet who withheld his own prophecy and didn't want to prophecy to the Gentiles. (103)

Sonya is deeply compelled by Dr. Schimmelmann's modernist, secular literalism. Schimmelmann's Bible is a godless Bible where theological questions are replaced by political and national concerns. Defined by the Greek term *biblia* rather than by the Hebrew term *Torah*, it has the freshness of the antiestablishment Zionism that Sonya goes on to speak of with enthusiasm, whose activities are "carried out mostly by young men and women" (104). It is the kind of Bible she can endorse, for it is not the sole property of the male realm of *talmidey hakhamim* (Torah scholars) but rather the topic of a cutting-edge series of lectures given by Schimmelmann to a group of young women in Jaffa, Sonya being but one of them.

Several ironic lines intersect in this passage. First, there is an ironic gap between Isaac's infatuation with Sonya's intellectual world and his lack of awareness of the erotic longings that inflame his craving to "swallow" her words. Second, there is a good deal of irony in the juxtaposition of Sonya's lack of interest in newspapers or history and her excitement over the political relevance of the prophets who were, as Schimmelmann put it, the journalists and orators of biblical times. Third, for all his modernism and reliance on the scientific findings of biblical criticism, the doctor's German name, "Schimmelmann," means "a moldy man."[36] Neither Sonya nor Schimmelmann, Agnon seems to intimate, realizes that there is nothing new in their desire to view biblical characters as if they "were people like you and me." Ironically, they follow in the footsteps of many generations of readers who sought to read the Bible anew, making the ancient text compatible with current norms and sensibilities.

Much has been written on Agnon's masterful use of irony, but Leah Goldberg's observations in this connection remain among the most insightful and succinct. She points to the ways in which Agnon oscillates between the naive and the ironic, unwilling to surrender either one of these modes. Through his naive characters he expresses the cravings for Eden, even in a world in which it is lost. Irony, in turn, allows him to expose the drawbacks and dangers of naive belief. Commenting on *Only Yesterday* with its prototypically naive protagonist, Goldberg depicts Agnon's "little demon of irony" laughing as he looks at Isaac's childlike picture of the Land of Israel destroyed by the "cruel sun" of reality. "Then comes the artist," she writes, "and folds the old picture, the horrible sun, and the laughing demon, and turns them, with his magic, into the art whose name is: Shmuel Yosef Agnon."[37] Agnon's irony, for Goldberg, is thus primarily a means for maintaining a multiplicity of perspectives while flaunting the split, sober authorial gaze behind the scenes.

Following Goldberg's imaginative rendition of the Agnonian scene of writing, one could imagine Agnon's "little demon of irony"—or rather Balak in his demonic embodiment of the Zionist Bible and heretical ghosting of the sacred Hebrew letters on his back—laughing at the naive reformulation of scriptural texts in Jaffa of the Second Aliyah. But Agnon's ironic stance (no exegetical trend is spared in *Only Yesterday*) does not stop him from probing the intricacies of this new exegetical phenomenon and juggling various perspectives at once.[38]

To pursue all of Agnon's metacommentaries on the Zionist Bible would have been as impossible as chasing Balak. I single out the Song of Songs both because of its privileged position within Agnon's exegetical imagination and within Israeli culture.

ZIONIST ALLEGORIES OF THE SONG

The virtuosity of Agnon's exploration of Israeli biblicism reaches a peak in his response to the Zionist reception of the Song of Songs. No other biblical text provides him with the same kind of tumultuous exegetical history that could set in relief the ambiguities and paradoxes of secular Zionism. No other biblical text could offer such a rich turf for rethinking the interrelations between the religious and the secular while contemplating the ever-changing modes of literal and allegorical exegesis.

The Song of Songs was traditionally attributed to King Solomon, the king who composed "a thousand and five" songs (1 Kings 5:12), the king whose wisdom was unsurpassed. But the Solomonic seal did not suffice to pave the Song's road to the canon. We do not know what was the content of the rabbinic dispute regarding the sanctity of the ancient love poem. One can only assume that the Song's daring erotic character and the fact that God is not even mentioned in the text made its canonicity questionable. In a renowned moment in the Song's biography, Rabbi Akiva rescues the text by declaring: "Heaven forbid that any man in Israel ever disputed that the Song of Songs renders the hands unclean, for that the whole world is not worth the day on which the Song of Songs was given to Israel, for all the Writings are holy, and the Song of Songs is the Holy of Holies" (Mishnah Yadayim 3:5).[39]

Within the world of Jewish exegesis, Rabbi Akiva's declaration was the point of departure for allegorical readings of the text as a love poem between the Holy One, blessed be He and the Congregation of Israel. For many centuries, allegory was perceived as the only way of reading. Numerous commentaries—from Song of Songs Rabbah to the Zohar—were put forth in an attempt to decipher the text's latent meanings.[40]

A dramatic shift—one of the most dramatic exegetical shifts of all times—took place in the eighteenth century with the rise of a new reading of the Song as an exquisite, earthly dialogue between human lovers. The most prominent advocate of this literalist-aesthetic trend was Johann Gottfried Herder. Herder's translation of and commentary on the ancient love poem, *Lieder der Liebe*, published in 1778, marked a moment of radical departure from traditional allegorical readings of the text and had tremendous impact on the modern perception of the Song—first in European circles and later in Zionist ones.

When Ben-Gurion declared that the Bible needs to "shine in its own light," he set the Song of Songs on a pedestal as one of the key texts of the new secular literalism Israeli culture had invented. What made the Song a particularly compelling text was the fact that it required no de-theologizing, given the absence of God in these amorous dialogues. The primary task, claimed Ben-Gurion, was to remove the allegorical layers that had been piled upon it. Only then would the Song's original, secular grandeur, be laid bare, its celebration of an earthly love between two shepherds. Ben-Gurion's declaration was a culminating moment in a long process by which the biblical love poem had acquired its central cultural position. From the early twentieth century on, secular Zionism embraced the Song with unparalleled passion. The biblical love poem appeared in different forms in diverse cultural realms—from the many musical adaptations of the Song, to numerous artworks, folk dances, the Haggadot of the kibbutzim, and biblical scholarship.

Agnon, I want to argue, sets out to complicate the story of the Israeli Song of Songs. Chief among Agnon's sharp observations regarding the Zionist reception of the ancient love poem is the recognition that, as surprising as it may first seem, allegory has not disappeared from the Israeli secular scene. Although the Zionist return to the Bible was accompanied by a fervent adherence to literalism, Zionist exegetes were by no means innocent of allegorical inclinations. Wittingly and unwittingly, new national allegories, shaped via the Song, emerge with the rise of Zionism, providing modern forms of collective love, above all, the love between the community and the Land, which replaces the love between Israel and God.[41]

Only Yesterday is an indispensable prelude in this connection as well. In a chapter titled "Days of Grace" ("Yemey ratson"), Isaac Kumer rejoices in the luscious concreteness of the fruits of the Land of Israel. He first muses on the pleasurable apricots—fruits that were not mentioned in the Torah and were virtually unknown in Europe—and moves on to fruits that were known in biblical times but unaffordable back home: grapes and watermelons. Among the latter is the fig—sweet in exile—but all the more so in the Land "where it dwells," where one can savor the special taste of a fresh fig that "is eaten as it is," entering "your mouth unmediated" (80–81). The pomegranate, too, is only remotely akin to its European counterparts: "Before we came to the Land of Israel, the pomegranate served us as a parable, for instance, he ate its core and threw away its rind. When we came to the Land of Israel, that parable became reality" (81). Kurzweil was close to the mark when he defined this chapter as an exquisite "Song of Songs for the fruits of the Land of Israel."[42] Isaac does not evoke the Song explicitly, but the erotic quality of the fruit descriptions in the ancient love poem seems to color his sensuous, literal approach to the fruits at which he marvels. At this point of his stay in Jaffa, Isaac still cherishes some of the religious modes of thought upon which he had been raised (seeing divine providence in the goodness of the produce), but he also begins to adopt Zionist exegetical practices—at least for a while—taking part in cherishing the literal while forging a love for the Land of Israel via the Song. More specifically, like many Zionist exegetes, he seems to perceive the Song as a key to the delights of the Orient and relishes its vivid depictions of the unique tastes, sights, and fragrances of enchanting Eastern geographies.[43]

There is something compelling in the representations of Zionist literalism in *Only Yesterday*—be it of Sonya's enthusiastic response to Schimmelmann's teachings or Isaac's Song of fruits—but Agnon does not hesitate to ridicule secular Zionism's tendency, all the more so in the 1940s, to ignore its own role in shaping new allegories while adhering to the concrete. It is the people of Jaffa, after all, who are the first to insist on a parabolic reading of Balak. They differ on the interpretation of the parable but not on the very fact that a parable is at stake. Their exegetical imagination turns out to be as wild as that of the Hasid who in light of his reservations regarding the mad dog dreams of a lamb who wears a *shtrayml* on which a verse from Song 2:14 is carved: "O my dove, that art in the clefts of the rock" (491).

The question of the Zionist Song of Songs is addressed more directly in the narrator's ironic comment on the lack of love in Palestine: "Not every Amnon wins his Tamar, and not every Solomon finds a Shulamit. How much their hearts had hummed when they lived Outside the Land and read the novel *The Love of Zion* about the splendor of the excellent daughters of Zion. Now that they dwell in Jerusalem, they haven't yet seen that splendor. Perhaps the Sages were right when they interpreted the Song of Songs as a parable and an allegory" (263–64). The novel referenced here is Abraham Mapu's renowned *The Love of Zion* (*Ahavat Zion*; 1853), the first Hebrew novel and one of the cornerstones of Hebrew Enlightenment. This proto-Zionist novel—whose exegetical contours I discuss in greater detail in the next chapter—is the site of the inception of the Zionist literalization of the Song and of its re-allegorization. Mapu provides a lively love story between Amnon and Tamar, modeled on the mutual courting of the Shulamite and her lover in the Song. But this new literal rendition of the Song in Hebrew, set against the backdrop of the supposedly concrete, Oriental landscapes of Zion, is inextricably connected with a new allegorical configuration of the Love for the ancient Land.

In *Only Yesterday*, the Zionist dream of a new literal Song in the Land of Israel, with its underlying erotic, Oriental promise, is a fragile one. The "excellent daughters of Zion" are nowhere in sight. The only exegetical mode that prevails is ironically that of the "Sages," with its allegories of divine love, leaving room neither for the realization of erotic fantasies nor for the love of Zion.

"AND SOLOMON'S WISDOM EXCELLED": BETWEEN THE ZOHAR AND ROSENZWEIG

Agnon, however, is not merely an outside observer of the Zionist obsession with the Song. He fashions his own Song and his own biblical aesthetics through and against this peculiar exegetical scene. He plays teasingly with allegorical readings of the Song, both traditional and modern, deconstructs them, reconstructs them, daring his readers into contemplating the restless instability of interpretive endeavors. Let me suggest that his very interest in the Song of Songs as aesthetic touchstone is indebted to its incredibly diverse, and at times contradictory, exegetical potentialities.

A rather unknown piece by Agnon, "And Solomon's Wisdom Excelled" ("Vaterev hokhmat shlomo"; 1950), captures something of his intricate hermeneutic position vis-à-vis the ancient love poem. A cross between a midrash and a tale, this short piece is a remarkable example of how Agnon mimics his sources with a swerve. It begins with a quotation from 1 Kings 5:10–12: "And Solomon's wisdom excelled the wisdom of the children of the East, and all the wisdom of Egypt. For he was wiser than all men. . . . He also uttered three thousand proverbs and his songs were one thousand and five." Agnon then cites several commentaries on this verse, each attempting to explain the discrepancy between the account of numerous proverbs and songs written by Solomon and the fact that the Bible includes only three of his books: the Song of Songs, Proverbs, and Ecclesiastes. Thus Rabbi Yehuda the Hasid "explains that, had Solomon written down all his wisdom, people would have busied themselves solely with that, diminishing their study of the Torah"; Rabbi Gershom claims that the Song of Songs includes solely the "choicest of Solomon's songs"; and Rabbi David Kimche (Radak) "observes that many of the books were lost during Israel's periods of exile."[44] After paying dues to his precursors, Agnon continues in a mock-reverent manner: "The rabbis have left me space in which to elaborate. Not that I come, heaven forbid, to take issue with them.

But, just as one text lends itself to numerous readings, so each reading may be understood in various ways" (278). His primary assumption (in accordance with the commentaries he cites) is that the verse from Kings must be taken literally (*mamash*), but he ventures to veer off in speculating that Solomon's unknown oeuvre was not lost (as Radak would have it) but rather that the wise king hid the songs intentionally.

In construing the lacuna in Solomon's poetic corpus as a deliberate act of concealment, Agnon relies in part on a source he does not mention explicitly: the commentary on 1 Kings 5:12 in Zohar Shemot (*Terumah*), where the mystery of Solomon's hidden corpus is inextricably connected with the supernal secret of sexual union in the upper worlds. In *Kabbalah and Eros*, Moshe Idel points out that as the author of the erotic Song of Songs, the Zoharic Solomon is regarded as the one who can best induce the *hieros gamos* among the *sefirot*.[45] To do so, however, requires supernal wisdom and utmost care. Solomon must hide some of his oeuvre or rather conceal the esoteric parts of his Song (construed as a separate corpus of a thousand songs), while orchestrating an amorous encounter between the male and female facets of the godhead.[46]

Agnon draws on the Zohar, but doesn't hesitate to use the space "left" for him to create his own modernist midrash on Solomon's Song, concealment, and eros. He opens his tale "And Solomon's Wisdom Excelled" with the kind of exegetical questions commonly found both in the Midrash and the Zohar only to whimsically cast Solomon in zones of authorial anxieties that bear the mark of modern sensibilities.[47]

> Yet why would Solomon have wanted to hide them? When he was a young man and the divine inspiration was upon him, he composed the "Song of Songs"—a song greater than all other songs, the choicest of songs—combining both love and fear of heaven. There was one circle in Jerusalem, however, of good-for-nothing intellectuals who would take the holy words out of context and twist the plain meaning. Of these people Solomon observed: "Little foxes that spoil the vineyards" [Song 2:15]. To which vineyard does he refer? To none other than the vineyards of the Lord of Hosts, of the House of Israel. What did this circle of intellectuals say? "Look at Solomon! The people of Israel are building the Temple and he busies himself writing love songs!" These words reached Solomon. He placed his left hand beneath his head like a man examining his deeds. His songs came before him and he saw each was whole, without blemish or fault. He despaired of mankind and wished to flee. Thus said Solomon: "Flee my beloved." [Song 8:14]

So why did he not flee? Because all Israel had set him on the throne of David, his father, and needed him to consolidate the kingdom and to judge Israel . . . Solomon went up to the mountain of myrrh and the hill of frankincense, as it is written: "Before the day cools and the shadows flee, I will get me to the mountain of myrrh and to the hill of frankincense" [Song 4:6]. How do we know that he wanted to hide his songs? From the following verse: "You are fair, my love, there is no flaw in you" [Song 4:7]. What is it that is fair and without blemish? It is the Song of Songs . . .

When Solomon reached the mountain of myrrh and the hill of frankincense, he came upon the daughters of Jerusalem . . . Solomon feared that they would place his songs on a rock, like a bundle of myrrh . . .

He went to the apple tree; he saw young men, their love awakened. He descended to his garden to the bed of spices; he saw the shepherds with their flocks. Solomon became afraid lest the shepherds find his songs. He went down to his nut garden, but even there he did not hide his songs. And why not? Because the nut does not cover its roots during planting.

Solomon finally went to his vineyard at Ba'al Hammon [8:11] . . . Since he saw that it was well-guarded he went and hid his songs—all one thousand and four of them—in the ground. When the fifteenth of Av came and the daughters of Jerusalem went out to dance in the vineyards, Solomon's songs arose from the ground and were heard between the vines. The young maidens stood and listened. Their lips dripped like honeycomb as their love was aroused. Of this moment Solomon wrote: "I charge you, O, daughters of Jerusalem, by the gazelles and by the hinds of the fields. Do not stir up nor awaken love" [Song 3:5]. The young girls heard Solomon's oath and hid their songs in their hearts. Because they were hidden, so they became silent and since they were silent they were forgotten, and as they were forgotten no one remembered them." (278–79)

King Solomon is presented here as an author who strives in vain to control his audience's modes of reading. When Solomon proclaims "Little foxes that spoil the vineyards," he supposedly refers to "none other than the vineyards of the Lord of Hosts" (278).[48] But the "the good-for-nothing intellectuals" ignore Solomon's allegorical intensions and scorn the king for writing songs of earthly love and desire (*shirey heshek*), thus taking the "holy words out of context and twisting the plain meaning" (278). In a desperate attempt to prevent future distortions and misreadings, the king seeks a site in which to hide his songs so as to prevent them from falling "into unworthy hands." The literal meaning of his Song, however, continues to haunt him. Wandering in the landscapes of the ancient love poem—from "the mountain of myrrh and the hill of frankincense" to the "nut garden" (278–79)—Solomon is reminded time and again of the unabashed eroticism of the verses he had composed. When he finally buries his songs in his vineyard at Ba'al Hammon, perceiving it as a terrain where they would be safe, he discovers that during the feast of love (on the fifteenth of Av) the songs spring up from the ground, arousing the young maidens dancing there in search of love.

The literal and the allegorical readings of the Song are inextricably connected for Agnon. Much as he highlights the allegorical dimension of literalist readings of the Song, so too he strives to complicate the common Zionist perception of traditional commentaries as innocent of eroticism. His Solomon wrote a song that is the choicest of all songs precisely because it combines "both love and fear of heaven" (278).

The modernist thrust in Agnon's insistence on the interconnectedness of the literal and the allegorical may be elucidated through Rosenzweig's renowned observations on the biblical love poem in *The Star of Redemption*. Up to the eighteenth and nineteenth centuries, Rosenzweig writes, "the Song of Songs was recognized as a love lyric and precisely therewith simultaneously as a 'mystical' poem. One simply knew that the I and Thou of human discourse is without more ado also the I and Thou between God and man. One knew that the distinction between immanence and transcendence disappears in language."[49] Not despite but *because* the Song was a "real" love poem (that is, "worldly") was it received as a genuine "spiritual" poem regarding the human–divine love. Rosenzweig's comment is meant as a critique of the literalist approach to the Song. Herder and Goethe (who followed the Herderian line), claims Rosenzweig, highlighted the lyrical and literal qualities of the Song, but in doing so mistakenly overlooked the poem's special position between human and divine loves.[50]

Agnon also comes close to Rosenzweig in his interest in the language of love. For both, the language of the Song is where the distinction between immanence and transcendence collapses. The language of Solomon's Song in Agnon's piece is located in a concrete reality where the king wanders, but at the same time it bears a certain mystical streak in its position between the hidden and the revealed. What complicates it all is the fact that the songs become active components of the amorous landscapes they depict. Though buried, they "arose from the ground and were heard between the vines." It remains unclear, then, whether the king wanders in the actual sites of the Song or within the ghostly text itself. The enigma thickens due to the ambiguous materiality of the hidden corpus. Does Solomon bury a text or oral songs?[51]

But there is more. In Agnon's depiction of Solomon's Song, the ancient poem itself becomes the object of love and is seen as analogous to the Shulamite. Not unlike her, the king's Song is a model of perfection: "fair and without blemish." Agnon, in a sense, creates via the Song an allegory about literary passions whose intensity may be as overwhelming as any other love. But in accordance with his aesthetic-hermeneutic presuppositions, this allegory too has the magical touch of the concrete and the literal insofar as it is inextricably intertwined with earthly loves. It is, after all, Solomon's songs (rather than men) that have the power to awaken the dancing maidens, making their lips "drip with honeycomb."

If Rosenzweig provocatively sides with traditional exegesis in his critique of modern literalism, Agnon playfully sets them against each other. Agnon moves beyond traditional exegesis both in his solution to the hermeneutic problem and in the special position allotted to poetry. At the same time, he challenges Herder and his Zionist followers for literalizing the text and ignoring the ways in which the Song never ceases to generate allegorical readings—from the midrash to modern national and aesthetic allegories. Even if one were inclined to read the Song literally, that is not quite an option for a text that is replete with metaphors and sexual double entendres, with "little foxes" that call for a reading between the lines.

TWO TALES: SCHOLARLY LOVES

A few words about the scope and trajectory of this book are necessary. *Agnon's Moonstruck Lovers* focuses on Agnon's response to the Zionist Song of Songs in the years of the peak of Israeli biblicism in the 1940s and 1950s. There are other Agnonian readings of the Song that are not included within this historical context and as such remain beyond the scope of my book, or else are on its margins. Already in "Agunot" ("Forsaken Wives"; 1908), the first story Agnon published under the pen name "Agnon," the Song resonates with unmistakable force from the very opening.[52] To mention but a few more notable cases: the collection of love stories *Upon the Handles of the Lock* (*Al kapot ha-manul*; 1922)—whose title is a verse from the ancient love poem (Song 5:5); "In the Heart of the Seas" ("Bilvav yamim"; 1935), where a group of Hasidim travel to Israel to fulfill the verse "The King hath brought me into his chambers" (Song 1:4); and "The Sense of Smell" ("Hush ha-reah"; 1937), with its evocation of the Song in defining

Hebrew as the language of love.[53] Even as an anthologist, when Agnon ventures to invent a nonexistent source as cover for his own commentary in *Days of Awe* (1937), he chooses to call it *Kol dodi* (the Voice of My Beloved) and adds it to the bibliography as a "manuscript in the author's possession."[54]

My introduction has relied on *Only Yesterday* (1945) and "And Solomon's Wisdom Excelled" (1950) as a springboard for spelling out the broad counters of the Agnonian aesthetic-hermeneutic project during the golden age of Israeli biblical culture. Chapter 2, "The Song of Songs as Cultural Text: From the European Enlightenment to Israeli Biblicism," provides a more extensive historical background. I consider the debt of the Zionist Song to the Enlightenment Bible—Herder in particular—and provide a detailed account of the Song's reception in Israeli art, music, dance, and scholarship. The bulk of the book—Chapter 3, "Rechnitz's Botany of Love: The Song of Seaweed," and Chapter 4, "The Biblical Ethnographies of 'Edo and Enam' and the Quest for the Ultimate Song"—revolves around two of Agnon's most remarkable and extensive metacommentaries on the Song of Songs in Israeli culture: the novella *Betrothed* (1943) and the short story "Edo and Enam" (1950). The Epilogue provides a final consideration of Agnon's exegetical imagination via "Forevermore" ("Ad olam"; 1954) as well as a brief sketch of the reception of the Song in Israeli culture from the 1950s until today.

My choice to link *Betrothed* and "Edo and Enam" is not without reason. Both are tales of love, with dreamy, lunar sequences, about scholars (Dr. Rechnitz and Dr. Ginat) who are drawn by maddened, somnambulist women (Shoshana and Gemulah).[55] Agnon, in fact, invites us to consider the interconnection between the tales via an explicit cross reference (a common feature of the Agnonian fictional world). Gamzu, the rare books seller of "Edo and Enam," describes the inscribed leaves brought back from an Enamite mountain cave by his father-in-law, Gevariah, as belonging to the same enticing sphere of the seaweed Rechnitz draws up from the bottom of Jaffa's sea in *Betrothed*: "On the way back, he opened the jar and showed me a bundle of dry leaves unlike any I had ever seen; and on them were the strange characters of a script unlike any that I knew. . . . But as I stood gazing, the colors altered before my eyes and changed into the tints of seaweeds drawn from the depths, such weeds as Dr. Rechnitz drew up from the sea near Jaffa."[56]

What interests me in these scholars' tales are the ways in which Dr. Rechnitz, the marine botanist of *Betrothed*, and Dr. Ginat, the philologist and ethnographer of the ancient culture of Enam in "Edo and Enam," are involved, almost in spite of themselves, in the investigation of scriptural texts, the

Song of Songs holding special prominence among them.[57] Whether the cryptic lines on seaweed or the glittering lines on ancient magical leaves are the object of study, each scholar unwittingly tries to reveal the hidden meanings of the ancient love poem. Rechnitz and Ginat are estranged scholars who are entirely unaware of their fascination with their own cultural heritage, and the scriptural texts that compel them are strange Bibles: wondrous weeds and magical leaves with bizarre-looking letters and scripts. But it is precisely the defamiliarization at stake that makes the ambiguities and ironies of the Zionist pursuit of the Song all the more palpable.

If in *Only Yesterday* Schimmelmann, who "speaks like a prophet and researches like a professor" (*no'em hu ke-navi ve-hoker ke-professor*) (119), borders on a caricature of a Bible critic, in *Betrothed* and "Edo and Enam," Agnon plunges into the worlds of his scholarly protagonists and reflects on the intricacies of their lives, loves, and exegetical work.[58] Although Rechnitz and Ginat are not explicitly defined as biblical scholars, their work, I set out to show, needs to be read in relation to this field of interest. More specifically, I read Rechnitz's marine botany as an inversion of biblical botany, with its special focus on the Song's plantscapes, and Ginat's study of the songs of Enam as a comment on ethnographic studies of the contemporary East in quest of the authentic, Oriental, poetic forms of the ancient love poem.

Why Agnon chooses to explore the biblical culture of Zionism through scholarly pursuits is a complex question. In part, his choice has to do with the position of scholarship as a vital national enterprise and the intellectual spearhead of Israeli literalism and secularism in the 1940s and 1950s. But, in part, Agnon's interest in the enigma of scholarship has a distinct aesthetic dimension. Being an erudite, bookish writer and an avid anthologist, his aesthetic concerns are inextricably bound up with scholarly ones.[59] Commenting on Agnon's scholarly inclinations, Scholem remarks: "Agnon was never a scholar in the sense of a person dedicated to historical and critical analysis and to the study of phenomena within a conceptual framework. Nevertheless, he has always had a penchant for scholarship, enamored as he is of the study of primary sources."[60] Scholem's sober admiration for his friend's erudition is captured in an anecdote regarding one of his first encounters with Agnon. "Even before I came to know Agnon personally, I had often seen him in the reading room of the library of the Jewish community in Berlin, where he indefatigably leafed through the card index of the Hebrew catalog. I asked him later what he sought so intently there. He answered with a guileless-ironic wide-eyedness, 'Books that I have not yet read.'"[61]

My readings of *Betrothed* and "Edo and Enam" are located in the realm of semi-hidden texts and subtexts. I follow traces of the Song and traces of the scholarly explorations of the ancient love poem. As a contemporary of Sigmund Freud, claims Nitza Ben-Dov, Agnon ventures to explore modes of indirection, the indeterminate realms of dream language, where latent texts are more voluminous than those revealed.[62] "I am as lustful for knowledge and curious as a psychoanalyst" (*sakrani te'ev da'at, mamash ke-psychoanalytican*), says Adiel Amzeh, the protagonist of "Forevermore," yet another scholar within the Agnonian academic gallery.[63] Agnon may mock psychoanalytic aspirations, but he nonetheless shares the craving to probe the oneiric, half-articulated, paradoxical realms of the mind, the lingering impact of memories, and the blurred distinctions between dreams, daydreams, and reality.

Of Freud's different writings, *The Interpretation of Dreams* has the greatest stamp here as elsewhere. Agnon, as Arnold Band points out, must have been exposed to this monumental book early in life via Viennese newspapers (available in Buczacz), which offered extensive coverage of Freud's controversial theories.[64] Later, in Jerusalem of the thirties, he became more familiar with Freudian writings. In fact, Max Eitingon, a student of Freud and the founder of the Psychoanalytic Institute in Jerusalem, was among Agnon's scholarly friends as well as the therapist of his wife, Esther (an unimaginable combination in current times).

By way of introduction to the particularities of scholarly loves and pursuits in Agnon's tales, Freud's reading of Wilhelm Jensen's *Gradiva* is of special importance. The protagonist of *Gradiva*, the archeologist Norbert Hanold, sets out to visit Pompeii in a delusional quest for Gradiva (Latin for "the girl who steps along"), a graceful female figure from an ancient Roman bas-relief who had appeared in his dreams. But, in fact, Freud writes, he travels to Pompeii to search not so much for the young woman depicted on the bas-relief, as for his forgotten childhood beloved, Zoe. "Once he had made his own childhood coincide with the classical past (which it was so easy for him to do), there was a perfect similarity between the burial of Pompeii—the disappearance of the past combined with its preservation—and repression, of which he possessed a knowledge through what might be described as 'endopyschic' perception."[65] Freud lays bare Hanold's "endopsychic," internal psychic processes, through which the young archaeologist conflates his own past with that of Pompeii, attributing to Gradiva the splendid gait of Zoe. Pompeii thus turns out to be an inscape—a perfect metaphor for the repression of a lost love and its preservation in hidden archives.

Scholarship for both Freud and Agnon is not set in an objective sphere: erotic longings and choices may unwittingly determine scholarly passions and pursuits. Both are intrigued by the psychical dramas that accompany scientific inquiries of archaic modes of life; both are interested in the fragility of knowledge where it seems to be most advanced.

But there are notable differences. Agnon is far more skeptical than Freud about the capacity of psychoanalytic tools to cure maladies. Agnon's characters lack Zoe's therapeutic capacity to step as an apparition into the shadowy world of delusions and bring their loved ones back to reason and life. No one rescues Rechnitz and Ginat from the Faustian predicament of being hopelessly lost in the realm of love.

What is more, in Agnon's tales, scholars are blind not only to the mark of Eros in their work but also to their infatuation with the greatest Song of love. Sexual repression is inextricably connected with textual repression. Rechnitz and Ginat are haunted not only by apparitions of lost loves in the old-new Land of Israel (Agnon's counterpart of Pompeii) but also by ghosts of lost scripts.

The question of textual repression leads us to another pertinent Freudian text: *Moses and Monotheism* (a book Esther Agnon received as a gift from Max Eitingon shortly after its publication in 1939). In a renowned passage in the account of the omission of the murder of Moses from biblical narrative, Freud claims:

> The distortion of a text is not unlike a murder. The difficulty lies not in the execution of the deed but in the doing away with the traces. One could wish to give the word "distortion" the double meaning to which it has a right, although it is no longer used in this sense. It should mean not only "to change the appearance of," but also "to wrench apart," "to put in another place." That is why in so many textual distortions we may count on finding the suppressed and abnegated material hidden away somewhere, though in an altered shape and torn out of its original connection. Only it is not always easy to recognize it.[66]

What Freud adds to the understanding of biblical reception is the realization that cultural transmission and cultural formation are not necessarily linear or conscious. Ambivalence may generate circuitous ways of passing on memories, traditions, and texts. Moses's teachings may have been wrenched apart and forgotten, but their traces eventually gained enough force to return from the realm of the repressed and to serve as the base for monotheism.

In turning one of the key texts of Israeli biblicism into a semi-hidden Song, Agnon, not unlike Freud, is interested in exploring what usually goes unnoticed: the ghostly routes of biblical reception, by which abnegated materials may emerge in altered form, in unexpected ways. Canonical texts acquire cultural resonance precisely because they generate both overt and covert modes of circulation. At this crossroad of texts cut loose, between the concealed and the revealed, Agnon meets, as it were, with both Freud and Scholem, conducting a different dialogue with each, forever maintaining a sense of irony with respect to both psychoanalysis and Jewish mysticism.

"I SLEEP, BUT MY HEART WAKETH"

Scholarly characters underscore the blind spots of Zionist exegesis in *Betrothed* and "Edo and Enam," but they are by no means the only ones to take part in a Song of Songs drama. I would go so far as to suggest that all the principal characters in these tales—Rechnitz, Shoshana, Ginat, Gemulah, and Gamzu—are moonstruck lovers who, as it were, bear the Song of Songs on their back, subjected to its mesmerizing cadences, incapable of decoding the ancient poem. The Song turns out to be no less maddening than the inscription "mad dog," for the verses that loom large in these tales pertain to the dream sequences of the Shulamite in Chapter 3 and Chapter 5 of the Song. In both cases, the dreaming Shulamite seeks her loved one but cannot find him; in both, she ventures to search for him in the city streets at night, where the watchmen roam about. Chapter 5, however, is the more elaborate dream sequence, where the darker, maddening qualities of love are spelled out with unparalleled verve, and as such has greater resonance in Agnon's tales.

> I sleep, but my heart waketh;
> Hark! my beloved knocketh:
> "Open to me, my sister, my love, my dove, my undefiled;
> for my head is filled with dew, my locks with the drops of the night."
> I have put off my coat; how shall I put it on?
> I have washed my feet; how shall I defile them?
> My beloved put in his hand by the hole of the door,
> and my heart was moved for him.

I rose up to open to my beloved; and my hands dropped with myrrh,
and my fingers with flowing myrrh, upon the handles of the bar.
I opened to my beloved; but my beloved had turned away, and was gone.
My soul failed me when he spoke.
I sought him, but I could not find him;
I called him, but he gave me no answer.
The watchmen that go about the city found me,
they smote me, they wounded me;
the keepers of the walls took away my mantle from me.
"I adjure you, O daughters of Jerusalem,
if ye find my beloved, what will ye tell him?
that I am love-sick." (Song 5:2–8)[67]

The memorable verse "I sleep, but my heart waketh" (*'ani yeshena ve-libbi 'er*) underscores the paradoxical experience of dreams, split as they are between passive sleep and a wakefulness that may exceed that of daytime. But it is also a reminder of love's overwhelming capacity to rouse. The verb *'ur*—to wake, rouse, arouse—is one of the key words in the Song, most conspicuous in the recurrent adjuration of the Shulamite. Time and again she warns the daughters of Jerusalem not "to stir up love until it please" (2:7, 3:5, 8:4), suggesting that love is too strong a power to arouse without caution. For once this force is set into motion it does not cease to stir, whether one is awake or asleep.

The sleeping Shulamite, whose heart is wide awake, is beckoned by her lover to rise and "open to [him]." The door is never mentioned, which is why the lover's request calls for several readings. Is the lover, whose "head is filled with dew," asking his beloved to unlock a literal door, trying to gain access to her body, or both? The Shulamite is as seductive. Although she refrains from opening up, she teasingly admits to being undressed: "I have put off my coat; how shall I put it on?" Whether or not the Shulamite actually rises to speak to her lover or dreams of doing so, we have here a daringly erotic dialogue "upon the handles of the lock" between lovers who cannot quite dismantle the barrier between them.[68] Equally removed from both the abstract ideality of Platonic love and the blatant sexuality of pagan cultures, the Song revolves around a passionate, exhilarating pursuit—not quite consummation.[69]

When the Shulamite finally seeks her lover in the city streets at night (or is it still a dream?), she cannot find him: "I sought him, but I could not find him; I called him, but he gave me no answer" (compare with Song 3:2). Her voice is the one to embody most forcefully the tumultuous intensity of yearning in the Song. "Limpid, intense, divided, quick, upright, suffering, hoping," writes Julia Kristeva in *Tales of Love*, the Shulamite is the primary speaker of love and its split, conflicting modalities.[70] The character of this nocturnal meandering becomes even more nightmarish when the keepers of the wall (rather than her lover) find the Shulamite and smite her, stripping off her veil. Their violence, however, cannot silence her. She now calls upon the daughters of Jerusalem to join her in her search: "If ye find my beloved, what will ye tell him? that I am love-sick." Of all the amorous messages that the semi-sleeping, semi-awake, Shulamite could have wished to pass on to her absent lover, the announcement of lovesickness comes first.

Shoshana and Gemulah are the most distinct somnambulist Shulamites in these two tales, but gender reversals of various sorts make clear that Rechnitz, Ginat, and Gamzu are as bewildered as the women to whom they are drawn. If Agnon's positioning of his male characters in the role of the yearning Shulamite sounds like an aberration, one should bear in mind that it is compatible with one of the inaugurating moves of his aesthetic-hermeneutic project. In "Agunot," his preliminary midrash on the pen name "Agnon," he chooses to identify with none other than the *agunah*, the forsaken wife.[71] What is more, the longings of the forsaken lovers in the tale (both Dinah and Ben Uri) are conveyed through an intricate network of allusions to the Shulamite's yearnings. Agnon's very pen name thus marks his great debt to the Song's aesthetic of yearning, the beloved's dream sequences being its most poignant expression.[72]

With their oneiric, lunar aesthetics, *Betrothed* and "Edo and Enam" intensify the disturbing, nocturnal facets of Song 5. Whether on the moonlit shore of Jaffa's sea or on the moonlit roofs of Jerusalem, Agnon's somnambulist lovers forever wander about in quest of each other. Their erotic longings are never fully realized, and their loves are not only metaphorically analogous to the antithetical experiences of illness and death: they come tantalizingly close to both.[73]

And much as these lovers cannot quite decipher the literal dimension of the Song that is inscribed on their backs, so too they have no control over its allegorical implications. Collective loves, the national yearnings to renew the ancient bond with the Land, are by no means exempt from the darker hues of amorous entanglements in the Song. They too may verge on madness and sickness; they too may be slippery dreams, whose realization remains partial, hazardous, and questionable. Agnon's deep commitment to Zionism only propelled him, with a greater sense of urgency, to hold up a critical mirror to its underlying utopian and messianic delusions.

Agnon never ceases to remind us that no one can attain mastery over the meanings of a circulating text, not even the great Solomon who composed the ancient love poem. In adopting the Song as a founding text, Zionist exegetes sought to return to the literal, springlike, pastoral scenes of "Nitsanim nir'u ba-'arets" and the enchanting, Oriental scenes of "El ginat egoz"; they sought to find in the Land of Israel a Pompeii in which the actual biblical past was kept intact. Their quest for a new uplifting secular literalism, however, could not do away with the haunting presence of the more somber verses of the ancient love poem, nor could it limit the lingering impact of traditional allegorical configurations and the formation of new national allegories.

But the gravest mistake of literalist readers of the Song, as far as Agnon is concerned, is their underlying assumption that they hold the ultimate exegetical key. The savant Saadia likened the Song of Songs to a lock whose key had been lost, applying the verse "upon the handles of the lock," with its insatiable amorous passion, to the exegetical experience of reading the ancient love poem.[74] Agnon endorses this beautiful commentary, though he explores its relevance to a modern world of exegetes who had invented keys of which Saadia could have never even dreamed.

2

The Song of Songs as Cultural Text

FROM THE EUROPEAN ENLIGHTENMENT TO ISRAELI BIBLICISM

THE Song of Songs was embraced by secular Zionism with unparalleled passion from the early twentieth century on, and yet this thriving exegetical scene has hardly been investigated. There are, to be sure, other pivotal biblical texts in Zionist culture—among them "The Binding of Isaac," Exodus, and the Book of Joshua.[1] Each one of these highlights other cultural aspects. What makes the Song's reception unique is how it touches on the intricate nexus of aesthetics and hermeneutics while allowing for a consideration of a certain history of emotions—above all, a record of the fashioning of national love. My account of the adaptations of the Song in Israeli art, music, dance, and scholarship is by no means exhaustive. I trace the distinctive nuances of this rich canvas in broad strokes, probing the interpretive trends and realms that are particularly relevant to Agnon's preoccupations.

To better understand the Zionist Song of Songs, one needs to begin with its precursors in the European Enlightenment. The eighteenth century saw the initial forging of a new literal Song by various scholars and literati, both in England and in Germany. Johann Gottfried Herder was undoubtedly the most fervent and eloquent advocate of this exegetical revolution. In his *Lieder der Liebe* of 1778—a translation of the Song and a verse-by-verse commentary—he bluntly attacks the traditional allegorical reading of the ancient love poem.[2] After centuries of distorted readings, the time had come to admit the obvious: "What then is the content? What does it treat from beginning to end? . . . *Love, love*. It is simply . . . what it is and with every word suggests: a love song."[3] The literal character of the poem, its original meaning, was repressed by Jewish and Christian exegesis, Herder protested, and concealed by mystical allegories of divine love. "I read the book and can find in it not the tiniest sign, not the smallest hint that any other meaning is . . . the purpose of the book."[4]

Herder's literalist approach is inextricably connected to an aesthetic turn in biblical exegesis. He admires the Bible's earthly love song as an exemplary code of art within the great code of art. More specifically, he regards it as a superb product of the Bible's unparalleled Oriental imagination, a text whose subtle meanings are best understood in light of the culture and customs of the Orient.[5] His *Lieder der Liebe* calls for a relishing of the literal beauty of these ancient love songs through a "sympathetic" immersion in the Song's original, Oriental realities. "It has frequently been noted," writes Hans W. Frei, "that in Herder's hands interpretation is not a technical or critical analysis of aesthetic products but an empathetic submission to the author, his depictions, and the atmosphere out of which they arise."[6] Herder's well-known guidelines for readers of the Bible in *Briefe, das Studium der Theologie betreffend* offer a succinct formulation of such *Einfühlung* (empathy/sympathy). "Become with shepherds a shepherd, with a people of the sod a man of the land, with the ancients of the Orient an Easterner, if you wish to relish these writings in the atmosphere of their origin; and be on guard especially against abstractions of dull, new academic prisons, and even more against all so-called artistry which our social circles force and press on those sacred archetypes of the most ancient days."[7] To follow the Oriental "spirit" of the Song of Songs, for Herder, means to "become with shepherds a shepherd," to draw nearer to the actual cultural and geographic setting of its composition, to enter empathetically into the convivial realms of the folk imagination that produced these admirable love songs.

Such folk poetry (*Volkslied*, or "folk song")—the true poetry of Nature—that gives voice to the living experiences of common people, claims Herder, was superior to the polished, sophisticated poetry written in Germany at that time. "The more primitive, i.e. the more vivacious and uninhibited a nation is [. . .] the more primitively, vivaciously, freely, sensually, lyrically active must its songs be, if indeed it has songs! The more removed a nation is from artificial, scholarly thinking, language and letters, the less should its songs be prepared for paper, and its dead letters used as verses."[8] Against those among his contemporaries who regarded ancient Hebrew poetry as "barbaric," replete with jarring guttural sounds, Herder hails it as a feast for the heart and for the ear. Poetry such as that of the Song is not simply to be read silently but has the power of a text that can be heard with "the ear of the soul."[9] Herder goes so far as to suggest that this ancient, primary poetry with its unmistakable aural force is precisely the kind of poetry German culture needs to emulate if it has any aspirations for revival. "If only we could first fully *explain* their poetry on the basis of their national history; and thereupon begin to translate and emulate!"[10] Entering the biblical Oriental imagination turns out to be an act both of immersion and of distancing—or rather a sympathetic identification that has the potential to lead to the formation of a new national aesthetics.

If Johann David Michaelis—a distinguished eighteenth-century German Hebraist and another prominent proponent of the literalist approach—took the Song out of his Bible, seeing in it no mark of sanctity, Herder does not doubt its canonicity. "For Herder desacralized the particular text," as Samuel Moyn suggests, "only by sacralizing the more general genre in which he included it. To put the matter briefly, for Herder it is the humanity of the entire Bible that makes it what it is; therefore, nothing special follows from the discovery of the Song's humanity."[11] To reinforce the canonical status of the Song, Herder underscores the chastity of the lovers. Rebuking other eighteenth-century readers of the Song who venture to see in it the sensuous Oriental practices of harem life, he insists on the innocence and naïveté of the Hebrew love lyrics, making them more compatible with contemporary sexual norms. Thus he addresses the commentators who find sexual innuendoes in the verse "He brought me to the banqueting house, and his banner over me was love" (Song 2:4) with an exclamatory refutation: "Oh, morality of the Orient! Oh, propriety! Oh, love! Were the Orientals acquainted with fleshly love? . . . And would a song of love, such as the one we have here, sing of such a thing? . . . The banner of love is nothing more than the image of the tree."[12] Not every Oriental scene was, apparently, worth entering in reading the Song. The very aesthetic power of the Song depended on an *Einfühlung* that would be attuned to the innocent simplicity of the biblical shepherds.

Some of Herder's followers, however, were somewhat reluctant to endorse their mentor's "cultural theology." Goethe, who also translated the Song, expresses his debt to and departure from Herder in *West-östlicher Divan*:

> I linger for a moment with the Song of Songs as the tenderest and most inimitable thing that has come down from the expression of passionate and graceful love. . . . Throughout, there blows a gentle breeze from the loveliest area of Canaan; rustic, intimate relationships, viticulture, horticulture and the growing spices, something of urban limitation, but then a royal court with all

> its magnificence in the background. Yet the main theme remains the ardent feelings of young hearts who look for, find, repel and attract each other under a host of very innocent circumstances.[13]

The first shock waves of these continental trends made their way to the intellectual circles of Jewish Enlightenment in the late eighteenth century and early nineteenth century. A whole gallery of Jewish enlightened thinkers and writers (here too primarily in Germany and England) were engaged in redefining the Bible for a Jewish audience, through and against the studies of Christian Enlightenment.[14] The first to provide a Jewish adaptation of the aesthetic Song was Moses Mendelssohn, whose annotated translation of the Bible into German written in Hebrew characters, published from 1783 over a period of several years, the *Bi'ur*, includes the ancient love poem. Mendelssohn highlighted the aesthetic features of the Song, yet he was still somewhat reluctant to endorse the literalist dimension of this new exegetical trend and insisted on maintaining a traditional allegorical framework.

It was left to Shlomo Levisohn (1789–1821) to offer a more substantive introduction to the literalist-aesthetic reading of the Song within the Jewish Enlightenment milieu. His *Melitsat yeshurun* (1816)—a blend of biblical criticism and flowery poetic discourse (*melitsah*) written in semi–Biblical Hebrew—includes extensive adaptations of the writings of Herder and Robert Lowth (the greatest advocate of the literary Bible in the English Enlightenment) on various biblical texts, the Song of Songs among them. For Levisohn, the Song revolves around the turbulent, earthly love affair of the Shulamite and her rustic lover.[15] King Solomon, who forces the Shulamite to reside in his harem, wooing her fervently, does not succeed in preventing the chaste maiden from running off to meet her lover in the fields and vineyards time and again. Spurning every royal allurement, she ignores Solomon's call for her to return to the harem—"Return, return, O Shulamite! (Song 7:1)—and remains faithful to her humble shepherd.[16]

While providing a strikingly sensuous dramatization of this triangular amorous knot, Levisohn calls upon his readers to consider the poetic grandeur of the Song. At one point, he likens the ravishing beauty of the verses to the beloved's "sweet" mouth (Song 5:16).[17] To display such poetic sweetness, he provides elaborate aesthetic explanations. In keeping with Herder's observations in *Lieder der Liebe*, Levisohn claims that the similes and metaphors of the Song may seem strange—the beloved's hair could hardly be similar to a flock of sheep—but one needs to bear in mind that the grand biblical artist draws his inspiration from the realities of Oriental pastoral life.[18] The shepherd whose sheep and fields are his entire world uses everyday experience as a source for figurative language. Envious of the shepherd, even King Solomon occasionally uses pastoral images to lure the Shulamite.[19]

Among the admirers of Levisohn was Abraham Mapu (1808–1867), one of the most renowned writers of the Hebrew Enlightenment. His *The Love of Zion* (*Ahavat Zion*; 1853), the first Hebrew novel, relies not only on Levisohn's innovative use of biblical Hebrew and *melitsah* but also on his reading of the Song.[20] Like Levisohn, Mapu spells out the beauty of the earthly love of the Song, but does so via a larger canvas with greater poetic license. The two innocent lovers, Amnon and Tamar, first meet against the backdrop of Oriental, pastoral fields of a shepherd community at the outskirts of Bethlehem (a community in conflict with the corrupt authorities of Jerusalem). Their love at first sight is rendered through an excessive pastiche of verses from the ancient love poem.

> After resting a little while, Tamar, with her maid, went to explore the fields and see the dwelling of shepherds [*mishkenot ro'im*; Song 1:8]. When she passed them in her walk, the shepherds were astonished and said to one another, "Look! The most beautiful of all the daughters of Zion!" . . .
>
> The sun poured out its light and warmth over the dwelling of the shepherds [1:8]. The streams were murmuring, the leaves rustled in the soft breeze and the birds twittered on the branches; the sheep bleated in the fields, and the combined harmony of all these sounds . . . awoke in the shepherds a mood for singing; and the fields rang with the music of the flutes and the song of the shepherds.
>
> Tamar, upon her return from her walk, was attracted by all this music, and especially by the voice and song of Amnon. . . . "Hear Macha," said Tamar to her maid, . . . "listen, if you are not deaf, and look if you are not blind!" . . .
>
> "Look, Macha, at the shepherd boy who has just finished singing. See his locks! They are as black as the raven [5:11], and his forehead how white! . . . How rosy are his cheeks [5:13] and how sweet is his voice."[21]

Mapu never set foot in Palestine. But using the Bible—and the Song in particular—as a guide, combined with the help of nineteenth-century travel books and geographic studies of the Holy Land (among them Levisohn's *Mehkarey 'erets* [*Studies of the Land*], 1819), he managed to fashion a new Song of Songs in which Zion's pastoral landscapes seem to be a concrete part of the drama.[22]

Mapu's proto-Zionist *The Love of Zion* is *the* inaugural site of the Zionist literalist approach to the Song. But simultaneously, curiously enough, it is also where the Song's reallegorization begins. What is at stake here, after all, is not only a reenactment of the Song with a literalist punch but also a modern, allegorical configuration of the Love for Zion. The Love of Zion is by no means a biblical concept. In the biblical text it is the Love of God that matters: "And thou shalt love the LORD thy God with all thine heart, and with all thy soul, and with all thy might. And these words, which I command thee this day, shall be in thine heart" (Deuteronomy 6:5–6).[23] The Promised Land is a token of God's love, not quite an object of love in its own right. Mapu, however, turns the modern configuration of national love or the love for the Land into a natural ingredient of his biblical spectacle. In doing so, he forges a new allegory of the Song, where the Love between God and his people is replaced by an allegory of the Love between the people and the Land. And yet God does not disappear from this tale. He is often evoked in the dialogues between the characters and seems to endorse this new bond behind the scenes.

Mapu thus shares Herder's perception of biblical poetry as a platform for the fashioning of a new national aesthetics—he simply takes it a step further. Herder never tried to spell out the contours of a potential national adaptation of the Song, nor did he plunge into the realm of national allegories, but his Zionist followers surely did. The cultural translation of Herder, however, entailed revising the definition of the Bible's Oriental bent. Already in Herder's writings on the Bible, one can trace a critique of the derogatory configurations of the Jews as Easterners (as in his redefinition of the guttural sounds of Hebrew). But from a Zionist perspective, the reassessment of the Orient was all the more urgent and indispensable. The very possibility of national renaissance depended on it. The Orient, for Zionists, was not merely an exotic distant land but rather a mystery that included their own as Jews who were returning to the region of their biblical ancestors.[24]

ZIONIST ART: LANDSCAPES OF LOVE

With the rise of Zionism as a political movement, the tendency to literalize the Song as a backdrop to national awakening became a paramount interpretive move. Zionist exegetes in the early twentieth century did not necessarily read Herder (though many did), but they all read Mapu. The impact of Mapu's novel as a founding text in the Zionist history of emotions cannot be overestimated. Ben-Gurion is exemplary: in his memoirs, he mentions *Uncle Tom's Cabin* and *The Love of Zion* as the two books that greatly influenced him in his youth—the former "kindled his loathing for slavery and bondage; the latter had breathed life into biblical tales, sharpening his yearning for Zion."[25]

As a marked aesthetic touchstone, the Song had particular appeal in the realm of the arts in early Zionist culture. The Bezalel School of Arts and Crafts, founded by Boris Schatz in Jerusalem in 1906, played a major role in endowing the Bible with a distinctly Zionist look. One of the founding artists of Bezalel, the Art Nouveau illustrator Ephraim Moses Lilien (1874–1925), went so far as to give the angel in the illustration of the Garden of Eden in his 1908 edition of the Bible Theodor Herzl's distinctive features. And if this were not enough, only a long sword, held forcefully in front of the body, covers the angelic Herzl's muscular nudity. Richard I. Cohen defines this exegetical provocation as characteristic of Lilien's "secular imagination" and indicative of his sense of "artistic license to mold the Bible within his own ideological framework."[26] Herzl crops up in other scenes of Lilien's Bible as well—most notably as Moses, just before the breaking of the tablets. In the visionary Moses, Lilien seems to have found a precursor to Herzl's iconoclastic attempt to reinvent Judaism and fashion a new Jew.[27]

The Song of Songs was among the biblical texts Lilien chose to illustrate. Consider his drawing of the Shulamite as a shepherdess, with an Oriental robe and veil, holding a lamb in her hands (see fig. 2.1). This image could have served as an illustration in Mapu's *The Love of Zion* as well.

The pastoral simplicity and the palm trees in the background are common themes in Orientalist visual renditions of Holy Land landscapes. The Shulamite's innocence is underscored by the dreamy gaze in her dark eyes and the white lamb that she holds with great tenderness in her arms. Herzl does not appear in person as a shepherd beside her. But the petals of the lilies (a flower associated with the beloved in Song 2:1) are shaped as Stars of David—the symbol Herzl turned into a Zionist emblem already in the first congress.[28]

There is a curious mixture of triumphal literalism and a purposeful invention of a Zionist allegory in Lilien's Song. Allegories seem to grow with and through the literal flowers of the Song. The allegorical bent of Lilien's exegetical line is all the more apparent in an earlier piece: the cover illustration for the Zionist journal *Ost und West* (Berlin, October 1904) (see fig. 2.2). Holding the Rose of Jericho in her hands, the female figure at the center is a cross between the Shulamite—as a rose "among thorns" (2.1)—and the Daughter of

Figure 2.1: Ephraim Moses Lilien (Galician, 1874–1925). Illustration from the Song of Songs, in *Die Bücher der Bibel*, 1909. Engraving. Israel Museum, Jerusalem.

Zion, or Bat-Zion. The exegetical history of the Rose of Jericho is a circuitous one. Initially, the flower was a symbol of resurrection for Christian pilgrims in the Holy Land, who marveled at the magical qualities of the dry desert plant: on receiving a few drops of water (even after many years), its entangled knots open up and the ball-like seeds leap forth (the magic is indebted to its sophisticated propagation apparatus). In Zionist hands—Lilien is paradigmatic—the Song's beloved/Bat-Zion replaces Mary, and the Rose of Jericho becomes an emblem of Jewish national revival against all odds.[29]

Figure 2.2: The Daughter of Zion holding the Rose of Jericho. Ephraim Moses Lilien (Galician, 1874–1925). Cover illustration for *Ost und West*, Berlin, 1904.

The Daughter of Zion is a well-known allegorical configuration of the nation, from the biblical text onward. But, interestingly enough, here—as in the Song illustration of the 1906 Bible—Lilien's formation of Zionist allegories is no less indebted to Christian allegories (the roses, much like the lilies, are flowers of Mary, not to mention the white lamb). Note that the *Ost und West* drawing sets a dichotomy between the circular, barbwire-like thorn thicket as

Figure 2.3: Ze'ev Raban (Polish-born Israeli, 1890–1970). *I Am the Rose of the Sharon*, illustration from Song of Songs, 1923. Watercolor on paper, 12 × 17 cm. Collection of the Israel Museum, Jerusalem. © Estate of the artist.

a symbol of exile and the desert bud destined to flower like the Song's rose as a symbol of the new Zionist paradise—a dichotomy that will be further developed in Lilien's renowned *Allegorical Wedding* (1906).

The most elaborate visual interpretation of the Song in the Bezalel School of Arts and Crafts was provided by Ze'ev Raban (1890–1970) in an illuminated edition of the Song of Songs, published in 1922. In Raban's captivating illustrations of the Song, the lovers are positioned in highly sensuous scenes against the backdrop of Oriental settings (both pastoral and urban), and the Shulamite oscillates between being covered, semi-bare, and bare (see fig. 2.3). Raban's Oriental Shulamite is not as chaste as Herder's image of the biblical beloved, but she is not quite a harem girl either: she is somehow innocent and voluptuous at once.

The Zionist-Symbolist dimension of Raban's rendition of the ancient love poem acquires another twist in the poster he designed circa 1929 for the Society for the Promotion of Travel in the Holy Land, titled *Come to Palestine* (today it forms part of the permanent collection of modern Israeli art in the Israel Museum; see fig. 2.4).[30] The poster provides a colorful visual interpretation of the renowned verses of Song 2:11–12 that are inscribed as its base: "For, lo, the winter is past, the rain is over and gone; the flowers appear on the earth; the time of the singing of birds is come, and the voice of the turtle is heard in our land." Coming to Palestine, the poster seems to promise, entails a plunge into the glittering love scenes of the Song of Songs. The viewers are invited, as it were, to enter the golden Oriental gate that frames these amorous sights, to enter the Zionist spring, and to join the pastoral world of the shepherd and shepherdess who tend their flock in the green hills above the Sea of Galilee and Tiberias. The utopian dimension of this blissful scene as a resurrection of biblical times is reinforced by the two roundels on the golden gate: the Dome of the Rock (the site of the Temple) on the left and the Tower of David on the right.[31]

The Haggadot of the kibbutzim are another important source of Song of Songs images. Although the kibbutz was the most adamant outpost of secular Zionism, the Passover ceremony was a central cultural event in kibbutz life. No community has taken the reinterpretation of the traditional Haggadah more seriously than the kibbutz movement, which by 1965 produced an estimated seven hundred different versions.[32] While the Song of Songs is read in synagogues as part of the liturgy on Shabbat Hol Hamo'ed during Passover, it is seldom included in traditional Haggadot or in the Seder ceremony. By contrast, in the Haggadot of the kibbutzim it acquired unprecedented visibility. Selected verses—primarily those celebrating springtime—were quoted in the format of songs. For the kibbutzniks, who construed their own project as a renewal of the literal, agricultural life of biblical times, Passover was both a commemoration of national liberation and a holiday of spring (*hag 'aviv*).[33] The Song's vivid depictions of spring were seen as vital to retrieving the precious, lost natural ambience of the holiday.

Figure 2.4: Ze'ev Raban (Polish-born Israeli, 1890–1970). *Come to Palestine*, 1929, poster for the Society for the Promotion of Travel in the Holy Land. Lithograph, 99 × 63.5 cm. Collection of the Israel Museum, Jerusalem. Photograph © Israel Museum, Jerusalem, by Elie Posner. © Estate of the artist.

In the illustrations that accompany the quotations from the Song, one finds numerous drawings of blossoming flowers and fields of all sorts. The theme of spring was salient even in Bezalel art, but in the context of the kibbutz and its rituals it became all the more prominent. The most dominant aesthetic lines in this artistic corpus were those of socialist and naive art. Consider the image of the worker in the Haggadah of Kibbutz Ein Gev from the 1950s, whose right hand leans on the hillside as his left hand welcomes the rising spring sun, peeping from beyond the hills behind the houses and fields of the kibbutz, in a gesture commonly employed in Soviet posters (see fig. 2.5).

In highlighting the Song in their Haggadot, the kibbutz artists wholeheartedly endorsed Zionist literalism—and were among its most ardent proponents—but here too one can discern an allegorical streak. "Allegory" and "symbolism" are not quite part of the vocabulary of kibbutz art, as it is the case with Bezalelian art, but allegorical configurations hover in the background. Images of spring in the kibbutz Haggadot connote a Zionist renaissance—only within this context, it is more of a revolutionary spring, bearing the stamp of socialist ideals, than an Oriental one.

Figure 2.5: Anonymous Israeli artist. *I Am My Beloved's, and My Beloved Is Mine*. Haggadah from Kibbutz Ein Gev, ca. 1950. © Archives of Yad Tabenkin.

Such yoking of landscapes of spring to national life in readings of the Song, one should bear in mind, is nowhere to be found in the biblical love poem itself. When the lovers depict their natural surrounding or liken each other to flowers and trees, they are absorbed in a world set apart from any national event or concern whatsoever. "Only in the Song of Songs," writes Robert Alter, "is the writer's art directed to the imaginative realization of a world of uninhibited self-delighting play, without moral conflict, without the urgent context of history and nationhood and destiny, without the looming perspectives of a theological world-view."[34] The lovers' admiration of spring is an admiration of its beauty and its potential to serve as a mirror to their own metaphorical blossoming as humans, ripe for the act of love. Scenes of spring are both the literal settings within which the lovers meet and a favorite figurative component of their mutual courting. The intricacies of this discourse of love are worthy of a closer reading.

> Rise up, my love, my fair one, and come away.
> For, lo, the winter is past, the rain is over and gone;
> The flowers appear on the earth;
> the time of singing is come,
> and the voice of the turtle is heard in our land;
> The fig-tree putteth forth her green figs,
> and the vines in blossom give forth their fragrance.
> Arise, my love, my fair one, and come away. (Song 2:10–13)

The *dod*, the lover, calls upon his beloved to "rise up" (*kumi*) (another variation on the theme of "rousing" or "awakening" that we witnessed in Song 5) and rush outdoors, into the world of spring. The lover does not explicitly lure the Shulamite to an amorous encounter, but the blossoming fields and vineyards, with their intoxicating welding of sights, sounds, and fragrances, serve as an indirect seductive invitation to search for love while exploring the wonders of springtime.[35]

This double entendre is spelled out boldly by the Shulamite, who at a later point of the Song declares:

> Come, my beloved, let us go forth into the field;
> let us lodge in the villages.
> Let us get up early to the vineyards;
> let us see whether the vine hath budded,

whether the vine-blossom be opened,
and the pomegranates be in flower;
there will I give thee my love.
The mandrakes give forth fragrance,
and at our doors are all manner of precious fruits, new and old,
which I have laid up for thee, O my beloved. (7:12–14)

With the same kind of urgency that characterized her lover, the Shulamite too calls for a leap into spring life. But she ventures to make it ostensibly clear that to go forth into the vineyards and check whether the first buds of the vine blossom (*semadar*) or those of the pomegranate have opened up is a sign, or almost a lover's code, for the time of love: "there will I give thee my love." And yet it is not quite consummation but intense erotic yearning or daring fantasies that lie at the heart of the ancient love poem. Even when the Shulamite invites her lover to spend the night in the vineyards, her offer is set in the future (in something of a subjunctive mode) and verges on a dream of wish fulfillment.

In projecting the nation onto these intimate, dreamy landscapes of love, Zionist artists first quite wittingly and then mostly unwittingly (depending on background) followed in the footsteps of their precursors. If traditional exegetes superimpose God and the Nation on the ancient love poem—perceiving the *dod* as God and the Shulamite as Knesset Yisrael—Zionist exegetes ironically follow in their footsteps at least insofar as they add a national spirit to these scenes of amorous spring. What the nation meant for traditional exegetes was surely different from the modern nationalism underlying Zionist art, but nonetheless in both cases there is a similar reliance on the Song in the construction of collective loves.

MUSIC AND DANCE: SOUNDSCAPES OF LOVE

Nowhere was the adoption of the Song in the Israeli context more passionate and widespread than in the realm of music. Here too kibbutz culture had a decisive role. In the Haggadot of the kibbutzim one often finds instructions for the choir and handwritten notes of the *va'adat tarbut* (committee of cultural events) regarding the select musical adaptations of verses of the Song that need to be sung at different points of the ceremony (see fig. 2.6). There were in fact several kibbutzniks who composed some of the most resonant of these musical renditions. Matityahu Shelem (1904–1975), from Kibbutz

Ramat Yohanan, composed a series of spring songs—based on Song 2:11–12—such as "Pana ha-geshem" ("The Rain Is Over and Gone"; 1943) and "Hine ha-stav 'avar" ("For Lo, the Winter Is Past"; 1945–47).[36] Being a shepherd (his primary occupation in Ramat Yohanan), Shelem was particularly intrigued by the ways in which the Song captured the nuances of pastoral life in springtime. In a short essay, "Al shir ha-shirim" ("On the Song of Songs"), he singles out the unique expression *ha-ro'e ba-shoshanim* ("feedth/browses among the [roses]"—2:16; note that *ha-ro'e* means both "feedth/bowses" and "shepherd") and the ways in which it captures the elating experience of roaming about in the midst of blooming, pastoral turfs.[37] Indeed, some of his tunes set out to underscore the charm of the realities of shepherd life in the ancient love poem, among them "Samuni notera" ("They Made Me Keeper"), a musical adaptation of 1:6–8: "'[T]hey made me keeper of the vineyards; but mine own vineyard have I not kept.' Tell me, O thou whom my soul loveth, where thou feedest, where thou makest thy flock to rest at noon. . . ? If thou know not, O thou fairest among women, go thy way forth by the footsteps of the flock and

Figure 2.6: David Elef (Israeli). *Go Thy Way Forth in the Footsteps of the Flock.* Haggadah from Kibbutz Ayelet HaShahar, 1952. © Archives of Yad Tabenkin.

feed thy kids, beside the shepherds' tents." Already in Herder's *Lieder der Liebe* and in Mapu's *The Love of Zion* there were detailed accounts of the customs and songs of shepherd communities, but for Shelem, this was not merely a remote, glamorous scene but rather part and parcel of his daily routine. He literally becomes—to evoke Herder's words—"a shepherd with shepherds."

Nahum (Nahche) Heiman (b. 1934) was privileged to have Shelem as his mentor not only in the kibbutz pasture (where he worked in his teens) but also in the domain of music. Heiman composed one of the most popular Israeli spring songs of all times: "Nitsanim nir'u ba'arets" ("The Flowers Appear on the Earth"—Song 2:12; 1951). The anecdote regarding the moment of its composition, which Heiman jovially recounts in a rather recent interview, is telling.[38] Given his musical talent, Heiman gradually worked less as a shepherd and more as an accordionist, accompanying folk dance classes. During one of these sessions, the seventeen-year-old Heiman was carried away by his improvisations, incurring the wrath of the dance teacher. Infuriated by her demands, he dashed into an adjacent room where there was a Bible on the table, apparently left by members of the kibbutz Bible reading group. He opened the Bible, and his eyes "landed" upon the verse "Nitsanim nir'u ba'arets." Within a few minutes, Heiman claims, he turned the song written by his hero, King Solomon—the wise and "gigantic poet" (*meshorer 'anaki*) of biblical times—into a musical hit. Although Heiman depicts the discovery of the verse in the Bible as a sudden revelation, he was in fact following Shelem's exegetical preferences, though with a more upbeat version of Song 2:12.

Heiman's anecdote has its unique attributes, but it is also representative of Israeli culture's obsession with the Bible as a whole and the Song in particular. To begin with, it would not have happened had there not been a *hug tanakh*, a Bible reading group, in the cultural center of the kibbutz. What is more, the immediacy with which a rebellious, secular teenager would seek inspiration in the Bible, regarding it as his own, is characteristic of an entire generation. Solomon in this tale becomes a "cool" partner for whimsical musical experiments—but this is not the Solomon of Proverbs but rather the Solomon who wrote love songs and could capture the utter delight and freshness of springtime. In the tunes of Heiman, as in those of Shelem, one can also trace the echoes of shepherd songs and folk dance music of Eastern European traditions, as well as rhythms reminiscent of the *debka* (the traditional Arab folk dance).

Not only kibbutzniks sang "Pana ha-geshem" or "Nitsanim nir'u ba'arets" and danced to their tunes at the Seder ceremony and beyond. These songs became part and parcel of Israeli culture as a whole and formed part of an ever-growing body of musical adaptations of the Song. Between the 1930s and the 1950s, at least one hundred different musical adaptations of verses of the Song were composed (see the Appendix), not to mention songs such as "Erev shel shoshanim" ("An Evening of Roses") with more diffused echoes of the ancient love poem. The resonance of this exegetical scene is not only quantitative. Within this corpus one finds a whole array of Israeli classics, of songs that were among the most prevalent in "evenings of singing" (*'arvey shira*) and gatherings of folk dance.

Until the late 1950s, one of the major trends in musical interpretations of the Song was Orientalist. Oriental themes formed part of the music of Shelem and Heiman but were far more pronounced in renditions of the verse "I am black, but comely" (1:5), such as "Sheharhoret" ("Black One") or "Shehora 'ani ve-nava" ("I Am Black, but Comely").[39] Interestingly, some of the most well-known adaptations in this connection were written by Ashkenazi composers and sung by Yemenite female singers. Thus the music for "Ma dodekh mi-dod" ("What Is Thy Beloved More than Another Beloved"; 1943) and "Dodi yarad le-gano" ("My Beloved Is Gone Down into His Garden"; 1950) was composed by Moshe Vilenski and sung by Shoshana Damari, and that of "Pithi-li ahoti ra'ayati" ("Open to Me My Sister, My Love"; 1943) was composed by Nahum Nardi and sung by Chana Aharoni. The tunes were construed as Yemenite but in fact entailed hybrid blends of Eastern and Western patterns.[40]

Among the most phenomenal contributors to the invention of the Zionist Oriental soundscape of the Song was the choreographer and composer Sara Levi-Tanai (1911–2005). Levi-Tanai was born to a Yemenite family in Jerusalem, but after her mother's death she was sent to the predominantly Ashkenazi orphanage of Me'ir Shfeya.[41] She began her career as a composer while working as a teacher—first in Tel Aviv and later in Kibbutz Ramat HaKovesh. Songs were needed for the various kibbutz ceremonies, and she ventured to present her own work. In Passover of 1944, she directed a multimedia production of the Song of Songs (*masekhet shir ha-shirim*) in Ramat HaKovesh. It included a whole cycle of her musical adaptation of verses from the ancient love poem, among them the highly acclaimed "El ginat egoz" ("Into the Garden of Nuts"—6:11) and "Kol dodi" ("Hark! My Beloved"—2:8).[42] The songs were accompanied by dances that soon became foundational in the burgeoning realm of Israeli folk dance.[43] In fact, "El ginat egoz" with its "Yemenite step," is the most popular Israeli folk dance after the *hora* until today. The success of Levi-Tanai's Song of Songs project was such that she was invited to work on a production of the Book of Ruth (the other most Orientalized biblical text) for a Shavu'ot ceremony in Kibbutz Mishmar HaSharon. Levi-Tanai was Yemenite, but here too—given her oscillation between the Mizrahi and Ashkenazi worlds—Eastern and Western musical traditions mingled freely. Even "El ginat egoz"—the hallmark of her oeuvre—is not quite a Yemenite tune. It was received as such and became more palpably so in later arrangements of Levi-Tanai, or when sung by Yemenite singers such as Chana Aharoni.

Already in the late 1920s, while studying at the Levinsky Seminar for Teachers, Levi-Tanai was drawn to Yemenite culture and sought contact with the young singers of the Yemenite neighborhood of Tel Aviv, Kerem ha-teymanim ("Tse'irey ha-kerem," the "Kerem's Youngsters"), but her major exposure to Yemenite heritage took place only in 1949, through the encounter with the Yemenite *'olim* (immigrants) of the Magic Carpet Operation. She became infatuated with the music and dance world of the newcomers and engaged in studying their particular features. During that very year, Levi-Tanai founded the Inbal Dance Theater with dancers whom she selected from the new Yemenite community. Initially, the press regarded Inbal's work as staged folklore, but gradually Levi-Tanai's originality and intricate reshaping of Yemenite folk dances via a modern vocabulary (the "Inbal language") was acknowledged—all the more so once leading choreographers such as Jerome Robbins (the choreographer of *West Side Story*) and Anna Sokolow extolled this project.[44]

Throughout her career, Levi-Tanai regarded the Bible as a major source of inspiration. She upheld the "powerful language" (*leshono ha-'aza*) of the ancient text, "its unique rhythms, beating like distant drums, carried by an Eastern wind (*ruah kadim*), crushing, arousing, and paralyzing!"[45] The dancing Shulamite, however, was a primary model for her. "Is it not the eternal Shulamit, who crazes us in the dance of Mahanaim?" she asks while alluding to Song 7:1.[46] In particular, the Song was the source of inspiration for many of Inbal's shepherd dances (see fig. 2.7). "Be-'ikvey ha-tson" ("In the Footsteps of the Flock"; 1950), whose title is taken from Song 1:8, is one such dance. Note that the music for this piece was a coproduction of Levi-Tanai and Matityahu Shelem (whose interest in Song 1:8, as one recalls, begins with "Samuni notera").[47]

In all realms of Zionist art, music, and, above all, dance—the endorsement of the literal dimension of the Song meant greater emphasis on the body. Daniel Boyarin has taught us much about the Zionist disdain vis-à-vis the "unheroic" body of the Diaspora Jew and the attempt to construct a new model of "muscular Judaism," in Max Nordau's terms. Lilien's image of Moses as a

Figure 2.7: Photograph of the *Shepherds*, choreography by Sara Levi-Tanai, the Inbal Dance Theater, 1951. © Inbal Dance Theater.

muscular, virile Herzl is one of his primary examples.[48] Within the context of the reception of the Song, the break with the Diaspora body was less muscular and more sensual. The Song was a founding text for imagining a new erotic freedom in the Orient, for defining the liberation of the senses from stifling European norms.

James Joyce must have been aware of the prominent erotic role of the Song in the Zionist imagination. Bloom, the protagonist of *Ulysses* (1914), finds an ad for the Zionist Agendath Netaim in the newspaper in which the meat he buys is wrapped. Its images and rhythms seep into his thoughts throughout the day and even more so at night, in his exchange with the seductive Zoe. Bloom is swept away in an associative stream of Song of Songs fantasies: "*Gazelles are leaping, feeding on the mountains. Near are lakes. Round their shores file shadows black of cedargroves. Aroma rises, a strong hairgrowth of resin. It burns, the orient, a sky of sapphire, cleft by the bronze flight of eagles.*" In turn, Zoe responds: "*Schorach ani wenowach, benoith Hierushaloim*"—Joyce's transliteration of the Hebrew words for "I am black, but comely, O daughters of Jerusalem" (Song 1:5) in a mistaken Ashkenazi accent.[49] Joyce lays bare the ways in which the Song introduces an oneiric-erotic dimension into Zionist visions as it blends with other sexual fantasies regarding the "burning" Orient and its luscious, dark women.

The representation of the Song's eroticism, however, varied. In Raban's illustrations, as we have seen, the Shulamite is voluptuous and innocent at once. Such unabashed sensuality, though not as promiscuous as Joyce would have it, was unacceptable within the framework of the kibbutz culture and beyond. In early Zionism, as David Biale puts it, "doctrines of 'free love' and 'puritanism' coexisted in a peculiar dialectic, similar in many ways to the status of sexuality in the Soviet Union after the Bolshevik Revolution. In the Zionist case, the tension between sexual liberation and asceticism channeled erotic energies into the tasks of nation building."[50] This tension is particularly evident in the lively folk dance scene of the 1940s and 1950s. Gender divisions were abolished (both in the Hasidic world and in Mizrahi contexts, men and women danced separately), and the dancing of "El ginat egoz" and "Nitsanim nir'u ba'arets" was conducted with sheer sensuous pleasure on the kibbutz lawns or in city squares. However, these were group dances—not quite a couple's tango—and as such took part in creating a sense of communal eros.

The body held a far more crucial role in traditional exegesis of the Song (especially in mystical commentaries) than Zionists would have imagined; however, it was primarily recruited on behalf of divine love. In early Zionist exegesis, a reverse phenomenon may be discerned. The body was the cherished site par excellence, but its role in enhancing literalism did not preclude its contribution to the formation of national allegories and the definition of a new contact with the Land.

I emphasized the role of the Song in collective settings, but the individualistic perspective did not dissolve. The great resonance of the Song was, in a sense, due to its potential to serve both as a very personal, aesthetic touchstone and as a base for a national one. This is evident in the work of Lilien, Raban, Shelem, Heiman, and Levi-Tanai but has special relevance within the lyrical realm of modern Hebrew poetry. Poetry is another important artistic medium of the Israeli Song, but it remains beyond the scope of my historical account, being far too vast and variegated a field to cover within my limited canvas. Suffice it to say that there was hardly a modern Hebrew poet between the 1920s and the 1950s who did not evoke echoes of the Song in his or her oeuvre. To mention but a few examples: David Fogel's "Bintot ha-yom" ("At the End of Day"; 1923), Shaul Tschernichovky's "Ve-haya be-heshkhat ha-'erev" ("In the Darkness of Night") Rachel Blustein's *Gan na'ul* ("Locked Garden"; 1928) and "Be-gani neta'atikha" ("I Have Planted You in My Garden"; 1929), and Leah Goldberg's "Mahar" ("Tomorrow"; 1949) and "Ha-'ohavim 'al sefat ha-yam" ("The Lovers on the Beach"; 1955).[51] It is also noteworthy that some of the poetic renditions of the Song were set to music and became an important component of the text's musical reception. Hayim Nahman Bialik's "Yesh li gan" ("I Have a Garden"; 1907) is exemplary.[52] Most peculiarly, its melody is one of the quintessential Oriental melodies of this corpus given that it is based on a Syrian folk song (arrangement by Vilenski; sung by Shoshana Damari and Bracha Zefira).

SCHOLARSHIP: THE BIBLICAL BOTANY OF EPHRAIM HAREUVENI

Within the Israeli context, as in the European Enlightenment, the Song held a special place in scholarly inquiry as well. This scholarly endeavor did not have the same kind of cultural impact as did the exegetical scenes in the realms of art, music, and dance. Nonetheless, it provided illuminating formulations of the underlying presuppositions of the Israeli Song and had substantive resonance beyond academic circles. In fact, there were intriguing interrelations between the academic and artistic interpretive spheres between the 1920s and 1950s. To follow the history of the reception of biblical texts requires precisely such attention to the ways in which diverse cultural realms may be engaged in cross-exegetical exchanges.

The two Hebrew University scholars whose work, I believe, serves as a subtext of sorts in Agnon's *Betrothed* and "Edo and Enam" are the botanist Ephraim Hareuveni and the historian, ethnographer, and biblical critic Shlomo Dov Goitein.[53] In keeping with Agnon's preferences, I will devote substantive attention to these scholars. Instead of mapping out trends, I provide detailed vignettes of the lives and work of Hareuveni and Goitein, taking into account the ways in which their respective inquiries regarding the ancient love poem are set within a broader involvement in Israeli biblicism.

What makes these scholars all the more fascinating is the fact that while they were among the most influential scholarly advocates of the Bible as national epos in the Zionist context, their approach was by no means typical. For both, the obsession with the Bible did not rule out a great interest in postbiblical Jewish sources—from the Talmud onward; both were observant and yet immersed in secular culture; both were Orientalists who were close in their political opinions to Brit Shalom; both were scholars whose biblical research entailed a preoccupation with aesthetic questions.[54]

I begin with Ephraim Hareuveni (Rubinovitch) and biblical botany. Like any other branch of Israeli biblicism, Zionist biblical botany has its beginnings in the European Enlightenment Bible. For Enlightenment scholars such as Frederick Hasselquist, Carsten Niebuhr, and Johann David Michaelis, the objective was, as Sheehan points out, to provide a natural history of Palestine that would not be distorted by missionary prejudices and theological concerns.[55] While travelers and pilgrims in the sixteenth and seventeenth centuries noted plant life in the Holy Land as part of their religious experience, expeditions to the Orient during the Enlightenment sought to introduce scientific methods to the one land that seemed to lie beyond the realms of science. The purpose of this post-theological move was not quite to debunk the Bible but rather to come closer to the literal dimension of scriptural truths via a better understanding of the geography, customs, and natural history of the region. Such scientific investigations were expanded in the nineteenth century and early twentieth century by scholars such as Edmond Boissier (1810–1885) and G. H. Dalman (1855–1941), the founder of the Jerusalem Research Institute of the Holy Land (Das Deutsche Evangelische Institut für Altertumswissenschaft), who conducted numerous studies in botany, zoology, and local customs.

When Zionist botanists entered the realm of *Flora Palestina*, they regarded themselves as having a familiarity with Oriental plant life and plant lore not available to previous scholars, who had not resided in the region. Botany was, as Ariel Hirschfeld puts it, one of the "loudest mouthpieces" of Zionism, a mode of establishing a sense of belonging to the natural habitats of the Land and to their biblical underpinning.[56] If the artists of Bezalel sought to define their bond with the Land via plantscapes and kibbutzniks through agricultural work and shepherding, Zionist botanists aspired to do so through scholarly expeditions and herbarium sheets.

Ephraim Hareuveni (Rubinovitch) was one of the most passionate botanists of early Zionism. As the son of a progressive Ukrainian rabbi, Hareuveni received a general education alongside the study of Bible and Talmud. He first came to Palestine in 1906 and taught science in the high schools of some of the *moshavot* of the Second Aliyah. Between 1909 and 1914, he completed his doctorate in natural science in the universities of Lausanne and Prague, after which he returned to Palestine and became a high school teacher and a researcher. Hareuveni's botanical studies combined the two great loves of his life, "the world of flora and the world of Torah," entailing a unique interdisciplinary approach in its mixture of natural science, Bible, Talmud, philology, history, and Arab plant lore.[57] Strictly speaking, Hareuveni's botany was not merely biblical, given that the Talmud was very much part of the project. But he regarded Talmudic texts as an extension of biblical culture and at times as exegetical keys to the identification of biblical plants.

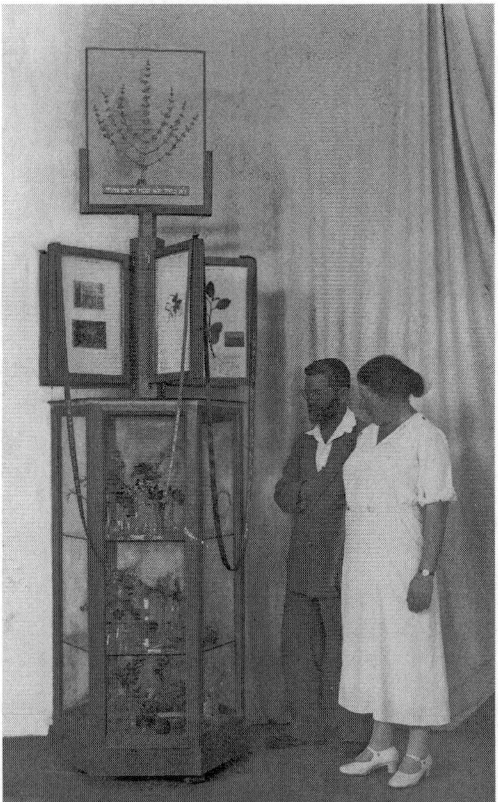

Figure 2.8: Ephraim and Hannah Hareuveni standing by a showcase of the Museum of Biblical Botany displayed at the Levant Fair, Tel Aviv, early 1930s. Neot Kedumim Archive.

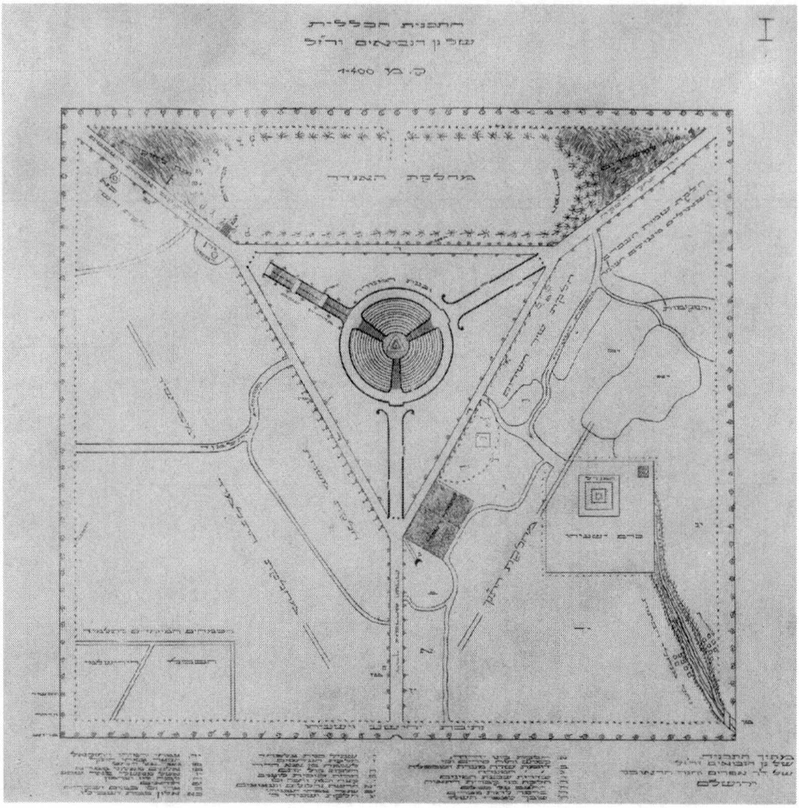

Figure 2.9: “Plan for the Garden of the Prophets and Sages,” 1927. Neot Kedumim Archive.

Although Ephraim was the spokesperson, Hannah, his wife and partner, was no less involved in the different botanical explorations, having a background in agriculture, much experience in inventing Hebrew names for local plants, and a great passion for hiking.[58] One of the couple’s primary objectives was to found a botanical museum. Initially, the Hareuvenis set up a small museum in their own apartment in Shkhunat HaBucharim in Jerusalem, where they developed a unique method for embalming plants (the secret of their preservation technique was never disclosed). Shortly after the foundation of the Hebrew University, in 1926, they transferred their collection to Mount Scopus and became the directors of the Museum of Biblical and Talmudic Botany and of Arab Plant-Lore (see fig. 2.8).[59]

More ambitious than the museum were their plans for the Garden of the Prophets and Sages, described in detail in an article published in *Hatoren* in

November 1924 (see fig. 2.9).[60] Organized according to textual and thematic criteria, the garden was to include sections such as "The Song of Songs," "The Vineyard of Isaiah," "The World of the Talmud," and even "Exegetical Disputes." At the center of the garden, the Hareuvenis intended to place a botanical menorah—the *marvah*—a local flower whose shape, they argued, was the model for the Temple artists. The garden as a whole was envisioned as a Third Temple of sorts—opposite the site of the original one—where the prophets and the sages could meet their returning descendants, where (in no less of a utopian flavor) literary critics, historians, archeologists, and philologists could leisurely converse with artists and poets. What is more, it was meant to serve as an emblem of peace in its insistence on the deep "spiritual cords" between Jewish and Arab plant lore.

The Hareuvenis were avid shapers of the new Zionist literalism. Their garden was to be a distinct embodiment of the sensual realities of ancient times. "We may not be capable of hearing the words of the prophets," they write, "but we can see what they saw, smell what they smelled, and listen to the murmur of the plants they listened to, approaching, in this manner, their lofty ideas and feelings as well as their ties with the world of vegetation and creation."[61] They defined the plants as "memory plants" (*tsimhey zikaron*), as "living witnesses" (*'edey hayim*), capable of passing on in full precious scenes of biblical and postbiblical plant life.[62] And yet this passionate quest for the literal did not hinder their interest in symbolic configurations, so much so that one of the sections in the garden was called "Symbols." Within the framework of the Hareuvenis' botanical exegesis, symbols were organic constructs, in which the material plant and its spiritual bearing were one. "Every plant is covered with a robe, embroidered by the prophets and the people from the very core of their soul."[63] With symbols growing from the earth—reminiscent of Lilien's Magen David lilies—the leap to allegorical configurations of national renewal via botany seemed to entail no departure from the literalism they cherished.

The Hebrew University's support of these projects gradually diminished. For botanists who wanted to adhere to "pure botany," Ephraim Hareuveni's approach was too close to Jewish Studies and deficient in scientific rigor.[64] The museum remained, but the blueprint for the garden was never endorsed. Instead of supporting the Garden of the Prophets and Sages, the university ended up allocating funds for constructing the botanical garden of Otto Warburg and Alexander Eig, the heads of the Botany department. Inaugurated in 1931, this new botanical garden on Mount Scopus (a botanical gem till this very day) was dedicated to the indigenous vegetation of "Palestine and its surroundings" and was organized according to an ecological-phytosocial concept (the principal plant communities were represented as they appear in their natural geographic regions).[65] That year, alongside the inauguration of this garden, Alexander Eig, Michael Zohary, and Naomi Feinbrun published their monumental tome, *The Plants of Palestine*. If more subtly, Warburg, Eig, Feinbrun, and Zohary were, to be sure, also part of the Zionist initiative of becoming acculturated in the region via the knowledge of Palestine's vegetation.[66]

In the nonacademic cultural arena, however, the enterprise of Ephraim and Hannah Hareuveni found an ever-growing number of notable supporters. Bialik's enthusiastic letter, following his visit to the museum in 1932, captures the appeal of such biblical botany to Zionist thinkers and writers (see fig. 2.10).[67]

> My dear sirs,
> My visit to the plants collection—the fruit of your hands—in the museum at the Hebrew University of Jerusalem, gave me great pleasure. I am not an expert in the matter, but my heart tells me that the path you have chosen is the true one. You approach our plants not as foreigners and lodgers, but as *relatives* and old friends who have been separated from their heart's beloved, and return to them after many days, full of love and longing sevenfold more powerful than before. In bridging the gap between the world of plants and our ancient literature—you renew the covenant between the soul of the people and their plants on the basis of youthful love and precious, holy memories from days of old—memories shared by both sides. I have no doubt that your way is the true and faithful path of *creativity*, the only path that will bring us to our goal: to revitalize the connection between the people and the nature of its land in ever-lasting bond. Walk in this path and you shall succeed.[68]

Bialik accentuates the power of the project to create a link between "our ancient literature" and the flora of the Land of Israel, thus leading both to a revival of the biblical text and to a renewal of that primal national love in the wilderness that Jeremiah called "youthful love" (*hesed ne'urayikh*; 2:2). Following the Hareuvenis' definition of the local vegetation as "memory plants," Bialik imagines this new encounter between the people and the biblical plants as an exhilarating event in which memories of both sides (!) resurge in breathtaking ways, leading to a new "path of creativity" (*derekh yetsira*).

The artistic potential of the biblical botany of the Hareuvenis did not escape Boris Schatz. In October 1920, upon seeing the botanical museum while it was

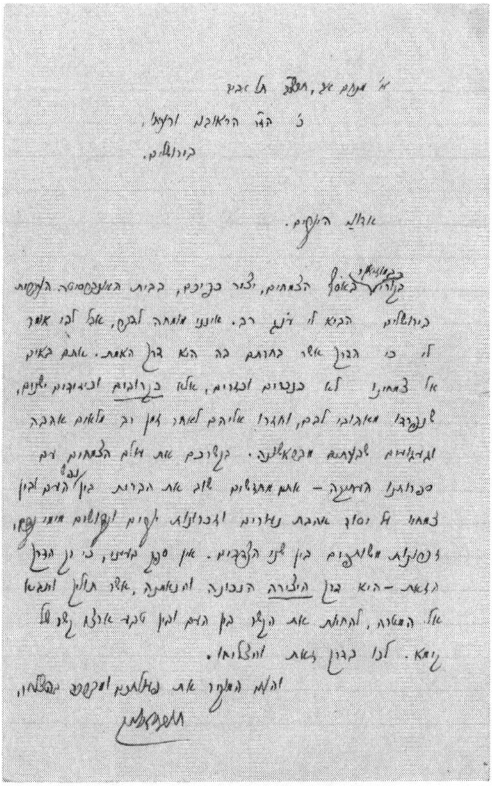

Figure 2.10: Letter of support written by Haim Nahman Bialik to the Hareuvenis, 1932. Neot Kedumim Archive.

still located in their household, the Bezalel director wrote: "I discerned a keen sense of art and beauty in your work. . . . Just as your scientific endeavors train people, so the artistic side of your labor will educate many others and foster the general public's good taste and love of flora, things that we are in dire need of in this land."[69] The paths of the Hareuvenis and the Bezalel School crossed in more substantive ways, when the former invited the Bezalel artist Shmuel Charuvi to prepare illustrations for an encyclopedia, the *Floral Treasury of the Land of Israel*, during the 1920s and the 1930s. The project of the two botanists, as Tamar Manor-Friedman notes, corroborated the Bezalelian belief that the new Zionist art ought to record the particular features of biblical flora and fauna in Palestine, finding in them visual symbols for Jewish national revival.[70] Indeed, there was a small museum of natural history at Bezalel, and students were required to draw biblical plants as part of their curriculum.

Though the Hareuvenis set out to trace every biblical plant mentioned in the Bible, the Song of Songs held a privileged position in their work. No other biblical text presents such a great variety of flora. But this salience is also indebted to the diffused ways in which Herderian notions of the Song found their way into Zionist scholarship. Indeed, the Hareuvenis shared Herder's perception of the Song as a key to Nature and Nature as the key to the Song and to the hearts of the folk who composed it.

In the Hareuvenis' description of the Garden of the Prophets and Sages in *Hatoren*, they foresee their garden as a site in which the Book of Books and the Song of Songs will be read anew in "the letters and the colors" of nature, the letters and colors through which "the Book of Books and the source of all poetry are written."[71] The superlative name of the ancient love poem—its designation as the ultimate Song—marks it as the epitome of the botanical revival of the ultimate Book. It is no coincidence, then, that an entire section of the garden is devoted to the Song and its plants. Similarly, an entire hillside is assigned to the plants and perfumes of the ancient love poem in Neot Kedumim, the Biblical Landscape Reserve in Israel—Noga

Figure 2.11: Herbarium sheet of the Hareuvenis; common narcissus identified as "rose of the valleys" (*shoshanat ha-'amkim*) of the Song of Songs 1930. Courtesy of the Israel Museum.

Hareuveni's later implementation of his parents' vision.[72]

The Hareuvenis added their own curious classification of the Song's flora to the long line of inquiries made by renowned botanists such as Hasselquist and Dalman. For the Hareuvenis, *shoshanat ha-'amakim* (the rose of the valleys) was to be regarded as narcissus and *havatselet ha-Sharon* (the lily of Sharon) as sun's-eye tulip (see figs. 2.11 and 2.12). In explaining the latter choice, they refute the identification of the *havatselet* as *Colchicum steveni* and declare that anyone who had actually explored the region would know that such flowers do not grow in the Sharon but rather in mountainous zones.[73] Accordingly, their herbarium sheets of these flowers from 1930 and 1931 show pictures of a narcissus and a tulip. "From Our Ancient Literature" ("Mi-sifrutenu ha-'atika") is the header of these sheets, and below there are three columns with handwritten notations regarding the botanical name, common name, family, locality, habitat of each flower, and the date on which it was inspected, in Hebrew, Arabic, and English.

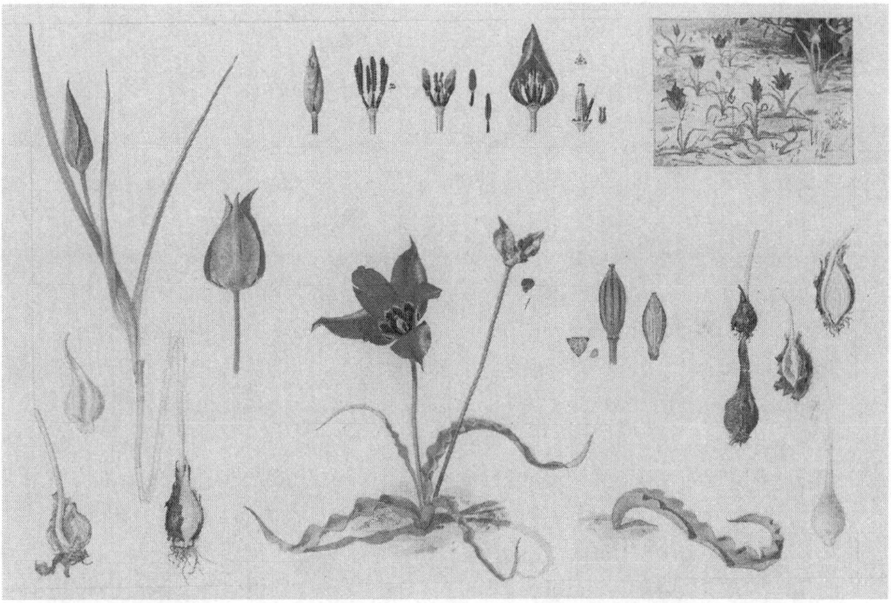

Figure 2.12: Shmuel Charuvi, (Ukrainian-born Israeli, 1897–1965). Sun's-eye tulip—identified as the lily of the Sharon (*havatselet ha-Sharon*), from *The Floral Treasury of the Land of Israel,* by Ephraim and Hanna Hareuveni, 1923–27. Pencil and watercolor on paper, 25.5 × 35.5 cm. Gift of Sheila and Nahum Gelber, Monaco. Israel Museum, Jerusalem. Photograph © Israel Museum, Jerusalem.

The Hareuvenis did not officially collaborate on a Song of Songs project with the Bezalel School, but their involvement in this exegetical nexus is unmistakable. Schatz underscores the connection in his depiction of a botany class in his utopian novel *Rebuilt Jerusalem* (1924). The teacher (bearing some resemblance to Ephraim Hareuveni) holds a *havatselet* in his hand and asks the attentive Bezalel students to consider the delicate and modest form of the flower . . . and innocent song of the Shulamite: "I am the lily of the Sharon." In speaking of a "lily" rather than a "tulip," Schatz does not quite accept the Hareuvenis' classification, but he is well attuned to the affinity between his own blend of literalism with Zionist utopia and that of his botanist friends, whose article in *Hatoren* was published during the same year.

Moving from the biblical botany of the Hareuvenis to the biblical ethnography of Goitein is not that sharp of a transition, given that in the former's research there is an Orientalist, ethnographic dimension as well. But whereas for the Hareuvenis, Arab plant lore served as a window to ancient times, in Goitein's research the primary path to the biblical world was made possible via the Jewish Yemenite community.

SHLOMO DOV GOITEIN: BIBLICAL ETHNOGRAPHY

Shlomo Dov Goitein was born in 1900 in the little village of Burgkundstat in southern Germany.[75] He was given both a thorough Jewish and secular education. On completing his dissertation in Islamic Studies in 1923 at the University of Frankfurt, he immigrated to Palestine (by curious coincidence, on the same ship with Gershom Scholem). His first position in Palestine was that of a teacher at the Reali (Haifa's renowned high school), where he taught Bible and history. In 1928, Goitein joined the faculty of the newly established Hebrew University and became one of the founding figures of Islamic Studies in Jerusalem.

Shortly after taking a position at the Hebrew University, Goitein began to do field work in Yemenite communities, a research endeavor that intensified with the Magic Carpet mass migration in 1949–52. His inquiries, as he recounts in "Research among the Yemenites," were initially linguistic. He was eager to discover unknown dialects and explore the "Hebrew elements in the vernacular of an autochthonous community, which was little exposed to inter-Jewish migrations."[76] But eventually "the linguist became an *ethnolinguist*," finding the rich world of tales, songs, and proverbs of his interlocutors too compelling and pertinent to leave untouched.[77]

Goitein's claim to fame—all the more so after the publication of Amitav Ghosh's *In an Antique Land* and Adina Hoffman and Peter Cole's *Sacred Trash*—was his Geniza research.[78] Discovered only at the end of the nineteenth century, the Geniza documents—comprising the largest and most diverse collection of medieval manuscripts ever to be found—include innumerable leaves of biblical manuscripts, rabbinic commentaries, and ancient *piyyutim* (liturgical poetry) as well as fragments of letters, legal documents, and hastily written notes. Goitein's first encounter with Geniza manuscript fragments was during a trip to Budapest in 1948, where he had the opportunity to examine the collection of the late-nineteenth-century scholar David Kaufmann. Thus began a preoccupation that would last for the remainder of his life, the bulk of which he conducted in the United States (from the late fifties on), first at the University of Pennsylvania and later at the Institute for Advanced Studies at Princeton. Goitein's monumental study, based on his investigation of the Cairo Geniza, *A Mediterranean Society*, has been regarded as a landmark in medieval scholarship ever since the publication of the first of its five volumes in 1967.

There is, however, a lesser-known realm of Goitein's work today: his biblical books. He published three major books on the Bible: *Omanut ha-sipur bamikra* (*The Art of Biblical Narrative*; 1956), *Hora'at ha-tanakh* (*The Teaching of the Bible*; 1957), and *Iyunim bamikra* (*Bible Studies*; 1957).[79] These books offer a mélange of literary, historical, and ethnographic approaches to the Bible and are written in an accessible form with a broad audience in mind. They reflect Goitein's commitment to pedagogical questions that he saw as central to Israeli society—the study of the Bible being one of them. He was indeed involved in shaping the curriculum for Bible studies in schools, first as a pedagogical supervisor during the British Mandate and then as a member of various pedagogical committees of the Israeli Ministry of Education.

Goitein was one of the greatest advocates of the Zionist Bible. In his essays on the teaching of the Bible in high schools (some of the chapters of *The Teaching of the Bible* were published as essays in the late thirties and forties), he accentuates the great importance of the biblical text to Zionism, paving, as it does, the road back to the homeland and to the "smell" of the soil.[80] Quoting Tolstoy's comment on Zionism—"I do not understand the Jews. They have the most beautiful homeland in the world, the Bible, and they insist on seeking another homeland"—Goitein remarks that the Russian novelist speaks with the carelessness of someone who is rooted in his land.[81] The Bible indeed wandered with the Jews in exile, enfolding within the treasures of the homeland—but now that they have returned, it is high time to open up these treasures and use them as guides to the literal Land of Israel. Instead of the imaginary abstract Bible of the Diaspora, he claims, we must now foster a new understanding of the Bible that will be attuned to the particular historical aspects of Eastern lifestyles and to the biblical accounts of early national history in the region.[82]

In many ways, Goitein was part of Ben-Gurion's "Bible-mania" (note that all of his biblical books were published in the 1950s). His approach, however, had a distinct critical edge. He never approved of the Zionist neglect of post-biblical traditions or of the tendency to disregard the religious dimension of the text.[83] What is more, the great value of the Bible for Goitein lay not merely in its national historiography but also in its privileged position as "World Literature." When teaching the Bible, writes Goitein, we do not worship the "idol of nationalism," but rather we provide our children with a taste of one of the finest masterpieces of all literature, with a book that has been admired for its outstanding literary power and human insights by leading thinkers and writers such as Herder and Goethe.

Goitein's work on the Song begins with a brief essay titled "On the Song of Songs" ("Al shir ha-shirim"), published in *Davar* on April 23, 1943. Later, in *Bible Studies* (*Iyunim bamikra*), he pursues some of his initial intuitions in two interrelated chapters: "Women as Creators of Biblical Genres" and "The Literary Character and Symbolic Interpretation of the Song of Songs." His primary premise is that women were the inventors of various biblical genres, among them dirges and love lyrics such as those of the Song of Songs.[84] In an introductory section, Goitein recounts that his impetus to investigate the question of female poetic traditions in the Bible stemmed from his extensive research on the Yemenite Jews who had come to Israel during the Magic Carpet wave of immigration from "over a thousand locations, most of which were not yet marked on any map, and in many of these the most ancient ways of life still prevailed."[85] Fascinated in particular by the singing of gifted Yemenite women singers/composers—known as *meshorerot* or *menagnot* (due to the musical accompaniment of their singing)—he marveled at the biblical echoes within their performance.[86] Goitein does not hesitate to admit that there are notable differences between contemporary Yemenite women and women of ancient Israel, but the comparison seems fruitful to him given that it sheds light on the ways in which women, regardless of their social marginality, may have a prominent role in Eastern oral/folk culture.

"What would be more natural," asks Goitein, "than for Solomon, the great women-lover, to ask one of the female singers of his court to gather for him the best of current Israelite poetry?" At a point where his study sounds like a tale of *One Thousand and One Nights*, he conjectures that the singer was a *bat-nadiv*, "daughter of a nobleman" (a designation that appears in Song 7:2), an admirable poetess, who was capable of creating a unique blend of popular love lyrics while "weaving" her own story within the framework of her composite work. That the Song is attributed to Solomon rather than to its female composer needs to be seen as characteristic of court procedures. Thus, in Islamic cultures, books that were dedicated to rulers were often named after them. "We can even imagine," writes Goitein, "that the alteration was made during Solomon's lifetime: the king became so enthusiastic about the composition handed to him that he was not satisfied until it carried his name."[87]

Goitein is not the first to ascribe female authorship to certain biblical texts, but he is the first to make this claim in reference to the Song. More persuasive than the intriguing speculation regarding the *bat-nadiv*'s role as composer and singer in Solomon's court is his poignant attention to the female-centered features of the Song—from the dominance of the Shulamite's voice, to the female chorus, and the recurrent use of the unusual term "mother's house." That an excerpt of this study was included as a proto-feminist piece in *A Feminist Companion to the Song of Songs* attests to the ways in which Goitein was ahead of his times.[88]

But the contemporary Orient—whether the Jewish-Yemenite or Islamic—does not suffice for Goitein. He also explores the relevance of the ancient Near East, claiming to find there a more substantive corpus of love poetry by women. In unearthing a polytheistic parallel of the Song, he endorses the practices of what Marvin H. Pope calls the "cultic" approach.[89] As far back as 1920, T. J. Meek drew comparisons between the Song and the liturgy of the Ishtar-Tammuz cult of fertility. S. N. Kramer further developed this thesis in his work on the Song and the ancient hymns of Sumer in the 1950s and 1960s. Goitein primarily refers to ancient Egyptian poetry, but he does mention Kramer's work in discussing the dirges of the biblical women who weep for Tammuz in Ezekiel 8:14.[90]

More relevant to our concerns are Goitein's ethnographic precursors. In tracing biblical echoes of the Song in the singing of Yemenite women, Goitein follows in the footsteps of various Orientalist scholars: first and foremost, J. G. Wetzstein, the German consul in Damascus and the most renowned nineteenth-century ethnographer of the Song. Influenced by Herder's writings, Wetzstein conducted a study in 1873 of praise songs—the *wasf*—sung in village weddings in Syria and used it as a key to understanding the profusion of laudatory depictions in the dialogue between the two biblical lovers.[91] These rural weddings in which the bride and groom were treated as a royal couple and praised as such, he contends, could also shed light on the dual roles of the lover in the Song as both rustic shepherd and king. G. H. Dalman and S. H. Stephan followed suit in the early twentieth century, exploring ethnographic parallels to the Song of Songs in Palestine (Goitein refers to all three ethnographers).[92]

The interest in Yemenite languages and customs as an invaluable ethnographic archive for biblical research may be traced back to Michaelis's work on Yemen. Given its isolation, the interior of Arabia represented, in his view, a remarkably preserved archive. Only in Yemen, he argued, where the Mosaic Law was exaggerated, "one could literally touch ancient Judaism"; only there "the biblical customs made dusty and dilapidated by the passing of time would be found, shining in their original alien splendor."[93]

Goitein's ethnographic study of the Song had an unmistakable Zionist stamp. He was among the Hebrew University scholars who were eager to make Mizrahi folklore part of the new Israeli culture, while aspiring, as Galit Hasan-Rokem puts it, to hold an "ethnographic mirror" that would enhance particular ethnic identities."[94] The retrieval of a biblical tradition via the customs of Yemenite women who had just immigrated to Israel exposed an ancient layer that was common to *all* Jewish communities; yet due to the special conditions of Yemen and the unique traditions of Yemenite Jewry, here it shone forth with exceptional visibility. The Magic Carpet Operation of the Yemenites could thus bring back what Ashkenazi Jews had lost in their years of exile, adding an unexpected vitality to the new biblical culture of Zionism—an inter-Jewish variation on what he defines as "creative symbiosis" within the framework of Jewish-Arab relations.[95]

Goitein's "national midrash" is not as overt as that of Hareuveni, but he too partakes in the formation of a Zionist allegorical configuration of the Song.[96] Interestingly enough, his project is comparable not only to other scholarly projects but also to the Orientalist trend in popular Zionist music. If the Hareuvenis were the scholarly compliment to Bezalel's visual renditions of the Song, Goitein was the counterpart to the composers and singers who set out to retrieve the authentic musical cadences of the ancient love poem through Yemenite or semi-Yemenite melodies. More specifically—not unlike Vilenski, Nardi, and Levi-Tanai—he deemed female Yemenite singers and composers as having a special role in conjuring up the music of the biblical past. In this case the exchange between the academic and artistic exegetical worlds is not as direct as that between Hareuveni and Schatz or Charuvi, but its more subtle character does not make it less forceful.

In the next two chapters we will follow Agnon's metacommentaries on the Israeli Song of Songs in *Betrothed* and in "Edo and Enam." If Agnon is particularly drawn to the exegetical scene of the Song, it is because here he finds an incredibly rich turf for exploring the paradoxes and ambiguities of Zionist biblicism as it oscillates between fashioning a new literalism and constructing new allegories. What is more, this is the one realm of Zionist biblical reception whose principal axis is distinctly aesthetic—not only within the artistic media of art, music, and dance but also within the framework of scholarship. As such, it provides Agnon with an extraordinary screen via which to explore aesthetic-hermeneutic sensibilities of others as well as his own.

One final remark before moving on to Agnon's tales. Lest my detailed account of the Zionist reception of the ancient love poem create the impression that cultural issues are the sole concern of these two tales, let me point out that in being a writer, rather than a historian, Agnon has the privilege of moving freely between individual loves and collective ones. His moonstruck lovers are by no means schematic representatives of cultural phenomena, but fully fledged characters with their own idiosyncratic biographies and peculiar amorous obsessions.

Agnon would have agreed with Rosenzweig's observation regarding the fashioning of subjectivity in the Song. "Comparatively speaking," writes Rosenzweig, "the word 'I' occurs this frequently in no other book in the Bible. . . . Like a single sustained organ note, it runs under the whole melodic-harmonic texture of mezzo-sopranos and sopranos."[97] In his renditions of the Song, Agnon pursues this singular, sustained "note," but while doing so he also aspires to trace the melodies of a national choir, as it were. He is forever interested in the ways in which individual loves are inscribed in collective loves and vice versa. With exceptional psychological acumen, he oscillates between the two realms and probes the intricate ways in which the Song may be used to capture the maddening intensities of both individual and cultural phenomena.

3

Rechnitz's Botany of Love

THE SONG OF SEAWEED

THE novella *Betrothed* (*Shevu'at emunim*), hailed as a masterpiece already on its publication in 1943, opens with a memorable depiction of Jaffa as a city "of beautiful seas": *yafo yefat yamim*.[1] The resonant alliteration of *y f m* augments the sensuality of a feminized city of legendary beauty, whose shores are "kissed" by the waves of the great sea (3). Among those compelled by Jaffa's sea is Jacob (Ya'acov) Rechnitz, a young marine botanist from Vienna. Although Rechnitz comes to Palestine as a traveler, with no intention of settling there, he ends up staying in Jaffa for a while, dedicating himself to the exploration of local seaweed. "Each day he would go out to take whatever the sea offered him. . . . Plying his net and his iron implements, drawing up specimens of seaweed not found along the beach, his heart beat like a hunter's at the chase" (8). Every time he embarks on his scientific expeditions, he lovingly says to the seaweed he collects, "My orchard, my vineyard" (8), echoing the renowned landscapes and metaphors of the Song of Songs.[2] He seems to go so far as to regard the lowly, forlorn plants of the sea as if they were exquisite plants of the upper, earthly world; more, as if they were the ultimate objects of love, precious relics of an ancient, primary, amorous chase.

As the tale unfolds in Jaffa of the Second Aliyah, we discover that Rechnitz's intellectual passions are set against, though bound up with, other competing amorous lines. There are six young maidens (*ne'arot*) in Jaffa with whom he strolls occasionally, finding each one of them attractive in a different way. But the woman who seems to lure him most is Shoshana Ehrlich, his childhood love. When Shoshana arrives in Jaffa with her father, the Consul, she awakens memories of a "betrothal oath" (the very oath that appears in the Hebrew title), opening the enigma of that early bond in the enchanting

Viennese garden of the Ehrlichs.[3] Whether or not the oath between Jacob and Shoshana could or should be rekindled now that they are adults is a question that remains tantalizingly unresolved. Whenever the two lovers draw close, they hasten to drift apart. The novella ends with a nocturnal race along the beach after which Shoshana supposedly reaffirms their bond as she places a crown of the young botanist's seaweed on her head. But this somnambulist encounter by the moonlit sea, with its curious intermingling of Rechnitz's botany of love and love for Shoshana, seems closer to a precarious, maddened dream of wish fulfillment than to an actual event.

There have been several attempts to decipher the scholarly context of Rechnitz's research. Arnold Band, in one of the most interesting accounts of the matter, points to certain affinities between the scientific portrait of Rechnitz and that of another Viennese scholar: Sigmund Freud.[4] Like Freud, he claims, Rechnitz is an assimilated, secular scholar who studied at the University of Vienna. Even their fields of interest are more akin than meets the eye. Freud's first publications were on eels (creatures as primitive and as watery as seaweed)—his primary research goal was to discover whether or not eels have sexual organs—and, in turn, Rechnitz's fascination with the unseen phenomena of the lower worlds of marine botany is analogous to the psychoanalyst's preoccupation with the darker, submerged strata of the mind.[5]

A reading that is, in a way, closer to my interest in Israeli biblicism is that of Israel Asael in a rather early piece on *Betrothed* titled "A Midrash of Seaweed." Asael regards Rechnitz as a modern biblical critic whose Bible research is as futile and detached as seaweed. A follower of Meshulam Tochner, Asael reads this tale as representative of Agnon's sharp critique of secular modern scholarship: it may strive to cure Judaism from stagnation but actually offers a disastrously pointless approach that overlooks the true vitality of traditional Jewish sources.[6] Asael's primary justification for linking Rechnitz's scholarly pursuits with biblical criticism is the passage from "Edo and Enam," where our two tales intersect, in which Gamzu, the book dealer and storyteller, associates the magical, inscribed leaves of Enam with the seaweed Rechnitz hauls up from the bottom of the sea. The sudden shift in the hue of the inscribed leaves from "the primary colors of the rainbow" (165) to the dull grays of Rechnitz's seaweed is, Asael claims, an ironic configuration of the ways in which the scientific tools of biblical criticism have stifled the "spirit of the sacred sources."[7]

However perceptive at points, Asael's midrash overlooks the intricacies of Agnon's irony. There is no interpretive trend that escapes Agnon's "little demon of irony"—be it modern biblical scholarship or traditional commentaries. Such irony, however, by no means precludes a passionate probing of the ever-changing modes of biblical reception. A closer look at the leaves that play so crucial a role in Asael's reading makes clear that their unexpected transformation is not quite a disastrous fading (caused by modern intervention) but rather an enchanting, inexplicable aesthetic-hermeneutic event, where colors and scripts are forever shifting:

> On the way back, [Gemulah's father] opened the jar and showed me a bundle of dry leaves unlike any I had ever seen; and on them were the strange characters of a script unlike any that I knew; and the color of the characters, that is, the color of the ink in which they were written, was not like any color we know. At first sight I should have said that the scribe had mixed gold, azure and purple with all the primary colors of the rainbow and written with them. But as I stood gazing, the colors altered before my eyes and changed into the tints of seaweeds drawn from the depths, such weeds as Dr. Rechnitz drew up from the sea near Jaffa. Then again, they were like the silver strands we observe on the moon. . . . As I stood marveling, Gemulah's father replaced the leaves in the jar and spoke to me simply, with these words: "They are plants of the earth, and they have been given the power to influence the upper air." (165–66)

The change in the letters' color does not end with the transition from the rainbow hues to the shades of Rechnitz's weeds: it is followed by a no less dramatic leap from the young botanist's specimens to the silver strands of the moon. Pertaining to the bottom of the sea, Rechnitz's leaves differ from the Enamite "plants of the earth," but they too seem to have some kind of odd connection with the lunar spheres of the "upper air"; they too are somehow both botanical specimen and captivating scribal sheets (in Hebrew, as in English, the term for "leaves," *'alim*, can mean both).

In Rechnitz's marine leaves, I detect Agnon's response to a branch of modern biblical scholarship whose relevance to the tale has gone unnoticed: biblical botany. Agnon reflects on the charms, pretensions, and pitfalls of the scientific endeavors of biblical botany, but he is also intrigued by its broader cultural implications in the exegetical scene of the Second Aliyah and beyond, a milieu in which biblical plantscapes—above all, those of the Song of Songs—were perceived as indispensable relics of biblical times and a vital means for the renewal of the bond between the people and the Land.

In *Betrothed*, Agnon shapes a grand Song of Songs through and against this exegetical botanical scene. If Zionist botanists were searching for biblical flora in the Land of Israel, Rechnitz moves in the opposite, or even heretical, direction in his attempt to collect and identify unknown specimens of seaweed from the sea. And much as the Song had a pivotal role within the framework of Zionist biblical botany, so too it colors Rechnitz's marine expeditions, though the assimilated Viennese scholar does not quite discern the hidden biblical layers of his inquiries.

Agnon's ironic inversion of biblical botany allows him to explore some of the paradoxes and ambiguities of the biblical culture of secular Zionism. Although Zionist botanists were eager to shape a new literal Song that would be grounded in botanical realities, their quest for literalism and for an authentic, erotic landscape of biblical times, Agnon intimates, does not quite lead to terra firma. What is more, for all its literalism, their botany is replete with allegorical innuendoes. Agnon playfully juxtaposes the new Zionist allegories invented via biblical flora with traditional allegories of the Song's roses, mocking normative distinctions between the secular and the sacred.

But what makes Agnon's rendering of the Song in *Betrothed* a virtuoso interpretive gem are the nuanced ways in which all the loves in the tale are interwoven. The Song reverberates through all realms—the scholarly, the personal, and the national—engulfing every imaginable dimension of life in a whirlpool of love. Rechnitz's obsession with seaweeds is deeply embedded within the intricate plot of his past and present amorous entanglements with Shoshana. These two loves, in turn, are set against the backdrop of the Second Aliyah and the new Zionist allegory of love for the Promised Land.

On the margins of this amorous network is yet another, less apparent, love: the love for art and for the Song itself. The nexus between botany and the visual arts was an integral part of the field from its very inception, as is apparent in the drawings that accompanied the scientific records of the anatomy of plants. Agnon takes the dependence of botany on art a step further by blurring the demarcation between Rechnitz's scientific passions and hidden artistic inclinations. As such, Rechnitz's marine botany also serves as a springboard for a meditation on the intensity of aesthetic attractions as a whole and those generated by the ancient love poem in particular.

How familiar was Agnon with the Zionist botanical world I sketched out in the previous chapter? There was hardly a scholar in Jerusalem whom Agnon did not know. In fact, scholars were among his closest friends and acquaintances. In the small, intimate Jerusalem of the forties and fifties, where the bulk of intellectual life was conducted in four (almost) adjacent neighborhoods—Rehavia, Talbiya, Beit Ha-Kerem, and Talpiyot (Agnon's neighborhood)—formal and mostly informal encounters with prominent scholarly figures such as Gershom Scholem, Shlomo Dov Goitein, Martin Buber, Dov Sadan, and Ephraim E. Urbach were very much part of Agnon's daily routine. Ephraim Hareuveni was not one of Agnon's close friends but was definitely an acquaintance, as two letters in the Agnon archive at the National Library make clear. Referring to a flower Agnon had asked about, Hareuveni writes: "I'm sending you the flower so that you can see its color and shape." He goes on to explain that he decided to name the flower (whose scientific name is *Colchicum stevenii*) *bar yoreh* ("the son of the first rain") because of the season in which it blooms.[8] (The dried flower of the *bar yoreh*—known today as *sitvanit*—may still be found in the envelope of this letter.) Language—the coining of new names and the revival of old ones—was at the core of Hareuveni's project, making his work of special interest for poets and writers as different as Bialik and Agnon.

My aim is not to identify Rechnitz with a sole botanist. I will read him primarily in relation to the life and work of Hareuveni, but he also has something in common with Alexander Eig, the "pure" botanist of the Hebrew University, and even with Shmuel Charuvi, the botanical artist of Bezalel. Like other scholars in Agnon's detailed representations of academic life, Rechnitz is an ironic blend of various historical figures—and much more than that. And although I focus on Rechnitz's affiliation with biblical botany, I will offer a consideration of the impact of Freud's portrait behind the scenes and the ways in which the interpretive practices of botanists in this novella tend to intersect with psychoanalytic exegesis. This psychoanalytic prism, in effect, deepens Agnon's study of the darker, disturbing facets of love in the Song and is relevant to all the different amorous ties in the tale.

THE QUESTION OF PURE SCIENCE

Rechnitz, in many ways, is the very antithesis of Ephraim Hareuveni: he is a researcher and a teacher who endorses no Zionist or Jewish pedagogical vision whatsoever. In stark contrast to other scholars of the Second Aliyah, the narrator assures us, who were immersed in either studies of the Land of Israel or studies of the Bible (*miktsatam 'asku be-heker ha-aretz u-miktsatam be-hikrey mikra*) and whose research was yoked to national, social, and religious agendas, Rechnitz "subordinated his work to no other consideration [*lo*

ʿasah ʾet ʿavodato snif le-shum davar aher]. He took trouble and pains solely in the cause of pure knowledge" (98).[9] Devoted to his marine plants, he goes out to the sea to collect new specimens in all seasons, regardless of weather hazards, despite the fact that no one in his vicinity—not even his students in the local high school where he teaches—has any interest in his findings. His work is acknowledged only abroad—either by European scholars who admire his contribution to the extent of naming one of the seaweeds he had discovered after him *Colorafa Rechnitzia* or by American academics who bestow upon him the title of professor and offer him a distinguished post.

Should Rechnitz then be considered as closer to the "pure" botanists? That the debate regarding "pure science" at the Hebrew University is of relevance to this tale is made clear in the speech the school principal delivers in the farewell party in honor of Rechnitz. The principal speaks in fictional time from a point in history before the foundation of the Hebrew University, but one can trace the voice-over of later perspective. "Why is Rechnitz departing?"—asks the principal in a mock pedagogical gesture—"Because we have no university here. If there were one, he would not have to leave us." Rebuking all those who do not believe in the possibility of founding a university in the Land of Israel, he moves on to the final pitch:

> Let me say in conclusion that I hope we, too, will achieve a university before long. . . . What a great university that will be, when all the scholars of Israel, from all the universities of the world, gather in Jerusalem, on the Temple Mount, to teach wisdom and knowledge! . . . But it follows of necessity that I mean no mere seminary for [Jewish] studies. We have enough already of this [Judaism] stuffed into us morning, noon and night. When I say university, I mean a real one, where all the forms of knowledge to be found in other centers of learning will be taught. (116–17)

Agnon ridicules those who insist on turning every science into Jewish Studies or Zionist lore, creating a stifling overdose of Judaism.[10] But at the same time, he mocks scholars who think that they can develop a "pure science" and remain objectively removed from their cultural milieu. The principal's protest against the imposition of a Jewish angle on all fields of knowledge does not stop him from envisioning the new, secular, Zionist university on the Temple Mount, of all places, or from defining its mission in prophetic, eschatological terms as a "light unto the nations."

A peculiar blend of secular and religious overtones was in fact evident in late December 1924 at the formal opening of the Institute of Jewish Studies at the Hebrew University. Judah Magnes declared that it was "a sanctuary in which to learn and teach, without fear or hatred, all that Judaism has made and created from the time of the Bible until our days" and then ventured to conflate the goals of modern and traditional research: "We exult in the ideal of pure science; and there is no place in the world with a *genius loci* as suitable for Torah as Jerusalem."[11] "The sentiment of the day," David Myers comments, "was perhaps best captured in the frequent expression of hope, drawn from a traditional liturgical refrain, that 'from Zion will go forth Torah.'"[12]

Rechnitz accentuates the fragility of "pure science" at the Hebrew University and beyond. Though respected for his rigorous research, the young botanist is far from being an emblem of objectivity, as is already evident on the dramatic night (during his student years in Vienna) when he first realizes that his vocation lies in the vast expanses of the sea.

> When he first entered the university he chose no special subject but applied himself to all the sciences, and particularly the natural sciences, for these had drawn his heart. He already thought of himself as an eternal student, one who would never leave the walls of the academy. But one night he was reading Homer. He heard a voice like the voice of the waves, though he had never yet set eyes on the sea. He shut his book and raised his ears to listen. And the voice exploded, leaping like the sound of many waters. He stood up and looked outside. The moon hung in the middle air, between the clouds and stars; the earth was still. He went back to his book and read. Again he heard the same voice. He put down the book and lay on his bed. The voices died away, but that sea whose call he had heard spread itself out before him, endlessly, while the moon hovered over the face of the waters, cool and sweet and terrible. Next day Rechnitz felt as lost as a man whom the waves have cast up on a desolate island, and so it was for all the days that followed. He began to study less and read books about sea voyages; and all that he read only added to his longing, he might as well have drunk seawater to relieve [the] thirst. The next step was to cast about for a profession connected with the sea. (10)

A Romantic scholar more than a follower of *Wissenschaft*, Rechnitz falls in love, as it were, with his object of investigation against the mysterious backdrop of the moon and the sea. And although he is drawn to the natural sciences rather than to the humanities, what seems to spur him to become a marine botanist is an encounter not with the sea but rather with literature:

hearing the irresistible sound of the sea while reading Homer.

Rechnitz reads Homer on that night, but he could just as well have been reading another text of antiquity: the Bible.[13] Behind the sound of the Homeric sea, one can hear the distinct echoes of numerous biblical scenes—the initiation scenes of Samuel and Ezekiel mingled with the aquatic moment in Genesis 1, with the spirit "hovering upon the water," images of God's voice exploding like *mayim rabim*, "many waters" in Psalms (29:3, 93:4) and Ezekiel (1:24, 43:2), and the "many waters" of the Song that cannot extinguish the fire of love (8:7). This is, indeed, a mock initiation scene that underscores Rechnitz's blindness to the impact of his own cultural waters on his professional choices.

Later, in Jaffa's sea, when Rechnitz admiringly notes the great beauty of the local seaweed, he seems to be equally unaware of the biblical ghost that hovers upon his stream of associations. The stamp of the Song is evident not only in his daily address to the seaweed—"My orchard, my vineyard"—but also in a whole array of exquisite images, of diverse colors and textures, that floods Rechnitz's mind just before he utters these words of love. This botanical underworld is anything but dull and gray. Rechnitz perceives the mysteries beneath the waters as "growing like gardens, like thickets, like shadowed woods among the waters, their color like the yellow of sulphur, like royal purple, like living flesh, like white pearls, like olives, like coral, like a peacock's feathers, clinging to the reefs, to the rocks, and the cliffs."[14] Unbeknownst to him, he fashions a condensed version of the ancient love poem, which despite its marine character comes close to some of its unique, aesthetic features. The Song's excessive, dreamy stream of similes and metaphors from different semantic fields (the gardens, the moon, a crimson thread, walls and towers, gazelles)—no figure of speech seems to suffice in depicting love—is rendered here through a breathless, unending list of similes (note the rhythmic repetitions of "like"), pertaining to all realms (gardens, woods, pearls, corals, peacock feathers). And much as in the Song every simile is charged with erotic overtones, here too there is a sensuous, anthropomorphic quality to the gardens of the deep: the seductive eye and the "living flesh" (*ka-basar ha-hay*).

Agnon derides scientific pretensions of objectivity, but he is nonetheless intrigued by scholarly passions, especially when they verge on art and coincide with his own exegetical obsessions. The interrelations between science and art, between the quest for an unbound science and the quest for an unbound art, become all the more conspicuous in the description of Rechnitz's album:

> But in his time, no one had a collection to match that of Rechnitz. There they were, dried, attached to their sheets, placed in the album. At first glance you would think you were looking into an artist's sketch book, each line was drawn with such exquisite care and beauty; for the way of seaweeds is to adhere to paper, become absorbed in it, and not protrude from the surface. But once you drop a little water on them, they grow soft and you see before you living plants, the work of the Creator who cares as much for each humble object as He does for what is high and mighty. There were times when Rechnitz dropped a tear in his rapture, which fell on the plant and brought it to life again. (118)

Likened to "an artist's sketch book," Rechnitz's album calls to mind the drawings of Charuvi and the herbarium sheets of the Hareuvenis, perhaps even something of their mysterious embalming techniques. Yet it departs from such botanical endeavors in moving beyond the constricting agendas and geographies of its practitioners—be they the scholars of the Hebrew University or the artists of Bezalel. Inasmuch as scholars, artists, or writers (for the sheets of paper with their marks resemble writing as well) assume the position of the Creator, they should be open to consider even lowly plants as objects of wonder and love. The miracle of a plant that comes back to life on receiving a few drops of water (or tears in this case) is not necessarily limited to terrestrial zones. In Rechnitz's inverted botanical world, seaweeds hold the magical qualities of the Rose of Jericho, though the name of the Rose does not resurge in his thoughts as he attaches the specimens he had collected to the sheets of his album.

MEMORIES OF A LOST GARDEN: THE BETROTHAL OATH REVISITED

In the human realm, Rechnitz's Song primarily revolves around Shoshana. If in the ancient love poem, "rose" is a metaphor for the Shulamite as well as part of the plantscape where the lovers meet, in Agnon's tale, the beloved is named after the flower she supposedly resembles ("Shoshana" means "rose"). Shoshana's name, we discover time and again, is not merely a dead metaphor for Rechnitz. In his visit as a boy to the Consul's office in Vienna, he sees a portrait of Frau Ehrlich and a portrait of Shoshana on the wall. In the latter, Shoshana is seen in a dress that "reached only to her knees and her legs seemed to tremble lightly," as if she were running. There are two additional pictures of the mother and daughter on the desk, and "before them was set a moist rose in a glass of clear water." When these portraits merge in his daydreams, he seems to be viewing a silent film in which Frau Ehrlich vanishes into the mists and Shoshana runs "on and on with a wet rose in her mouth" (13–14). The "wet rose" in the glass supposedly soars into the picture, or rather into Shoshana's mouth, transforming the running girl whose name means "rose" into a sensuous bearer of an actual wet rose.

In Rechnitz's memories, his childhood Rose is placed in the bright, Song of Songs garden of the Ehrlichs in Vienna.[15] When he hears of the forthcoming trip of the Consul and Shoshana to Jaffa, he recalls their blissful encounters in this garden as children: picking flowers, preparing garlands for each other, skating on the frozen pond. "In his thoughts all the seasons merged, and all the goodness and grace in them became one" (24).

Upon Shoshana's arrival in Jaffa, memories of a more pivotal scene in this enchanted garden are set into motion: the declaration of the love oath. They resurge with particular intensity one day as the two walk by the sea. The sea was calm that day, and its hue was deep blue; "the waves broke over one another, raising their crests as if held back from mingling with the waters beneath" (55–56). And much as the waters do not mingle, so Rechnitz and Shoshana drift apart. "Jacob would have given all the expanse of the earth in return for something that might draw Shoshana's attention. But nothing in the world could awaken this sleeping princess [*bat malka menamnemet*] who walked by his side, insensible to his presence."[16] His desperate longing for her attention leads him to recall better times when they fed the goldfish in the pond at the Ehrlichs' garden. Yet as he "watched the sea and the lonely fisherman standing up to his waist in water, he could not bring himself to speak of things past" (56). Just then, Shoshana halts suddenly and says:

> "Do you remember how you and I used to play in our garden?"
>
> He answered in a whisper, "I remember."
>
> "Good," said Shoshana. "Let's go on."
>
> Then again she stopped. "Do you remember what games we played?"
>
> Jacob began to recount them to her as he walked. She nodded her head at every detail, saying, "That's right . . . That's right . . . I thought you had forgotten."
>
> He laid his hand over his heart, as if to say, "How could anyone forget such things?" . . .

. . . "Do you remember that vow we made together?"

"I remember," said Jacob.

She looked at him steadily for a moment. "Do you remember the words of the vow?"

"I remember them," said Jacob.

"Word for word?"

"Yes, word for word."

"If you remember the vow, repeat it."

Jacob repeated the substance of what they had sworn.

"But you told me . . . that you remember it word for word." . . .

He hesitated, sighed, and at last said: "We swear by fire and by water, by the hair of our heads, by the blood of our hearts, that we shall marry one another and be husband and wife, and no power on earth can cancel our vow, for ever and ever." (56–57)

The garden of the Ehrlichs' is remembered as a playful paradise. It is a garden where love blossoms and oaths of eternal love may be delivered with the seriousness that accompanies children's games.

But such blissful gardens of the past are bound to be lost. Shoshana forces Jacob to reiterate the oath verbatim (no paraphrase is accepted) and later asks whether their oath still holds. And although he follows her subsequent whim as well and declares, "I am prepared, I am prepared, I am prepared" (*mukhan 'ani, mukhan 'ani, mukhan 'ani*), while committing himself to marrying her, it isn't that clear whether the reenactment of the speech act has actual power in a present fraught with moments of estrangement and illness.[17]

Shoshana is not quite a Shulamite who is awakened by love, but rather an ailing "sleeping princess," who perks up occasionally but then falls asleep again (the link between the Song and the folktale of Sleeping Beauty is made apparent in the German title: *Dornroeschen*, meaning "the rose among the thorns").[18] Rechnitz, in turn, is neither a Prince Charming who can rescue his beloved from the world of slumber nor a *dod* who can lure her with songs of love. He mostly walks silently by her side, groping for words he cannot find or else repeating words of times past (he is surely more imaginative when talking with the seaweed). Their relationship as adults, in fact, seems a distorted Song of Songs in which the more somber aspects of the ancient love poem are set in relief.

LOVESICKNESS: THE FREUDIAN UNDERCURRENTS

"I am love-sick"—*holat 'ahava 'ani*—sounds like a cliché (it is one of the most resonant lexicalized expressions of the Song), but it is in fact part of a remarkably intricate metaphoric network in the Song. The expression emerges in Chapter 2 after a sequence of plant metaphors:

> I am a [lily] of Sharon, a [*shoshana*] of the valleys.
> As a [*shoshana*] among thorns, so is my love among the daughters.
> As an apple-tree among the trees of the wood, so is my beloved among the sons.
>   Under its shadow I delighted to sit, and its fruit was sweet to my taste.
> He hath brought me to the banqueting-house, and his banner over me is love.
> "Stay ye me with dainties, refresh me with apples; for I am love-sick."
> (Song 2:1–5)[19]

In a breathtaking juggling of metaphors, the Shulamite likens herself to a rose and a lily, and then, adhering to the same semantic field of vegetation, she casts her loved one in the role of an apple tree. Plunging into this imaginary landscape, she makes it semi-concrete by sitting under the apple tree and relishing its shade and sweet fruit (the metaphor extends to the extent of becoming a conceit). Here and elsewhere in the Song, as Robert Alter points out, there is a distinct blurring of figurative landscapes and real ones.[20] Metaphoric language is an intrinsic element of the courtship and is continuously made seductive by double entendres. Is she actually sitting under an apple tree, or should her eating of the ravishing fruit be construed as a provocative metaphoric sequence through which she imagines the pleasures of love?

In verse 5, the Shulamite momentarily leaves the natural scenery and shifts to a very different semantic field: illness. Addressing her listeners, she now declares that she is "love-sick." Expressing love requires not only an unending stream of metaphors but also antithetical metaphors that can approach the puzzling paradoxes of the amorous experience: the sudden oscillations between pleasure and pain, power and utter powerlessness. What complicates it all is the thin line between bodily experiences and emotional ones. Is the Shulamite physically ill, or is it an inner event that is likened to a bodily disease—or both? She requests a bedding of apples to alleviate her sickness. But given that she had just described her loved one as an apple tree, is she seeking a soothing apple-bed or yearning for him? Love, rather than its absence, turns out to be, at times, the very source of sickness—not quite a cure. Overbearing in its radical wakefulness, it leads the Shulamite to desperately utter: "I adjure you, O daughters of Jerusalem, by the gazelles, and by the hinds of the field, that ye awaken not, nor stir up love, until it please" (2:7).

The Shulamite's declaration of sickness reappears in the nocturnal, dreamlike sequence of Chapter 5. On hearing her lover speak behind the door (or upon recalling that earlier experience), the beloved depicts her *nefesh* as departing: *nafshi yatsa' ve-dabro* (5:6). This verse has been translated in a variety of ways, primarily because of the multiple meanings of *nefesh* in biblical Hebrew: "breath of life," "life," "innermost feelings," and "soul." The KJV, among earlier translations informed by allegorical readings, sought to underline the soul: "my soul failed when he spake." In the Blochs' recent translation, the spiritual routes are avoided and desire is foregrounded: "How I wanted him when he spoke."[21] What gets lost in both translations is how close these acute longings are to death. The Shulamite does not merely "want" her lover: she dies, as it were, on hearing the voice of her unreachable *dod* (the shades of another somber metaphor of the Song—or rather simile—are already apparent here: "for love is strong as death"—8:6). But as her *nefesh*, her breath of life, goes out, it curiously has the freedom and pleasure that her body lacks: of being outdoors where her loved one roams (this is not a Platonic soul). When the beloved actually ventures to go outdoors, the guardians of the walls bruise her, adding external violence to her sense of inner turmoil. It is at this point that she yet again adjures the daughters of Jerusalem and sighs that she is "love-sick" (5:8). If in Chapter 2, lovesickness dismantles the boundaries between the body and the *nefesh*, here the split between the two is set up only to be obliterated again by a love that comes close to death in its intensity.

Shoshana's illness, like that of the Shulamite, remains a mystery. Love isn't quite the origin of Shoshana's malady (and definitely not the remedy), but her attacks break out in the context of her renewed amorous ties with Rechnitz. Here too illness is of the body and of the mind, though it is morbidly troubling in both realms. The only desire that prevails in Shoshana's world is the desire to sleep. Her sleeping disease is "a sickness which had not been heard of before in Palestine. Her head was dizzy and she had lost full control of her legs, which tottered as she moved about. When she spoke, her voice was indistinct and sounded like someone talking in his sleep; indeed, her only desire was for sleep" (105). The local doctor, Zablodovsky, prescribes various medicines, but his greatest achievement is to make sure Shoshana is put to bed with careful supervision.

There are distinct melancholy underpinnings to her lethargic conduct. During dinner at the Jaffa hotel one evening, Shoshana's *nefesh* seems to have withdrawn inward or to have fled her body altogether (*nafsha ke-'ilu nitcansa le-tokha o ke-'ilu barha mi-gufa*).[22] Agnon invokes the words of the Song, but in this highly distorted split between the body and the soul, the term *nefesh* also acquires the connotations of the modern expression *holat nefesh*—"mentally ill." Just then the Consul ponders over the coffee that is served: "Every age has its own customs: our forefathers used to take drinks that put them to sleep, but now we try to keep ourselves awake. After all, is there anything in the world worth staying awake for?—Those scents from the garden are most exhilarating: a mixture of jasmine and orange blossom, isn't it?" (51). His comment sounds like a parody of the wakefulness that stirs the enamored Shulamite's heart even in her sleep. Coffee, rather than love, is the stimulus that arouses people in modern times, and the question of whether or not there is something for which to be awake does not receive a decisive answer. The Consul seems to find some pleasure in the intoxicating scents that blow from the citrus orchards into the dining room, the kind of scents that awaken the sea of Jaffa and "enliven the soul" (*she-mehayim 'et ha-nefesh*),[23] the kind of warm, spring scents of jasmine and orange blossom that have the potential of forming part of a new, Oriental Song of Songs garden, but his daughter is only "put to sleep" by them (51).

In her mixed somatic and mental symptoms, Shoshana bears some resemblance to Freud's hysterical patients. Like many of them, she comes from an affluent Viennese family, holding the necessary means to afford psychoanalytic treatment. Given that such treatment is not available in Jaffa, the Consul thinks of consulting Nothnagel, a Viennese doctor who happens to be a historical figure: none other than one of Freud's teachers.[24] The voice-over of a later period may be traced here as well. In Jaffa of the Second Aliyah there were no psychoanalysts, but in Jerusalem of the forties there was a thriving Psychoanalytic Institute, founded by one of Freud's students: Max Eitingon.[25]

To the extent that Agnon writes a case study of Shoshana, he evokes Freud's theories with characteristic irony. As with biblical botany and other modern exegetical trends, he is both fascinated and amusedly critical. Psychoanalysis offers new methods for exploring the *nefesh* that appeal to Agnon in their emphasis on dreams and the darker, uncontrollable aspects of the mind, yet he cannot but ridicule Freud's overriding assumption that psychoanalysis holds the decisive key to the psyche. His skepticism merges with that of Shoshana at different points, most notably when she recounts one of her dreams. She dreams not of her lover knocking or calling her "upon the handles of the lock" but rather of the seductions of emotional numbness and death. "I dreamed that I was dead," she notes. "I wasn't happy, I wasn't sad, but my body felt such rest as no one knows in the land of the living. And this was the best of it, that I wanted nothing, I asked for nothing, it just felt as if I were disappearing into blue distances that would never end." But then she sarcastically adds: "Next morning I opened a book and read in it that nobody dreams of himself as dead" (94–95). The untitled book, one may assume, is *The Interpretation of Dreams*. Freud's analysis of dreams as wish fulfillments in this monumental work does not quite account for Shoshana's dream, where her own death is the greatest wish of all.[26]

ARZAF'S EMBALMED WORLD: INCESTUOUS FANTASIES

The young botanist could also be put on the psychoanalytic couch—and indeed he has. Gershon Shaked defines him as a neurotic who is beset by oedipal fixations.[27] Against common readings that define Rechnitz's inability to fully commit himself to Shoshana as his paramount failure—involved as he is in ongoing flirtation with the six maidens of Jaffa—Shaked calls attention to the pathological qualities of this return to a childhood love. Above all, he highlights the incestuous dimension of Rechnitz's attraction to Shoshana (they were raised as siblings of sorts) and the ways in which Shoshana and her mother, Frau Ehrlich, often blend in his mind.

Incest is not absent from the world of the Song. The lover calls his beloved "sister," and the term *dod* means both "lover" and "uncle." What is more, the Shulamite, at one point, revives the lexicalized metaphor of brother as lover on exclaiming: "O that thou wert as my brother / that sucked the breasts of my mother!" (*mi yitenkha ke-'ah li yonek shedei 'imi*; 8:1). She imagines her lover as a brother in seeking a way to stroll in the streets with him without being scorned. Yet her fantasy of a more acceptable encounter discloses a wish for an even more illicit love: one that entails incest and a highly erotic sucking of the mother's breasts. Not unlike illness and death, incest, in the ancient love poem, conveys a certain maddening intensity of a love that remains, in a sense, impossible.

Rechnitz's incestuous cravings are more than a luring sideline: they pose a surplus of stimuli he cannot quite endure. Sitting with Shoshana in the hotel garden, yet another garden with a potential of turning into a new Song of Songs garden, Rechnitz's thoughts drift from Shoshana's hands to a memory of how he used to "long to touch" her mother's hands with his lips (90). Out of this childhood recollection emerges another unexpected memory of a visit to the abode of Arzaf in Ein Rogel. Shmuel Werses regards Arzaf, the taxidermist (one of the marginal characters in both *Betrothed* and *Only Yesterday*), as an ironic replica of Israel Aharoni: the half-crazed biblical zoologist of both Bezalel and the Hebrew University, the zoological counterpart of Hareuveni.[28] Aharoni, in fact, was the first to call attention to this connection. He went so far as to claim that the name Arzaf is an acronym for "Aharoni the head [*rosh*] of zoology in Palestine." Agnon whimsically responded that he would have never thought of using the term "Palestine" rather than the "Land of Israel."[29]

Rechnitz recalls watching the hands of Arzaf stretching an animal skin on a board. The sequence between these three sets of hands (which surprises Rechnitz) lays bare a deep attraction coupled with an equally deep disgust. The young botanist tries to block his incestuous fantasies by thinking of a supposedly remote topic—Arzaf—but eros returns through the back door. Unwittingly, he identifies with Arzaf, whose eccentric love for animals is defined as that which "[gives] them life even after their death" (64). He would have liked to embalm his childhood love and her mother, as it were, much as Arzaf embalms his animals, or much as he himself, in the analogous botanical practice, dries, glues, and draws seaweed in his album. It is a way of touching that is supposedly less threatening in the control it seems to promise over the embalmed.

Given her own morbid wishes, Shoshana plays along with Rechnitz's latent fantasy. On hearing of Arzaf (Rechnitz eventually mentions his thoughts about the zoologist, though he censors their erotic dimension), she exclaims: "Cattle and wild beasts may enjoy a privilege granted to no man except the mummies in Egypt. . . . Our days on earth are like a shadow, and the time of our affliction is the length of our days. How fortunate are those mummies, laid in the ground and freed from all trouble and toil. If I could only be like one of them!" (91). She craves nothing less than to be one of Arzaf's taxidermic specimens or an Egyptian mummy. But her wish to be embalmed does not provide Rechnitz with much tranquility. The ill Shulamite never stops dragging the young botanist, ever more forcefully, into vortexes of love, incest, and death.

A SUDDEN INSIGHT: PLUNGING INTO THE POND

The connection between Rechnitz's love for marine botany and his love for Shoshana is intimated at various points throughout the tale—from the wet rose in Shoshana's mouth to his ruminations on Arzaf—but is addressed openly in Rechnitz's response to the Consul's questions about his choice of profession. Initially, the young botanist doesn't really explain his choice: instead, he depicts his gradual decision to turn from the botany of "upper plants" to the botany of "lower" ones. But then the Consul goes on to ask whether the plants that he investigates "also have their characteristic diseases" (103). "There isn't a single thing in creation that is not liable to disease," Rechnitz replies (104). And as he ruminates on botanical maladies, his thoughts wander off to the ill Shoshana: it suddenly dawns on him that the reason for his particular professional preferences may lie in a forgotten episode on the day of the betrothal oath at the Ehrlichs' garden.

> Suddenly Jacob's eyes grew round with wonder. A new perspective opened up beyond the one he saw before him, like the vision of a painter. . . . The pond in the Consul's garden, whose water plants used to fascinate and amaze him, came back into his memory. Perhaps, after all, his heart had been drawn to these plants since those very days? Twenty years and more had passed since he had first gone down with Shoshana to the pond and drawn up the wet vegetation; the strange thing about it was that in all those years the thought had never come back into his mind. At that moment he saw before his eyes the same circular pond set in the garden among the shrubs and the flowers, with Shoshana picking flowers and braiding garlands; now Shoshana jumped into the pond and disappeared; and now she rose again, covered with wet seaweed like a mermaid, the water streaming from her hair. As he thought of her hair, he thought, too, of how on that same day Shoshana had taken a curl from her curls and, with it, a lock of his forelock, and mingled them and burned them together and they had eaten the ashes and sworn to be faithful to each other. (104)

This is one of the most climactic moments in the tale. It has the sudden, revelatory force of an exhilarating Proustian scene of recollection; it has the freshness of a retrieved lost memory whose emergence opens up unknown realms of the past. Rechnitz is likened to an artist, in this case, not because of the sketches in his album but because his sudden insight resembles that of "a painter struggling to apprehend what his eyes have never seen" (104). If visual terms prevail in the depiction of this moment, it is because he now plunges back into a magical, childhood sight: one in which Shoshana emerges out of the pond, like a mermaid or a siren (*bat galim*) with wet seaweed streaming down her hair.

Once again Rechnitz recalls the blissful Song of Songs garden of his childhood, but this time around the aquatic qualities of that garden are more apparent, calling to mind the blending of vegetation and water in the *dod*'s playful punning: "A garden shut up [*gan na'ul*] is my sister, my bride; a spring shut up [*gal na'ul*], a fountain sealed" (4:12). The locked garden and the locked spring (literally "wave"), drawn from the surrounding sites, serve as metaphors for the vitality and virginity of the Shulamite. But the dripping of myrrh from the beloved's body onto the "handles of the lock" shortly afterward, in the dream sequence of Chapter 5, intimates that the fountain may not be as sealed as it first seems. For once, Rechnitz seems to be attuned to the tension in the Song between chastity and unabashed sensuality. Shoshana in the pond of the Ehrlichs' garden is no longer merely an innocent, chaste girl (modeled on Herderian notions of the Shulamite) but a wildly sensuous and seductive mermaid/siren who teasingly disappears in the water and then rises up again.

Band reads the pond scene as a kind of dream and sees Rechnitz as its Freudian interpreter. In accordance with the psychoanalytic exegetical practices of *The Interpretation of Dreams*, the young botanist moves from the overt to the covert—following a stream of associations from the seaweed of the deep to the seaweed on Shoshana's hair—and much as Freud was preoccupied with decoding childhood memories that appear only in fragmentary forms in dreams, so too Rechnitz is immersed in a search after the hidden spheres of his childhood games.[30] To top it all, Freud too defined his vocation as involving a heretical move from the upper worlds to the lower ones, as the evocation of the *Aeneid* in the epigraph to *The Interpretation of Dreams* makes clear: "If I can sway / No heavenly hearts I'll rouse the world below" (7:425–26).[31]

Gradiva's gait may also be traced in this scene. In fact, this is her most pronounced appearance in Agnon's tales. Both *Betrothed* and Freud's study of *Gradiva*, as Erella Brown points out, probe the impact of lingering memories of childhood loves on later professional choices.[32] If Norbert Hanold becomes an archaeologist in reenactment of his childhood infatuation with Zoe, Rechnitz becomes a marine botanist, charmed by those dripping weeds on Shoshana's hair. In both cases, there is an unconscious attempt to both preserve and escape primary erotic experiences. "Archaeology took hold of [Norbert Hanold]," remarks Freud,

> and left him with an interest only in woman of marble and bronze. His childhood friendship, instead of being strengthened into passion, was dissolved, and his memories of it passed into profound forgetfulness. . . . What is

> repressed cannot, it is true, as a rule make its way into memory without more ado; but it retains a capacity for effective action, and, under the influence of some external event, it may one day bring about psychical consequences which can be regarded as products of a modification of the forgotten memory and as derivatives of it and which remain unintelligible unless we take this view of them.[33]

In Agnon's tale of a Pompeii-like Jaffa, it is the scholar himself who retrieves repressed memories while gaining insight into the link between his childhood love and professional passions. He is positioned, for a brief moment at least, in the role of the analyst. But how successful is Rechnitz's probing into the mysteries of the mind's underworld? In a famous section in *The Interpretation of Dreams*, Freud writes:

> There is often a passage in even the most thoroughly interpreted dream which has to be left obscure; this is because we become aware during the work of interpretation that at that point there is a tangle of dream-thoughts which cannot be unravelled and which moreover adds nothing to our knowledge of the content of the dream. This is the dream's navel, the spot where it reaches down into the unknown. The dream-thoughts to which we are led by interpretation cannot, from the nature of things, have any definite endings; they are bound to branch out in every direction into the intricate network of our world of thought. It is at some point where this meshwork is particularly close that the dream-wish grows up, like a mushroom out of its mycelium.[34]

For all his certainty concerning his capacity to solve oneiric puzzles, Freud does not hesitate to acknowledge the hermeneutic limits of psychoanalytic inquiry. In an admirable move, he goes so far as to define the obscure, impenetrable passage of the dream as its very navel. The metaphor of the navel leads to the maternal body and the moment of birth, to the inscrutable site of human origin. But Freud does not remain in the human realm for long. Harking back to his interest in the natural sciences, he adds a semi-botanical image to his explication as he depicts in detail the intricacies of the mushroom growing out of its mycelium, branching out in all directions, having no "definite endings." Both the navel and the mushroom mark the dark, unknowable "spot" where our quest for interpretive insight fails. Any notion of human mastery is mitigated by a humbling reminder of the embeddedness of the mind in the body and of humanity in the evolutionary chain.

Agnon goes with Freud beyond Freud into more skeptical zones. There is much that remains concealed and uninterpretable in this "locked spring" of Rechnitz's childhood. Seaweeds no less than mushrooms, and perhaps even more so—as they are among the most ancient species and lower in the evolutionary scale—reach down to the unknown and as such allow Agnon to underscore the partiality of Rechnitz's new perspective. This scene of remembrance may seem to offer a deeper explanation for Rechnitz's choice of profession than the legendary Homeric scene of initiation, but here too the young botanist still thinks in terms of classical and European myths (the sirens and mermaids), unaware of his latent attraction to his own cultural heritage and to the underlying Song of his life; here too he is at a loss when it comes to understanding the one love of his life that neither botany nor psychoanalysis can make truly graspable.[35]

ALLEGORICAL ROSES: NATIONAL LOVES

Betrothed has generated numerous allegorical readings. Avraham Kariv, among its early reviewers, regards the novella as an uplifting allegory of national renewal, embodied in the reaffirmed oath of Yaacov Rechnitz as Israel and Shoshana as the Shekhinah of the Shabbat (the six maidens turn out to be the six secular days of the week).[36] By contrast, Dov Sadan, in one of the first monumental books to dismantle the common notion of Agnon as a pious writer, aptly calls for a more nuanced understanding of allegory in the novella—one that does not overlook the literal dimension. The *mashal* and the *nimshal*, he argues, each has its own "wondrous autonomy."[37] The beauty of the piece lies precisely in that the literal love story is not simply yoked to the allegorical one but rather stands in its own right. Sadan goes on to complicate the allegorical dimension of the tale. He calls attention to the tale's oscillation between non-Jewish texts—from classical literature to the folktale "Sleeping Beauty" and the novels of Knut Hamsun—and Jewish subtexts, among them, the allegorical network created by the combination of the names of the two protagonists: *shoshanat Ya'acov* (the "Rose of Jacob," a traditional designation for the Jewish people).

If Sadan questions Kariv's overemphasis on the Jewish sources of *Betrothed* and calls attention to their presence as hidden subtext, Hannan Hever, in a more recent essay, has challenged the tendency to view the novella as an uncomplicated allegory about Zionist renewal. In contradistinction to the Zionist tendency to relegate the sea to the margins and regard it as a subordinate geography whose primary role is to lead to the sanctified land, Agnon, Hever suggests, inverts these hierarchies. He places the sea at the center of all events and exposes the instability of terrestrial attachments.[38]

The discussion regarding the allegorical dimension of the novella has had its twists and turns—from Kariv to Hever—but it has not touched on the exegetical issues I've been addressing in my consideration of Agnon's response to the Zionist adaptation of biblical botany and of the Song.[39] Walter Benjamin's redefinition of the distinctions between allegory and symbol is vital to the understanding of Agnon's take on the allegorical underpinning of biblical botany. "Whereas in the symbol," writes Benjamin, "destruction is idealized and the transfigured face of nature is fleetingly revealed in the light of redemption, in allegory the observer is confronted with the *facies hippocratica* of history as a petrified, primordial landscape."[40]

For Agnon, who shares Benjamin's critique of the illusionary, organic wholeness of the symbol and its redemptive light, biblical plants are as arbitrary a sign as seaweed.[41] There is, after all, no guarantee that the scientific identification of biblical plants is an actual retrieval of an authentic, botanical past (if it were decisively so, there would not be so many disputes regarding the correct identification and translation). Seaweeds that do not pertain to the world of biblical flora may be associated with the Song no less than terrestrial plants. When botanists such as the Hareuvenis regard biblical plants as "natural" symbols and a concrete bridge to the biblical past and to national renewal, they are, Agnon reminds us, in the realm of sheer, inorganic allegory.

To highlight the absurdity of the Zionist quest for the concrete biblical plantscapes of the Land of Israel, Agnon playfully evokes a series of traditional allegories of the Rose (the Rose of Jacob is but one specimen). The *shoshana* is first constructed as a metaphor for national renewal in Hosea 14:6—"I will be as the dew unto Israel; he shall blossom as the [*shoshana*]." Following Hosea, the commentators of Song of Songs Rabbah interpret the "rose among the thorns" as an allegorical representation of the chosenness and glory of the nation, blessed as it is by divine dew (2:14). The Zohar, in turn, endorses the midrash on Song 2:2 and uses it as a springboard for a mystical reading: "Rabbi Hizkiya opened: '*Like a rose among thorns, so is my beloved among the maidens*. . . . Who is *a rose*? Assembly of Israel. For there is a rose, and then there is a rose! Just as a rose among thorns is colored red and white, so Assembly of Israel includes judgment and compassion. Just as a rose has thirteen petals, so Assembly of Israel has thirteen qualities of compassion surrounding Her on every side'" (1:1a).[42] If in the midrash the Assembly of Israel (Knesset Yisrael) refers to the earthly community of the people of Israel, in the Zohar it primarily designates the Shekhinah, the divine feminine counterpart of the people, here in her configuration as Rose.[43]

To this traditional line of roses Agnon adds a touch of the Zionist Rose of Jericho, capable of being revived by the slightest rain, even after many years of exile. With its promise of national renewal in modern times, the Rose of Jericho turns out to be yet another intricate chapter in the history of allegorical readings of the Song's *shoshana.*

The wet roses of *Betrothed* are saturated by all these different allegorical roses. Their overall allegorical hue is, however, distinctly darker. To the extent that Shoshana is an ill Rose who cannot quite be awakened, Agnon seems to challenge the very possibility of glittering allegories of national renewal—both old and new.

With his incredibly broad, panoramic view of the numerous, often contradictory, commentaries of the Song, Agnon sets the rosy, dreamy allegories of the Song against one of the more ominous ones: that of the Three Oaths. The Three Oaths (*shalosh ha-shevu'ot*) are based on an allegorical reading of the verse "awaken not, nor stir up love, until it please" as a warning against any attempt to rebuild Zion before Messianic times. This allegory has its beginnings in the Talmud but is still endorsed in current times by some Ultra-Orthodox and Hasidic communities, where it is used to oppose Zionism as a pseudo-messianic movement.[44] Whether the national love oath of biblical times—the covenantal scenes of Mount Sinai and beyond, which are construed by Hosea as an act of betrothal ("And I will betroth thee unto Me in faithfulness"; 2:22)—should be reenacted or replaced by a counter-oath of the *shevu'ot* is a question that underlies the ambivalence with which Rechnitz and Shoshana open up their childhood bond.

The warm, Oriental Song of Songs gardens of Jaffa in springtime, with all their intoxicating fragrance and promise of a new Paradise, are not quite a national cure in *Betrothed.* Shoshana and Rechnitz seem to stroll in an entirely different planet. More often than not, they wander in their minds and memories in the Eden-like Song of Songs gardens of Vienna rather than in the resurrected Song of Songs landscapes of the Zionist spring.

To evoke the Freudian connection yet again, this time via Freud's *Moses and Monotheism*, I would add that Agnon's suspension of belief in allegorical roses is accompanied by a suspension of belief in the value of awaking repressed collective memories. In *Moses and Monotheism*, the return of the repressed has its unmistakable dangers but is ultimately construed as a vital "progress in spirituality" that eventually leads to the reemergence of the Mosaic text and the monotheistic nation.[45] Agnon renders the lure of rekindling past memories but is keener on probing the pathological fixations at stake—in both the individual and the collective spheres. Whether or not biblical plants are "memory plants"—in Hareuvenis' terms—or bearers of traces of biblical events (a botanical version of Freud's phylogenetic perception of human memory), it remains unclear why such memories should propel a whole community to search for a sense of belonging in biblical lands.

Writing in 1943, against the backdrop of the Second World War, Agnon's preoccupation with the founding dreams of Zionism had special urgency. In one of the most moving moments in the novella, Rechnitz looks at Shoshana with dismay, wondering how such an ill, melancholy woman could expect him to marry her. But just as he approaches the point of leaving Shoshana behind, he cannot but admit to himself that without her, he feels "as if the whole world is taken from him" (*she-be-lo 'ima kol ha-'olam menutal mimenu*).[46] In Agnon's multifaceted allegorical framework, national passions may be construed as an equally impossible love—one that can be neither followed nor relinquished. Rechnitz cannot quite commit himself to Palestine, but he is, nonetheless, compelled by the seaweeds of Jaffa rather than by those of Ithaca.

"THE TALE OF THE SCRIBE"

In his unending exegetical experiments, Agnon juggles yet another traditional allegory of the Song in this novella: the Torah as Rose and the concomitant configuration of the study of the Torah as "picking roses" (*lilkot shoshanim*) (6:2). This allegorical line, whose most renowned advocate was Rashi, appears explicitly in Agnon's "The Tale of the Scribe" ("Agadat ha-sofer") at the moment in which Rafael, the scribe, decides to write and embellish a Torah scroll in memory of his late wife, Miriam.

> Rafael was a great gardener. He planted beautiful Torah scrolls in the world. And whoever was invited to appear before the King . . . took a Torah scroll with him. And now that Miriam's time had come to appear before the King—the Holy One, blessed be He—Raphael immediately went down to his garden—that is, to his pure and holy table—and picked roses—that is, the letters of the Torah scroll he wrote.[47]

Rafael's thoughts seem pious in character. He wants to create a Torah as beautiful as a rose so that his wife would be able to bring it along with her as she approaches the Ultimate Gardener upon her death. "While the story appears to take at face value Rafael's devotion," Hoffman writes, "there are subtle indications that his excess is not simply to be understood as piety."[48] Rafael's relentless, erotic immersion in his work comes at the expense of his relationship with his wife. He can unite with Miriam only after her death, in a highly sensual, ecstatic dance with the Torah scroll he had made on her behalf.

Asael, who calls attention to this passage from "The Tale of the Scribe" in his reading of *Betrothed*, misses this irony. According to Asael, Rechnitz is doomed because he chooses to adhere, like a biblical critic, to the secular studies of the sources instead of clinging to Shoshana, the Rose of the true Torah. Focusing solely on Agnon's irony vis-à-vis biblical criticism and modern scholarly trends, he neglects to take into account the blunt questioning of the exegetical practices of the orthodox world as well.[49]

But Agnon's irony is even more complex given that he is deeply interested in the similarities between modern scholars and the *talmidey hakhamim* from whom they wish to depart. Regardless of the palpable differences between their respective worlds, both Rafael and Rechnitz are so trapped in their passion for their work that they lose touch with the women whom they love. Their love for the Song itself and for picking roses—be they scribal or scientific—seems at times to reach troubling proportions.

In depicting happy days for Rechnitz, when he ends up withdrawing both from Shoshana and from the *ne'arot* of Jaffa—devoting himself, in "an undistracted love" solely to the study of seaweed—the narrator whimsically defines "wisdom" (*ha-hokhma*) as a conveniently "pleasant wife" (*ra'aya noha*).[50] Agnon deliberately uses the term "wisdom" (with its biblical, midrashic, and mystical echoes) rather than "research"—in order to underline questions of continuity between traditional exegesis and modern scholarship. But how long can such happiness last when the "good gods" (121) are envious of Rechnitz's tranquility and the women of Jaffa of his scholarly solitude?

THE SOMNAMBULIST RACE

The somnambulist race with which the novella ends is the grand finale of Agnon's dramatization of the dream sequences of the Song. On the night of the race, when Rechnitz is alone in his room, Tamara, one of the six *ne'arot* of Jaffa, ventures to knock on his door, with "her lips trembl[ing] like petals touched with morning dew" (122), assuming the role of the dew-drenched *dod* (Song 5:2) with lips as roses—*siftotav shoshanim*—"dripping with flowing myrrh" (5:13). Rechnitz longs to take her into his arms, but desire remains unfulfilled, for Rachel and Leah suddenly appear and shortly after the other maidens. Once they all have gathered together, they go outdoors and stroll by the moonlit sea.

> The sea lay down on an unending bed, with moon-whitened waves as its nightgown. The shores had lengthened and the moon shone over the sands and the sea. And a benevolent spirit hovered over Rechnitz and the six maidens. . . . Sea and sky, heaven and earth, and all the space between became one body which is not a body but rather a luminous calm enveloped by azure, or an azure transparent as air. Up above, and under the surface of the sea, the moon raced as a somnambulist. . . . Even the sands were moonstruck and seemed to be walking on and on. Like the sands, like the entire surrounding air, the maidens, and with them Rechnitz, stood as if dream-struck. If they looked above, there was the moon running her race, and if they looked out toward the sea, there she was again hovering upon the face of the waters.[51]

All are swept into the Shulamite's nocturnal imaginings—not only Rechnitz and his female companions but also the personified sea, who lies in bed with a dreamy, unending, moonlit gown. Agnon uses the feminine term for "moon," *levana*, and plays with its adjectival meaning: "white" (in the feminine form). The *levana* whitens the waves and engulfs them with her lunar magic, but then goes on to spellbind the entire cosmos. If the sands become "moonstruck" (*mukey yareah*), Rechnitz and the maidens become "dream-struck" (*mukey halom*), surrounded as they are by the race of the moon in heaven above and her reflection "upon the face of the waters."[52]

This lunar race is contagious, for it leads the *ne'arot*, one by one, to dance:

> Rachel took Leah's hand, Leah the hand of Asnat and Asnat that of Raya, and Raya took Mira's, and Mira Tamara's and Tamara took Rachel's; they encircled Rechnitz and danced around him—danced until Rachel broke from their ring and knelt down facing the sea with her eyes uplifted to the moon. Asnat stood still, stretched out her hands in the air and played inaudible notes on an unseen keyboard. "Listen, Tamara," said Mira, "if I had a horse, I would go galloping from one end of the world to the other!" (129)

The dancers form an enchanting ring around Rechnitz. And although the young botanist seems to be the center of attention, the young women are as absorbed in one another in a playful, imaginary game that doesn't remain within the confines of the circle or the confines of normative conduct. First, Rachel breaks from the ring and kneels before the *levana*, as if she were paying homage to the goddess of this magical dance by the sea. Then, Asnat comes along and accompanies her by playing an inaudible melody on an unseen piano. Finally, Mira, caught by the same wild whim, ventures to imagine herself galloping like an unstoppable knight "from one end of the world to the other."

The gender reversal that begins with Tamara's knocking on Rechnitz's door and continues with Mira's fantasy about the gallant galloping reaches its peak when the *ne'arot* propose an earthly race in which they will compete over Rechnitz's hand. The winner and future bride will then be crowned with a garland made out of Rechnitz's seaweed.

> "Do you see this garland?" said Leah. "We've all agreed that the fastest runner will win and wear this wreath, made of Dr. Rechnitz's weeds. Do you agree, Dr. Rechnitz?"
>
> Rechnitz nodded, saying, "Yes." But his face grew pale and his heart began to quake.
>
> Leah insisted, "The Greeks had the men run, not the girls."
>
> Asnat answered, "But since all those young men are dead and we are alive, let's do their running ourselves." (133)

The race, with its Greek stamp, continues the idolatrous moon worshipping in the dance that preceded it. But despite the pagan qualities of the race, it is inextricably intertwined with the rhythms of the Song and the intoxicated movement that characterizes the Shulamite, from her call upon her lover to rush in the opening verses of the biblical poem—"Draw me, we will run after thee" (1:4)—to her somnambulist wanderings at night in Chapter 5. Rosenzweig's depiction of the Song's speech of love in *The Star of Redemption* is most pertinent in this connection:

> The speech of love is all present: dream and reality, sleep of the limbs and awaking of the heart, intertwine indistinguishably. Everything is equally present, equally fleeting and equally alive—"like a gazelle or a young stag upon the mountains." A downpour of imperatives descends on this evergreen

> pasture of the present and vitalizes it. The imperatives sound different but always mean the same thing: "Draw me after you, open to me, arise, come away, hurry"—it is always one and the same imperative of love.[53]

A similar mixture of dream and wakefulness, a similar kind of speed, of urgency, of fleeting images, a similar sense of an all-encompassing vivacity are characteristic of the final sequences of *Betrothed*.[54]

When the semi-awake, semi-dreaming Rechnitz approaches the running maidens at the last stretch of the race, he suddenly sees dashing past them the figure of the somnambulist Shoshana in her white nightgown.

> Neither Leah nor Rachel nor Asnat nor Raya nor Mira nor Tamara had seen her running, yet each of them had been aware in the course of the race that someone was ahead of her, without knowing this someone as Shoshana Ehrlich, Jacob's friend, who for many days and weeks had been asleep, never rising from her bed. With fear in their souls they forgot the garland and their agreement with Jacob. And Jacob, too, forgot all this as he stood before Shoshana.
>
> Suddenly there was a voice calling him by name, a voice that came, as it were, from beneath Shoshana's eyelashes. Jacob shut his eyes and replied in a whisper, "Shoshana, are you here?"
>
> Shoshana's eyelashes signaled assent. She put out her hands, took the crown from Jacob's arm and placed it on her head. (138–39)

As a "rose among thorns," Shoshana outdoes the other *ne'urot* in the race. She places the "crown/diadem," *'atara*, of seaweed upon her head to mark her victory. The use of the term *'atara*, which appears in the Song in the context of Solomon's wedding ("Go forth, O ye daughters of Zion, and gaze upon king Solomon, even upon the crown [*'atara*] wherewith his mother hath crowned him in the day of his espousals"—3:11), endows the scene with nuptial overtones. It seems for a moment a happy ending that combines elements of the Song with the scene of awakening in the Sleeping Beauty legend. Above all, this encounter by the vast sea that "grew even vaster" (138) as they draw nearer to each other is a remarkably intensified reenactment of several childhood scenes that now blend together: Shoshana's running with a wet rose in her mouth, the love oath in the Viennese garden, and that other more hidden scene in the pond, when Shoshana arose from the water with seaweed streaming down her hair.

But what if the reunion between Shoshana and Rechnitz takes place only in the dream zone between his "shut eyes" and her semi-closed "eyelashes," from whence her voice emerges? Is it Rechnitz's dream of wish fulfillment, where his two loves—the love for Shoshana and the love for marine botany—are wedded via the crown of seaweed? Or is it a more somber ceremony on the threshold of a love that yields to death (not unlike the *Liebestod* of Rafael and Miriam in "The Tale of the Scribe")? Alter suggests that "Agnon is careful to draw a veil of ambiguity over the conclusion" and points to the deadly qualities of this nocturnal scene: Are Shoshana's "night clothes her shroud? Has she arisen from a sickbed or a grave to fulfill her pact with Jacob?"[55]

The open-endedness of the literal love story of Rechnitz and Shoshana is accompanied by a final insistence on ambiguity on the allegorical level as well. The revival of the national Rose doesn't seem less complicated at the conclusion. Dashing miraculously ahead of the maidens and then setting the *'atara* upon her head, Shoshana seems almost celestial. She basks in the light of three of the Shekhinah's designations/symbols (all drawn from the Song): the Rose (*shoshana*), the Diadem (*'atara*), and the Moon (*levana*).[56] And yet Agnon's Shekhinah has a dubious dimension: the Rose is ill, the Diadem is made of seaweeds, and the *levana* "races like a somnambulist" and is associated with pagan rituals. National loves are set in this final race in a maddening, semi-heretical moonstruck world of enchanting dreams, equally removed from a naively hopeful perspective or an apocalyptic scenario.

A PRECARIOUS AESTHETICS OF RENEWAL

In a moment of uncharacteristic optimism, Kurzweil speaks of the ending of *Betrothed* as an exhilarating episode in which the "Song of Songs of true love" emerges with great resonance (*'ole u-metsaltsel*).[57] Poetry appears sporadically in Rechnitz's mesmerized gaze at the seaweed and in the different scenes of remembrance, but here, indeed, a whole section has something of the intensity and force of sheer poetry. Lunar light seems to entrance not only the characters of this novella but also its narrator. More than ever before, the tale breaks away from prose and moves beyond normative genre boundaries, into poetry, as if moving even closer to the original mode of the Song of Songs.

Is Agnon intimating that whether or not the Song can offer renewal at the personal or national spheres it has the capacity to serve as a base for aesthetic renewal? To some extent this is the underlying melody of the final sequence. But for the forever ironic Agnon—who steers away from the flamboyant praises of aesthetic renaissance one finds in the writings of the Hareuvenis, Schatz, and Bialik—prose remains the predominant genre even when he experiments with poetry.[58] The very final note of the story is accordingly a prosaic, ironic coda of the narrator: "Here, for the time being, we have brought to an end our account of the affairs of Jacob Rechnitz and Shoshana Ehrlich. These are the same Shoshana and Jacob who were betrothed to one another through a solemn vow. Because of it, we have called this whole account 'Betrothed,' though at first we had thought to call it 'The Seven Maidens'" (139). Agnon flaunts the artistic work behind the scenes and treats authorial choices with pseudo-naive, ironic recognition that they are not as innate as they may seem at first. There is always the ghost of another potential title or plot, of another potential love. I would add that there is also a sense of another potential genre, of a latent Poem, which was ultimately replaced by prose.

In a famous passage from his banquet speech on receiving the Nobel Prize in 1966 (quoted on the Israeli fifty-shekel note), Agnon recounts:

> As a result of the historic catastrophe in which Titus of Rome destroyed Jerusalem and Israel was exiled from its land, I was born in one of the cities of the Exile. But always I regarded myself as one who was born in Jerusalem. In a dream, in a vision of the night, I saw myself standing with my brother-Levites in the Holy Temple, singing with them the songs of David, King of Israel, melodies such as no ear has heard since the day our city was destroyed and its people went into exile. I suspect that the angels in charge of the Shrine of Music, fearful lest I sing in wakefulness what I had sung in dream, made me forget by day what I had sung at night; for if my brethren, the sons of my people, were to hear, they would be unable to bear their grief over the happiness they have lost. To console me for having prevented me from singing with my mouth, they enable me to compose songs in writing.[59]

Agnon regards biblical songs (he refers to David's songs, but Solomon's Song hovers in the background) as a primary, legendary genre that may appear in the world of dreams but not in daylight.[60] In his wakefulness, in the exilic world that follows catastrophe, Agnon can only grieve over the poetic "happiness" that had been lost and find some consolation in composing "songs in writing." He supposedly distinguishes between "song" and "poem" (in Hebrew the term *shir* refers to both), between oral culture and written culture. But given that Agnon is primarily a writer rather than a poet, he seems to imply that prose—or prose that aspires to be "songs in writing"—is the most suitable mode of expression in a fallen world where truly divine songs can no longer be heard or uttered.

In his renowned "Revealment and Concealment in Language," Bialik compares the "masters of prose" to "one who crosses a river walking on hard ice frozen into a solid block. Such a man can divert his attention completely from the covered depths flowing underneath his feet." Conversely the "masters of poetry" are likened to "one who crosses a river when it is breaking up, by stepping across floating, moving blocks of ice. He dare not set his foot on any block for longer than it takes him to leap from one block to the next. . . . Between the breaches the void looms, the foot slips, danger is close."[61] Agnon reverses Bialik's distinction: poetry may well be located on the brink, but it is above all the writing of prose that resembles the precarious experience of leaping from one block of ice to the next, far from any sense of security. Closer to Hegel, Agnon treats prose as a belated genre that is more attuned to the modern rift of loss and disenchantment. "The world of prose," writes Hegel, is "a world of finitude and mutability, of entanglement in the relative, of the pressure of necessity from which the individual is in no position to withdraw."[62]

On preferring prose in his renderings of the Song, Agnon underscores his exilic position and the limits and pressures of the prosaic world. Even if one were to reiterate the words of the Song verbatim, as Shoshana asks Rechnitz to reiterate the oath, such speech acts, he intimates, couldn't possibly provide access to the "real" sounds and hues of the ancient gardens of love. And yet Agnon, as we have seen, doesn't entirely relinquish poetry. He is intrigued by the interdependence of prose and poetry and by the ways in which they may haunt each other.[63] Through the rare moments in which poetry suddenly erupts in *Betrothed*, battering against the surrounding prose, against all odds, Agnon ventures to capture the tremendous craving for an aesthetic renewal, the wondrous vitality of the race for a new Song, even in a world in which it is lost.[64]

4

The Biblical Ethnographies of "Edo and Enam" and the Quest for the Ultimate Song

"Edo and Enam," one of Agnon's most enigmatic tales, a renowned Agnonian riddle that has generated as many readings as the dog Balak, opens with the narrator's puzzlement at finding his friends, the Greifenbachs, "so dark and distracted" before traveling abroad. The story takes place in Jerusalem under the British Mandate (after "the war"), a time of instability, and the Greifenbachs, who are about to leave for a vacation in Europe, fear that their house will be plundered during their absence (143). They do have a tenant, Dr. Ginat, but given that he is constantly on field trips connected with his philological-ethnographic researches, he is rarely at home. The narrator's heart beats fast on listening to his friends. Both Ginat and his famous discovery of the Enamite hymns move him with unexpected force. Ginat, he informs us, published articles on the grammar of Edo, but what made him "truly famous was his discovery of the Enamite Hymns . . . they were not only a new-found link in a chain that bound the beginnings of recorded history to the ages before, but—in themselves—splendid and incisive poetry." One thing, however, surprised the narrator. "All these scholars affirmed that the gods of Enam and their priests were male; how was it that they did not catch in the hymns the cadence of a woman's song?" (145–46).

Although Ginat's studies do not address the question of female poetic traditions, there is, we discover at the very end, a woman singer behind his findings. Her identity is revealed on a mysterious night in which all the principal characters of the tale meet, unexpectedly, at the Greifenbachs' abode. The narrator happens to be there because he had promised the Greifenbachs to keep an eye on their house. On hearing a woman singing, he approaches Ginat's moonlit room, where he sees "a young woman wrapped in white, her feet bare, her hair disheveled, her eyes closed. And a young man sat at the table by the window and wrote in ink on paper all that she spoke" (220). The man turns out to be Ginat, and the woman is Gemulah, Gamzu's Mizrahi (Eastern-Jewish) wife, who was brought up in contemporary Enam—way out in the deserts of the Orient—but left its rocky mountains and followed her husband to Jerusalem. She is now revealed as Ginat's primary informant, the source of his knowledge of the Enamite hymns and of the inscrutable language of Edo. But this is not merely an ethnographic scene of writing. It is also the dramatic moment in which all the desperate loves of the tale intersect. Gamzu begs Gemulah to return to him; Gemulah, in turn, rejects her husband and attempts to lure the young scholar: "Let me stay with you," she says to Ginat, "and I shall sing you the song of the bird Grofit, which she sings only once in her lifetime" (221–22).[1] Ginat succumbs for a moment and says "sing" but later urges her to follow her husband. At the tale's end, Gemulah and Ginat fall to their deaths when the young scholar tries to prevent the moonstruck Gemulah from walking on the roof.

Agnon wrote "Edo and Enam" sometime between March and October of 1949, when he was staying at the apartment of Gershom and Fania Scholem in Rehavia while his friends were in the United States for a visit. Many have consequently read Dr. Ginat and his mysterious preoccupation with ancient esoteric texts as a comment on Gershom Scholem and the academic study of Kabbalah. Tochner regards the tale as a critique of the rational, cold manner in which the modern scholarship of the Kabbalah treats Jewish sources.[2] More recently, Tzachi Weiss has suggested that the tale calls into question Scholem's attempt to define his research as a detached "pure science," supposedly untainted by the mystical materials it sets out to explore.[3]

When Dan Miron asked Scholem in an interview in 1982 whether he saw himself as Dr. Ginat of "Edo and Enam," Scholem was infuriated. "That interpretation," he exclaimed, "is wrong from start to finish!"[4] Scholem, however, was not unaware of the great interest Agnon had in his scholarly friends—both in their work and in their lives. "As a matter of fact," Scholem writes in his "Reflections on S. Y. Agnon," "Agnon never felt as comfortable in the company of writers as he did in that of scholars who, surprisingly enough, appear as central figures in some of his strangest stories. The calling of the writer seems to have held no mysteries, whereas the utter and largely hopeless devotion of the scholar obviously filled him with sinister fascination."[5] In the Hebrew and German versions of this essay, he actually refers to "Edo and Enam" as exemplary in this connection and defines it as "an enigmatic story about the greatness and failure of scholarship."[6]

My reading of "Edo and Enam" follows the traces of another scholar and close friend of Agnon: the ethnographer-philologist, historian, and biblical critic Shlomo Dov Goitein. Here, as in the previous chapter, my objective is not merely to identify yet another possible face (or partial face) behind the portrait of an Agnonian scholar. The Goitein connection serves as a point of departure for a broader consideration of Agnon's response to Israeli biblicism and to the privileged position of the Song of Songs in this connection. More specifically, I read "Edo and Enam" in relation to a plethora of modern ethnographic studies of the Song—from Wetzstein's study of Syrian wedding songs to Goitein's essays from the 1940s and 1950s.

The relevance of biblical criticism to Ginat's research is by no means explicit. Ginat's official field of interest is, after all, the ancient, Eastern culture of Enam. But a scholar who is wholly immersed in a search for the wondrous, ultimate songs of the past and whose name is "Ginat"—the first word of the construct form *ginat egoz* (the "nut garden" of the Song)—can hardly be innocent of hidden passions for the ancient biblical love poem.[7] That scholars have blind spots is something to which the narrator calls our attention from the very outset on wondering why no investigator of Enam has managed to "catch in the hymns the cadence of a woman's song." Indeed, Ginat's lack of awareness to the resonance of his own cultural heritage in his work is inextricably connected to his failure to even hear, let alone cope with, the feminine lure of the ancient songs he collects. The dialogue with psychoanalysis is less elaborate in "Edo and Enam" than in *Betrothed*, but here too the dynamics of scholarly blindness is pivotal, and Enam has some of the qualities of Freud's Pompeii. One may also wonder whether the ancient Enamite culture also bears some resemblance to the hidden, matriarchal Minoan-Mycenaean civilization Freud discovers (to his surprise) behind Greek civilization in his exploration of female sexuality.[8]

The ironic discrepancy between the overt and covert aspects of Ginat's studies is accompanied by an ironic probing of the methodologies of biblical ethnography. The predominant tendency among biblical ethnographers of the Song was to regard the contemporary Orient as the ultimate exegetical key to the understanding of the actual love songs and rituals of biblical times. In his attempt to retrieve the authentic hymns of Enam through Gemulah's Mizrahi tunes, Ginat, as it were, follows such practices. But given that the question of the affinity between Gemulah's Oriental songs and the ancient Enamite hymns remains palpably open, Ginat's research seems, at times, closer to a wild goose chase or a grand artistic feat than to a rigorous scientific project.

Agnon reflects on such Orientalist research but is, as always, interested in the ways in which scholarship forms part of a broader cultural scene, in this case, the Zionist fascination with the Orient. The question of the Oriental features of the Song, which is only on the margins of the Jaffa gardens of *Betrothed* becomes central in "Edo and Enam." Appearing on no known map, Enam is something of an imaginary Eastern oasis, bearing a phonetic similarity to *teyman* (Yemen) and *'elam* (a biblical designation for Persia) as well as to *eynot* ("fountains") and *eynam* ("nonexistent"). It serves not only as a site through which to examine the ancient and contemporary culture of exilic, Eastern communities but also as a screen through which to explore the dreamy, allegorical zones of Zion—where national love is renewed within the Oriental, erotic-poetic, pastoral landscapes and music-scapes of the Song.

Agnon spells out large the magic of individual and collective dreams spun around the Orient but does not hesitate to flaunt their delusional qualities and the hazards they may entail. What is more, he ventures to add a meta-poetic dimension in which he meditates on the ways in which his own Song and quest for poetic epitome is set against, yet deeply embedded in, the imaginary realms of Gemulah's songs.

In "Edo and Enam," as in *Betrothed*, we witness a spectacular exegetical juggling. Here too Agnon points to the allegorical innuendoes embedded in the new Zionist literalism. Here too he offers a remarkable juxtaposition of literalist readings of the ancient love poem along with traditional and aesthetic allegories. And yet Agnon now ventures to develop his inquiry of the Song's reception in new contexts. His move from *Betrothed* to "Edo and Enam" entails a transition from biblical botany to biblical ethnography, from Zionism's craving for renewal via Nature to its craving for renewal via the Orient, from the Second Aliyah to the postwar years. But it also provides a different blend of traditional allegories of the Song. Whereas in *Betrothed* the Zohar is a vibrant backdrop, in "Edo and Enam" kabbalistic texts are boisterously foregrounded.

I focus on Goitein and his ethnographic precursors but also refer, at points, to the ways in which the interpretive practices of biblical ethnographers in "Edo and Enam" merge with kabbalistic exegetical pursuits. Accordingly, I will also consider, however partially, some aspects of the dialogue between Agnon and Scholem. Much as Agnon does not hesitate to cross the boundaries between marine botany and psychoanalysis, so too he allows biblical criticism and the Kabbalah to intersect in unexpected ways.

SHLOMO DOV GOITEIN: THE STORY OF A FRIENDSHIP

The friendship of Agnon and Goitein has become more visible lately with the publication of their correspondence.[9] Goitein was the Arabic teacher of Esther Marx (Agnon's wife) in Frankfurt and through her came to know Agnon (her Hebrew teacher at the time). Later on in Jerusalem, Agnon and Goitein met on a weekly basis. In its initial stages, Dan Laor comments, their close friendship "was nurtured by the literary ambitions of Goitein, who wished to become a playwright and saw Agnon as an astute advisor in this matter."[10] Goitein's play, *Pulcellina*, never acquired much acclaim, and he did not venture to write additional plays (though he occasionally published poems in *Haaretz*). His gift as a writer, however, is evident in his engagingly written academic publications, often punctuated with anecdotes and moments of dramatic spark.[11] Between Agnon's scholarly inclinations and Goitein's literary sensibilities, not to mention their unorthodox mingling of religiosity and secularism, their paths crossed in a variety of ways, making their friendship all the more intimate in the course of time.

Most of their correspondence is from the late fifties on, after Goitein had moved to the United States and founded the Geniza research, first at the University of Pennsylvania and then at the Institute for Advanced Studies at Princeton. It reveals a familiarity of each of them with the minute details of the other's familial and professional life. They exchanged notes on their work in progress and responded to each other's new publications. Agnon complains of interruptions in his work on *A City and the Fullness Thereof* (*Ir u-melo'a*), and Goitein reports: "The day before yesterday, I sent the second volume of my book *A Mediterranean Society* . . . to the publisher, 1078 pages (without index). . . . Never before have so many interesting sources on public life in Israel been collected in one volume."[12] In a letter from September 4, 1966, Agnon apologizes that his handwriting (which was notoriously illegible) is even more obscure than the Geniza fragments. Goitein, in turn, deciphers this letter with the same methods he used in examining Geniza documents (words he was sure of were marked in pen and the rest in pencil).

When Agnon won the Nobel Prize in 1966, Goitein was interviewed on various TV programs and was vital to the reception of Agnon's oeuvre in American literary circles.[13] In 1970, in a ceremony at Dropsie College commemorating Agnon's death, he spoke of his late friend with great admiration. "Since biblical times," he declared, "there has not been in Hebrew language a corpus of narrative prose of the magnitude, dignity, and meaningfulness of Agnon's creation. He has done for Hebrew prose what Yehuda Halevi has achieved in religious poetry. Halevi wrote in the forms and spirit of the 12th century. Agnon expressed the mood and refinement of the 20th. But both are the mouth-pieces of genuine and integral Judaism."[14]

Agnon could not have read Goitein's 1957 essays "Women as Creators of Biblical Genres" and "The Literary Character and Symbolic Interpretation of the Song of Songs" while writing "Edo and Enam," but he may have come across an earlier, very brief sketch titled "On the Song of Songs" ("Al shir hashirim"), published in *Davar* on April 23, 1943, where Goitein first speculates about the female poet who composed the Song. And given the ample intellectual exchange between the two, Agnon must have heard of Goitein's ideas in the late forties, at the time his friend's ethnographic work with Yemenite women singers led him to develop and substantiate his previous intuitions regarding the Song of Songs and female poetic traditions.

"AH, FOLKLORE, FOLKLORE!": THE QUESTION OF ETHNOGRAPHIC LITERALISM

What makes Ginat something of a Goitein? The fact that his name begins with *gimel* seems almost a prerequisite to becoming part of a tale where most names begin either with *gimel* or *ayin* (Agnon's implicit signature).[15] In fact, there is greater phonetic similarity given that in both names there is a *nun* and a *tet-taf* (the two Hebrew *t*'s are interchangeable).[16] Beyond the shared letters, there are, of course, more substantive points of affinity. Like Goitein, Ginat is an ethnographer, a philologist, and a biblical critic (if latently so) whose research entails a quest for the remnants of an ancient language, the collection of traditions of Jews from the lands of Islam, and an interest in scriptural leaves with mysterious inscriptions. The very root "*ganaz*" ("hidden"—the base of the term *geniza*) appears at various points, most significantly in the depiction of the "hidden," precious traditions that Gemulah's father had passed on to his daughter and in the account of the earth wondrously "opening up" and allowing for the discovery of the manuscripts that previous generations had concealed (*ganzu*) (214). But, above all, it is Goitein's Orientalist, ethnographic study of the Song that comes strikingly close to Ginat's research: in both cases, it is the singing of Mizrahi women that serves as a window to the songs of the past; in both one finds a leap from the contemporary Orient to the ancient one (biblical and prebiblical); in both there is an unknown female poetic tradition that protrudes between the lines.

Gamzu's amusing comments on biblical criticism, which implicitly refer to Ginat's work, convey, I suspect, something of Agnon's own critique of the pretensions of such scholarship. The observant Gamzu, the seller of rare manuscripts, admits that traditional exegetes, even "true *zaddikim*," may "twist the words of the Holy Writ," but whereas they do it "with the intention of serving heaven," Bible critics "who have not the merit of studying the Torah for its own sake, their teaching is perverted in accordance with the emptiness of their own spirit" (180–81). At a later point, he spells out his resentment with greater pathos: "Ah, folklore, folklore! Everything which is not material for scientific research they treat as folklore. Have they not made our holy Torah into either one or the other? People live out their lives according to the Torah, they lay down their lives for the heritage of their fathers; then along come the scientists, and make the Torah into "research material," and the ways of our fathers into—folklore" (210).

Gamzu's debunking of biblical folklore bears some resemblance to Rosenzweig's scathing account of Wetzstein's ethnographic research of the Song, though the latter engages in a theoretical debate that is, of course, foreign to the bookseller's vocabulary:

> The hopeless caprice and text-critical adventurousness of all those interpretations into the objective realm of the "musical drama" made the learned spirits receptive to a new view. . . . [I]t was suddenly discovered that among the peasants in Syria the wedding is celebrated on the analogy of a royal wedding to this day, with the groom as the king and the bride as the royal choice. . . . Now everything is once more enclosed in the lyrical duo-solitude of the lover and the beloved. And now, above all, the simile is brought back into the "most original" sense of the Songs . . . the shepherd who is bridegroom by the king whom he feels himself to be. This, however, is the point at which we are aiming. Love simply cannot be "purely human."[17]

In this climactic moment of Rosenzweig's "theological anti-historicism," to use David Myers terms, biblical ethnography is mocked for its fanciful, reductive so-called literalism.[18] The "objective realm" such scholars have found in Syrian weddings, the supposedly authentic, Oriental window to the "most original" historical sense of the Song, is nothing but an "adventurous" interpretation of "learned spirits" who ironically end up decontextualizing the biblical text in overlooking the inseparability of human and divine love.

The critique of Orientalism does not begin with Edward Said. Rosenzweig's reading of the Song, as Samuel Moyn points out, is an interesting example of an earlier critical assessment of a different bent.[19] Rosenzweig is not concerned with the political implications of the Western imposition on the East, but he is a precursor of Said in laying bare the misconceptions at stake.

Agnon would agree with Rosenzweig only to a point. He surely flaunts the absurdities and fallacies of ethnographic literalism. And yet it is precisely the paradoxical moves of scholars who have no intention to "serve heaven" but are compelled by the biblical text to the extent of seeking new exegetical methodologies that are of interest to him.

Gamzu's perspective is not the sole one. The narrator, the primary spokesperson of Agnon in the tale, the one who is moved even by the mention of Ginat's name, calls upon us, from the very outset, to see the charms of such ethnographic-philological studies and the aesthetic wonders of their object of investigation. Whether or not the Enamite hymns are authentic relics of the ancient Orient (the language of Edo is presented both as a real ancient tongue and as a language Gemulah and her father had invented to amuse themselves), they are exquisite poems that stir the heart. In being far more drawn to Ginat than to Gamzu, Gemulah, one should bear in mind, also testifies to the power and seductions of modern scholarship.

The inventiveness of biblical ethnographers could hardly bother Agnon as such. There is something about the imaginative dimension of scholarship that makes it refreshingly similar to literature. It is no coincidence that Agnon's closest scholarly friends—and this is true of both Goitein and Scholem—were also great writers. Projections (in the broad sense of the term), for Agnon, are indispensable for any literary feat, much as they are part and parcel of the most intriguing inner dramas of the mind. When Ginat seeks echoes of the hymns of ancient Enam in Gemulah's songs, his quest resembles that of Norbert Hanold and his search for the actual traces of Gradiva *rediviva* in the streets of contemporary Pompeii: "And 'traces' literally; for with her peculiar gait she must have left behind an imprint of her toes in the ashes distinct from all the rest."[20] At one point in his study of *Gradiva*, Freud comments on Hanold's "lively imagination" and claims: "This division between imagination and the intellect destined him to become an artist or a neurotic."[21] Hanold turns out to be the latter rather than the former, but his delusions shed light on artistic imagination as well as on the centrality of fantasy in the realm of love, not only among neurotics.

Inasmuch as Agnon is concerned with the darker aspects of the delusional dimension of ethnographic literalism, he strives to lay bare the hopeless blindness of scholars, their adherence to dreams of mastery while ignoring the utter fragility of any pursuit of knowledge, whether academic or not. Ginat may wish to remain an uninvolved observer, but, despite himself, he becomes trapped in the Song of Songs culture that he unwittingly investigates. For all his detached Western secularism, he cannot escape Gemulah, who, like the Shulamite, seeks her loved one desperately at night in the moonlit streets of Jerusalem. He is, in a sense, an Agnonian Faust (Gerda Greifenbach surmises that he may be writing the third volume of *Faust* for all she knows [150]) whose fervent, somewhat sinister, pursuit of knowledge leads him to an amorous brink.

In Agnon's biblical ethnographies, the one maddening inscription that all the characters in the tale—be they Mizrahi or Ashkenazi—seem to bear on their back, unbeknownst to them, are the dream sequences of the Song of Songs. The premise that Eastern communities are more authentic preservers of the biblical text seems groundless. I mentioned Gemulah and Ginat, but Gamzu too has a pivotal role in this drama. Echoes of the verse "I sought him, but I could not find him" (3:2 and 5:6) appear time and again in the depiction of his nocturnal searches for his moonstruck wife. On the first of these searches, he finds himself at the abode of the Greifenbachs, on another mysterious night when the narrator happens to be there. "'Forgive me' he said, 'for suddenly bursting in on you. Just imagine: I came home after the evening service at the synagogue to get my wife settled for the night and found the bed empty. I went off in search of her. 'Going to the south, turning to the north, turning turning goes the wind, and again to its circuit the wind returns.' Suddenly I found myself in this valley without knowing how I came here" (162–63). The Shulamite's search and meandering in the city—*asoveva va-'ir* (3:2) and *metsa'uni ha-shomrim ha-sovevim ba-'ir* (5:7)—blend with the melancholy, monotonous rhythms of Ecclesiastes ("turning turning goes the wind," *sovev sovev holekh ha-ruah*) in a combination of obsessive seeking and turning round and round in vain.[22] The only one Gamzu keeps finding, in a mock imitation of the Shulamite's meandering, is the narrator, who is always there ready to hear more tales.

The amorous entanglements of "Edo and Enam" underscore yet another mistaken premise of biblical ethnographers: a true literal reading of the ancient love poem cannot remain solely in the peaceful, pastoral zones of rural weddings or in the pleasurable setting of Solomon's court, where the *bat-nadiv* allegedly sings her songs. Here, the nightmarish, if magical, Jerusalemite nocturnal scenes of the Song are intensified. In the modern Jerusalem of the late 1940s, yearnings are never reciprocal and the amorous search is perpetual—Gamzu searches for Gemulah who searches for Ginat who searches for the ancient hymns of Enam.[23]

GINAT VERSUS GAMZU: IRONIC CONTINUITIES

If Rosenzweig sees the scientific approach to the Bible as distinctly secular (he even overlooks the more pronounced theological underpinnings of Herder's hermeneutic aesthetics), Agnon thrives on finding unexpected continuities between religious and secular scholarship. Historians have often located the origins of the human sciences to a gradual secularization of knowledge in the wake of the scientific revolution. Agnon's project entirely recasts this history. It calls attention to the domain of religious exegesis where these disciplines first took form.

In "Edo and Enam," the topic of ironic continuities is raised explicitly when the narrator responds to Greifenbach's observations regarding the mystery of the formation of languages—based on his philological readings of, among others, *Gesenius' Hebrew Grammar*, one of the major books of German biblical Orientalism—with a wry comment on the ways in which the Kabbalah "anticipated academic scholarship" in this matter (152).

The thrust of the irony is evident in the juxtaposition of Ginat, the quintessential modern scholar, and the traditionalist Gamzu, or rather in the questioning of the dichotomy at stake. From the little that we hear of the enigmatic Ginat (his inner world remains blocked throughout the tale), we learn that during his ethnographic field trips, the young scholar dresses as a Jerusalemite sage and is regarded by the Enamites as "the Sage Gideon" (Hakham Gideon).[24] This may be a strategy to disarm his informants, but it also discloses an unexpected familiarity with traditional Jewish modes of knowledge and a latent preoccupation with Jewish sources.

Gamzu, in turn, may passionately scorn biblical critics and ethnographers, but he himself is an avid collector of *piyyutim*.[25] In fact, he is so fond of traveling among remote Jewish communities in the East in pursuit of lost *piyyutim* and old manuscripts that he is driven out of the yeshiva (207). Better still, Gamzu provides detailed accounts of the manners and customs of Enamite Jews that come surprisingly close to biblical ethnographies. "If you had seen my father-in-law Gevariah when he stood on the peak of a rock," recounts Gamzu, "a sky-blue turban on his head, his complexion and beard set off by his flowing hair . . . his big toes striking the towering rock while he raised a song from the depths . . . and Gemulah his daughter sang . . . [trilling her voice] and between twenty-two and twenty-seven maidens danced, all of them beautiful and high born, then you would have seen a likeness of the festive days of ancient Israel, when the daughters of Israel went out to dance in the vineyards" (176). To travel to Enam, for Gamzu, means to step into an enchanting exegetical landscape of biblical texts, the Song of Songs among the most prominent among them.[26] Songs, shepherds, hopping over rocks, vineyards, and dancing maidens are very much part of the ancient love poem. Towering over the other maidens with her singing, Gemulah is allotted the role of the Shulamite whose exceptional voice is lauded by her loved one (*ki kolekh 'arev*—Song 2:14). To capture the exquisite, Oriental quality of Gemulah's singing, Gamzu depicts her as "trilling her voice" (*mena'an'at kola be-shir*), as if she were rocking her voice, with the spiral, rhythmic beats of a musical arabesque.[27] In using this expression, interestingly enough, the bookseller also harks back to Rabbi Akiva's famous admonition against those who venture to "trill their voice" while singing the Song of Songs in banquet houses, treating a song of divine love as if it were an earthly song.[28]

As one with a face "of a Jew out of the Middle Ages" (209), who has no interest in books that are "less than four hundred years old" (179), Gamzu's primary sources of inspiration, one may assume, are the travel narratives of Eldad the Danite (ninth century) and Binyamin of Tudela (twelfth century) as well as other early reports on the lost tribes of ancient Israel (he regards the Enamites as pertaining to the lost tribe of Gad). Modern ethnography, Agnon reminds us, did not invent the craving to explore remote communities, nor did it invent the desire to look for a window to biblical times through travel. What is more, biblical ethnographers were not the first to discover the literal dimension of the Song. In evoking the trace of a literalist tradition of singing the Song as a secular love song in Rabbi Akiva's times, Agnon highlights a somewhat forgotten precursor to modern literalism. The irony, then, is double-edged: Ginat is far more indebted to traditional exegetical modes than meets the eye, while Gamzu rejects modern scholarship without realizing that there are unforeseen similarities between the interpretive practices he is accustomed to and the new scholarly trends. To top it all, it is none other than Gamzu who sells old manuscripts and ancient leaves to scholars (among them Ginat), thus taking part in this modern desecration of scriptural texts.

In an essay published in the proceedings of the conference "Religion in a Religious Age," Goitein wonders whether as "sons of the secular age," scholars of today, can truly understand the religious culture of medieval times. "My trepidation," he claims, "is soothed somewhat by remembering that once I myself was a thoroughly medieval man, that is, one for whom religion is the overriding concern in life." "In the course of the years," he jokingly adds, he became a "medievalist" rather than a "medieval man," but that early experience never vanished, providing him with certain insights in his current scholarly work.[29] Whether or not Agnon was thinking of Goitein in turning Ginat and Gamzu into an oddly inseparable pair, his insistence on having their respective worlds implicated in each other complicates any attempt to regard the secular and the religious modes of erudition as distinct realms.

Leah Goldberg, with the admirably combined sensitivities of a critic and a poet, distinguishes between three circles in "Edo and Enam."[30] The first circle is that of the Greifenbachs, who live close to the sources of mystery and belief but can approach them only intellectually, grasping not even a speck of their power. When they hear the voice of Gemulah's singing burst forth from Ginat's room, they can only make jokes about it and find it a worthy topic for gossip. The second circle belongs to the dreamers (*ba'aley ha-dimyonot*)—Gamzu, Gemulah, and her entire tribe—who live in the world of their imagination, close to poetry, pain, and the depths of the soul (*tehomot ha-nefesh*). They own that invented tongue with which they can express the kind of things no human language can capture. On the border between the two circles, in the third circle, lives the artist. This artist has two faces. His revealed face is that of the narrator, who lives in the secular, mundane world but can hear the tales of Gamzu and the voice of Gemulah, sense the magic of the moon, and turn them all into a story. The artist's hidden face is that of Ginat. As a modern philologist of European background, he bears resemblance to Greifenbach, but he is nonetheless something of a unique Hakham as well, one who is capable of drawing Gemulah to him and turning her songs into a "tremendous artistic experience."[31]

In calling attention to the interrelations between the exegetical worlds of Ginat and Gamzu, I have somewhat redefined these circles. Both Ginat and Gamzu, I suggest, wander between the world of the Greifenbachs and the Enamites in a zone where scholarship and poetry meet, ancient cultures are explored, tales are spun, and lost poems are brought back to light. Both, if differently, are immersed in a passionate pursuit of a supreme Song and are helplessly drawn to the enchanting singing of Gemulah. Both, I would add, are immersed in their pursuits to the extent of losing sight of her flesh. In the scene in which Ginat urges the somnambulist Gemulah to return to her husband, the Enamite woman bluntly declares that she is nobody's wife. "Ask him," she implores, "if his eyes have ever seen my flesh" (*she'al 'oto 'im ra'u eynav 'et besari*).[32] And although Gemulah seduces Ginat, thinking him better than her husband, the young scholar can only disappoint her, for he too seems incapable of approaching the intensities of human love.

THE RESURGENCE OF MYSTICAL ALLEGORIES: REDEMPTIVE IMAGININGS

Gemulah holds a peculiarly paradoxical position: she is at once the primary window into the realities of the Song and the allegorical crux of the tale. Her name, accordingly, is linked to diverse words and worlds, among them to "Jamila," a common Arabic name meaning "beauty" (though Agnon denied the connection), to *gemul* (recompense), and to *ge'ulah* (redemption).[33] Characteristically, Agnon allows the literal and the allegorical lines in his tales to preserve their "wondrous autonomy" while playing them against each other.

Of the various traditional allegories of the Song that intersect in Gemulah, the Zohar has a distinct presence.[34] In adhering to the term *allegory* while speaking of kabbalistic readings of the Song, I primarily mean to locate them in the realm of commentaries that focus on divine love, but one should bear in mind the controversial position of the symbol/allegory contrast in Kabbalah studies. In *Major Trends in Jewish Mysticism*, Scholem regards the symbol—rather than allegory—as the privileged trope of the world of Kabbalism.

> In the mystical symbol a reality which in itself has, for us, no form or shape becomes transparent and, as it were, visible through the medium of another reality which clothes its content with visible expressible meaning. . . . The thing which becomes a symbol retains its original form and its original content. It does not become, so to speak, an empty shell into which another content is poured; in itself, through its own existence, it makes another reality transparent which cannot appear in any other form. If allegory can be defined as the representation of an expressible something by another expressible something, the mystical symbol is an expressible representation

> of something which lies beyond the sphere of expression and communication, something which comes from a sphere whose face is, as it were, turned inward and away from us.
>
> . . . The symbol "signifies" nothing and communicates nothing, but makes something transparent which is beyond all expression. Where deeper insight into the structure of the allegory uncovers fresh layers of meaning, the symbol is intuitively understood all at once or not at all.
>
> . . . The infinite shines through the finite and makes it more and not less real.[35]

Scholem shares Goethe's definition of the symbol as a living, instantaneous revelation of the inscrutable. For both Scholem and Goethe, as Susan Handelman puts it, the symbol is the "natural, intransitive, immediately intuitable, existing in and for itself as well as for what it signifies . . . an indirect expression of the inexpressible, a passage from the particular to the general via *participation* of the ideal in the object."[36] Allegory, by contrast, is a mechanical "empty shell" that is an arbitrary container of "another content," closer to the realm of meaning than to the infinite. Scholem, to be sure, does not do much justice to allegory: in the best allegories of all times, there is nothing mechanical or empty. His observations, however, can shed light on the ways in which kabbalistic hermeneutics strive to move beyond earlier, midrashic allegorical modes.

In previous chapters, I addressed Agnon's Benjaminian tendencies in discussing his redefinition of allegory and suspicion of the organic wholeness of the symbol. I would now like to suggest that while savoring the capacity of allegory to underscore the complication of signification in modernity with Benjamin, Agnon is at the same time gripped, like Scholem, by the tangibility of mystical language, by the poetic power of such language to create a different sense of reality—to create heavenly spheres more real than earthly ones, thus dismantling, more forcefully than midrashic allegorical configurations, the boundaries between immanence and transcendence in language.[37]

Gamzu's account of his first encounter with Gemulah is undoubtedly the most conspicuous kabbalistic moment in the tale. Gemulah (unlike Shoshana) is affiliated with the Shekhinah explicitly:

> When I saw her for the first time poised on a rock at the top of a mountain which not every man can climb, with the moon lighting up her face while

> she sang, "*Yiddal, yiddal, yiddal, vah, pah, mah*," I said to myself, If she is not one of the angels of the [Shekhinah] who have union with angels of the [Holy One, blessed be He], she must be one of the twelve constellations of the Zodiac, and none other than the constellation Virgo. (164–65)

This heavenly union, with its sudden shift to Aramaic, calls to mind the Aramaic formula *le-Shem Yihud Qudesha' Berikh Hu' u-Shekhinteih*, meaning "For the sake of the union of the Holy One, blessed be He, with His Divine Presence [the Shekhinah]." As Moshe Idel points out, this pivotal kabbalistic pronouncement reflects a supreme aim: "to induce the union, which means the sexual union, between a masculine divine attribute, on the one hand, described by various terms like *Tiferet*, 'the Holy One, blessed be He,' or 'the sixth sefirah' and, on the other hand, a feminine divine manifestation, designated by various terms like *Shekhinah*, *Malkhut*, *Knesset Israel*, *Atara*, and 'the tenth sefirah'"[38] The Song is the underlying text of this Aramaic formula. In fact it is the very base of all kabbalistic representations of the Shekhinah and theurgical inducements of divine eros.[39]

In Gamzu's tale of love at first sight, kabbalistic theurgical interventions are amusedly bidirectional, for divine eros is construed as an inspiring model for a sexual union on earth (he is determined to marry Gemulah). But he does follow the kabbalistic hermeneutic dictum of relying heavily on the Song in his depiction of Gemulah as Shekhinah. When Gemulah appears as a moonlit, larger-than-life Shekhinah, her enchanting song, "*Yiddal, yiddal, yiddal, vah, pah, mah*," though delivered in the incomprehensible, nonsensical language of Edo, bears echoes of the ancient love poem. Tochner contends that "*Yiddal, yiddal, yiddal, vah, pah, mah*" is based on a kabbalistic play on the initial letters of the Hebrew text of Song 4:16: "Let my beloved come to his garden and eat his pleasant fruits (*y*avo *d*odi *l*e-gano *v*eyokhal *p*ri *m*egadav).[40] Even without the kabbalistic letter juggling, this passage bears the stamp of a fascinating commentary on the Song in Zohar Shemot (*Terumah*), which is quoted in Agnon's compilation *Book, Writer, and Story*:

> Rabbi Yose opened, saying, "*Song of Songs, which is Solomon's* (Song of Songs 1:1). This song was aroused by Solomon when the Temple was built and all worlds were consummated, above and below, in single perfection. Although the Companions differ on this, still this song was uttered solely in completeness, when the moon became full and the Temple was constructed according to the pattern above. When the Temple was built below, since the day that the

world was created there has never been such joy before the blessed Holy One as on that day.[41]

In Song of Songs Rabbah 1:12 (on 1:2), Daniel C. Matt notes, "various opinions are offered as to where and when the Song of Songs was uttered: at the crossing of the Red Sea, at the giving of the Torah on Mount Sinai, as the Tabernacle was erected in the desert, or when the Temple was built. However, Rabbi Yose insists that this perfect song must have been composed and sung at the moment of perfection: when King Solomon completed the Temple and *Shekhinah* descended to dwell on earth."[42] The Zohar thus associates the first utterance of the Song with a perfect moment in the life of its composer, Solomon, in which the Shekhinah appears above the fully constructed Temple as a full moon (one of her prominent symbols), in an utterly joyful scene of redemption, reenacting another renowned verse of the ancient love poem: "Fair as the moon [*yafa kha-levana*] / Clear as the sun" (Song 6:10). Later, Gamzu will highlight this connection on longingly praising his wife's celestial radiance: "Perfect as the moon was Gemulah [*tama kha-levana hayta Gemula*]: her eyes were sparks of light; her face was like the morning star; her voice was sweet as the shades of evening" (200).[43]

Just as Gamzu oscillates between literal and allegorical perceptions of Gemulah, so too does Ginat. To the extent that Ginat, like Goitein, traces a new polytheistic dimension in the Song (the "cultic" approach), he too surely leaves the plain sense of the Song behind. Whether Gemulah is associated with the Shekhinah or with Ishtar, the "Queen of Heaven" (Gemulah has a peculiar craving to bake and eat *kavanim* [178], the kind of cakes idolatrous women prepare for the "Queen of Heaven" in Jeremiah 7:18; 44:17–20)—she transcends the human, earthly realm. What is more, as strange as it may seem, Ginat's research is comparable to kabbalistic hermeneutics. If the Kabbalah probed the mystery of the formation of languages long before *Gesenius* (as the narrator suggests), it also preceded biblical criticism in unabashedly highlighting the mythical layers of biblical texts. One of Scholem's projects was indeed to call attention to the eruption of myth—including the eruption of a divine feminine principle—within the kabbalistic godhead, a project that was further developed by Moshe Idel and Yehuda Liebes.[44]

But there is another mode of modern reallegorization of the Song that is of great interest to Agnon, one that will lead us from the blind spots of biblical critics to the fissures within Zionist literalism. Indeed, the ironic continuities between traditional and modern modes of scholarship in "Edo and Enam" set in relief the absurdities of the Zionist tendency to disavow interpretive modes that precede the Enlightenment. Against the Zionist rejection of traditional allegories, Agnon points to their ongoing relevance and to their reformulation in modern Israel. In singing "Kol dodi" and dancing to the so-called Mizrahi tunes of "El ginat egoz," Israelis in the 1940s may well have attempted to advocate secular literalism and retrieve the authentic, Oriental biblical past. But in their understanding of the ancient love poem as vital to scenes of national redemption and revival corresponding to poetic-musical perfection, Agnon intimates, they are far closer to the allegorists of the Zohar than one would expect.

The singing, radiant, Mizrahi Gemulah could have leaped out of the golden Oriental gate in Raban's *Come to Palestine* poster, with its inscription "For, lo, the winter is past, the rain is over and gone; the flowers appear on the earth; the time of the singing of birds is come, and the voice of the turtle is heard in our land," or out of the alluring Zionist publicity material Bloom ruminates on in *Ulysses*. Within the ever-growing allegorical zone of the tale, she is not only the embodiment of the Shekhinah and Ishtar but also a feminine personification of the Zionist quest for national renaissance within the Oriental habitat of the Song.

Agnon may also be referring to the somewhat forgotten earlier wave of immigration from Yemen, in 1882, known as *e'ele ve-tamar* ("I will climb up into the palm-tree"—Song 7:9). These Yemenite *'olim* envisioned their "ascent" to Palestine as a fulfillment of an allegorical reading of the ascent up to the palm tree in the ancient love poem (their choice was also based on a play of letters, *sikul otiyot*, between *ve-tamar* and the Hebrew year of their immigration, *tarmav*). While secular Zionism recruited Yemenite culture to enhance literalism, Yemenite immigrants—from *e'ele ve-tamar* to the Magic Carpet Operation—were actually very much immersed in religious modes of life and allegorical exegesis.

THE DIMINUTION OF THE MOON AND THE FALL OF THE NATIONAL HOME

Agnon's provocative juxtaposition of traditional, redemptive allegories of the Song with Zionist allegorical configurations is bound up with a sharp critique of the idealization at stake. Here, as in *Betrothed*, somnambulism—by and large enacted by a somnambulist woman—is the symptom that marks not only the enchantment of individual and collective dreams but also their proximity to illness. Gemulah is at once glorious as the *levana* and struck by her.

She is a somnambulist, sick woman who loses her capacity to sing on reaching Jerusalem, except on nights when the moon is full. Both Shoshana and Gemulah stand for the returning Zionist community as a whole, but whereas the former primarily represents the hardships of German-speaking newcomers (the Yekehs), the latter primarily underscores the estrangement and disillusionment of the Eastern Aliyot. As Ariel Hirschfeld points out, the dream of the "ingathering of exiles" turns out to be a colossal, erotic failure in "Edo and Enam."[45] Instead of leading to rejuvenation or to a "creative symbiosis," in Goitein's terms, the marriage of the Mizrahi Gemulah and the Ashkenazi Gamzu is never consummated.

Writing in 1949, right after the foundation of the State of Israel, Agnon is still haunted by doubts regarding the prospects of the Zionist enterprise. He seems to wonder whether Zionism has led to a construction of a national home that may be ruined or deserted in ways that are all too similar to the ancient catastrophe of the destruction of the Temple. Kurzweil rightly defines the literal, familial, and national "house/home" (*bayit*) as a central motif in the tale. All the leading characters of "Edo and Enam," he contends, are restlessly away from their home and spouses, dislocated in one way or another. Their return to the Land of Promise does not rid them of their inclinations to remain wandering Jews.[46] The quest for the archaic in Zionist culture is thus nothing less than a sign of "spiritual bankruptcy, an illusory attempt at renewal which is but a step in a process of decay."[47]

Agnon invents a powerful modern version of a whole array of bleak allegories of the Song, in which the ancient love poem accentuates the pain of destruction and the eclipse of God. "Woe how the Rose of Sharon sits alone," cries Elazar HaKalir in one of the famous *piyyutim* of Tish'a be'Av, where the Song of Songs and Lamentations merge into each other. There is a soundtrack of dirges underlying "Edo and Enam."[48] Gemulah is a great singer not only of love songs but also of dirges, the other major female tradition in the Bible that Goitein discusses.[49] "Gemulah mourned her father for seven days and nights, with songs of lamentation every day and night. At the end of her first week of mourning she made him great obsequies, with songs and dances full of dread and wonder" (203). And then there are dirges (reminiscent of those of Gemulah) that are sung by an unknown woman, wailing and weeping, while trilling her voice, over her deceased young lover in a funeral that happens to take place alongside the funerals of Gemulah and Ginat (229).

The Zohar is a rich source for mystical commentaries in this grim venue as well. Most relevant to Gemulah are commentaries on the diminution of the

Shekhinah in times of exile. In exilic times, when the sins of Israel deprive her of the bounty of the upper spheres, the Shekhinah's "voice separates from her," and her legendary, lunar light diminishes to the point of becoming an almost invisible, black point. At that dark moment, she declares, "I am black" (*shehora 'ani*), expressing her agony via the Shulamite's memorable words (Zohar 3:191a).[50]

It is precisely the minute black point of the Shekhinah that needs to be aroused, as Melila Hellner-Eshed puts it, in order to enhance redemption in kabbalistic theurgy.[51] But in Agnon's tale no one can handle the intense wakefulness of Gemulah.[52] The Three Oaths, with their admonition to refrain from awaking love "until it please," reappear in "Edo and Enam" within a mystical framework. Gemulah is, at times, a cross between the Shekhinah and a haunting golem who cannot be laid to rest. Indeed, the letters of Gemulah's name, may be "set free to recombine: a female golem," as Cynthia Ozick points out.[53] The golem, according to one legend, has the word *emet* ("truth") inscribed on his forehead. The only way to control the creature is by erasing the letter *alef*, thus forming the word *met* ("dead").[54] In imagining potential remedies for Gemulah's somnambulism, the narrator playfully raises the possibility of taking the letter *bet* out of *levana*, allowing the remaining verb *lana* ("she sleeps") to take its course.[55] His pun, however, remains imaginary and has no impact on Gemulah's conduct.

TEXTUAL EXTRAVAGANZA: THE LEAVES AND THE DREAM OF THE LUNAR SONG

In yet another breathtaking allegorical twist of the tale, Gemulah, much like the "mad dog" (*kelev meshuga*), is a text cut loose. When Gemulah dances in the rocky hills of Enam, there are approximately twenty-two maidens—the number of letters in the Hebrew alphabet—who accompany her.[56] Here, as in the pun on *levana-lana*, and the bewildering proliferation of the letters *ayin* and *gimel*, Agnon playfully relies on the primary premise of *Sefer Yetsirah* (Book of Creation), one of the earliest kabbalistic texts: that the Hebrew alphabet was the foundation of all creation. "All the real beings in the three strata of the cosmos: in the world, in time and in man's body . . . came into existence through the interconnectedness of the 22 letters."[57]

Beyond Gemulah's ties with the twenty-two letters–maidens and far more visibly, she is inextricably connected to the magical, inscribed leaves of Enam. We first hear of the leaves when Gamzu goes up a steep mountain, "the highest of the range of steep mountains that raised themselves up to heaven," with his future father-in-law, Gevariah. Gevariah, at one point, digs beneath a rock and lifts a stone, under which a cave opens up. He comes out of the cave holding an earthenware jar and lays bare the hidden leaves placed there. Let us consider yet again the passage in which our two tales intersect:

> On the way back, he opened the jar and showed me a bundle of dry leaves unlike any I had ever seen; and on them were the strange characters [letters] of a script unlike any that I knew; and the color of the characters, that is, the color of the ink in which they were written, was not like any color we know. At first sight I should have said that the scribe had mixed gold, azure and purple with all the primary colors of the rainbow and written with them. But as I stood gazing, the colors altered before my eyes and changed into the tints of seaweeds drawn from the depths, such weeds as Dr. Rechnitz drew up from the sea near Jaffa. Then again, they were like the silver strands we observe on the moon. I stared at the leaves, at the characters, at Gemulah's father. At that moment he seemed as if transported to another world. And then it became increasingly clear that what at first sight seemed an illusion was the truth itself. . . . And if I have no words to describe the experience, yet it was more distinct than anything one can explain in words. . . . As I stood marveling, Gemulah's father replaced the leaves in the jar and spoke to me simply, with these words: "They are plants of the earth, and they have been given power to influence the upper air." (165–66)

Gevariah reveals the leaves to his future son-in-law and designates them as an antidote against his daughter's somnambulism: in marrying Gemulah, Gamzu must bind himself to these leaves. But on an allegorical level, Gevariah is a Moses who brings down from the mountain a very strange Torah, "unlike any [we have] ever seen."[58] With its mysterious jars, caves, and magical leaves, this scene offers a unique mixture of a carnivalesque *One Thousand and One Nights* version of the revelation on Mount Sinai, a variation on Zohar Shemot's account of the spectacular moment in which the letters of the Torah were engraved, and an unexpected scientific dive into the depths from which Rechnitz draws up his wondrous weeds.[59] What the Holy Writ is depends on the eye of the beholder. Even a single beholder, if he is as wild an exegete as Gamzu, can wander between several perspectives at once—the fabulous, the mystical, and (in spite of himself) the scientific—admiring the ever-changing shifts in color.

Gemulah is a woman of many biblical leaves, but she is a grand embodiment of one leaf in particular: the Song of Songs. More specifically, she is an aesthetic allegory that probes the great intensities of the language of love and the love of language. The aesthetic, allegorical aspect of Gemulah is most apparent in the narrator's dreams. The narrator, a writer of sorts, falls asleep during one of his stays at the Greifenbachs and dreams of being on a train.[60]

> Sleep came quickly, and I knew nothing until I was roused by the sound of train wheels. The train reached Garmisch and stopped there. The door of the compartment opened and there was a view of high mountains and streams; I could hear a voice singing *yiddal, yiddal, yiddal, vah, pah, mah.* I was drawn by the voice and wanted to follow it. The door was shut against me. The moon came out and covered me with her light. I smiled at her with one eye and she smiled back with a grin that covered all her face.
>
> But there was no train. I was in bed at the Greifenbachs'. I turned over to one side and pulled the blanket over my eyes, because the moon was shining on my face. I was thinking of how the world has shut itself in so that none of us can go where he wishes, except for the moon, that wanders over all the earth, singing *yiddal, yiddal, yiddal, vah, pah, mah.* (182–83)

Gemulah herself does not appear in the dream. Instead, the moon is personified as a seductive woman who covers the narrator with her light and shines on his face while singing Gemulah's song. The Song, then, becomes the beloved as it becomes one with the Shulamite's moon metaphor. Something of the mystical reading of the Zohar resonates here, but in the narrator's dream-world the *levana* seems more of a teasingly, uninhibited song or an uninhibited singer/poetess than a divine being (note the unusual use of the term *meshoreret*—a term that means both "singing" and "poetess" but is more commonly used in the latter sense in Modern Hebrew—in the depiction of the "voice singing"). The flirtatious, singing moon lures the narrator through the shut door like the voice of the lover "upon the handles of the lock." And although the enchanting *levana* makes her way through the locks with the immense erotic tangibility of her dazzling light and voice, she remains high up in the sky, wandering "over all the earth," with a wide grin on her face, while the narrator's movement is obstructed as he is trapped in the train compartment below.

But why is the narrator in Garmisch (a town located in Bavaria)? In this context, the European qualities of Gemulah's song become more evident. It seems closer to a German shepherd tune (*yodilahihu*) than to an Oriental melody. Is this yet another moment in which Agnon lays bare the absurdities of the projection at the base of biblical ethnographies of the Song? What is even more vital for Agnon, I believe, is maintaining the mobility of any imagining whatsoever. One can be in Germany, like Herder, and imagine folk-life in the Orient, and one can lie in a bed at the Greifenbachs' and dream of Garmisch. The Song is not bound up with a particular culture or with a fixed geographic zone.

The linguistic-cultural multiplicity of Gemulah's Song does not end here. Given that there are no vowels in Hebrew, she could be singing *Yiddel, Yiddel, Yiddel, vah pa mah,* introducing into Garmisch's German a touch of Yiddish and a latent evocation of the Yiddish term for "Jew," *Yid.*[61]

Gender is as unstable as geographic and linguistic distinctions in this dream. The narrator is both the male lover and the dreaming Shulamite yearning for her loved one. Gender fluidity, as we have seen, is a central feature in the dramatization of Song 5 in the dreamy, lunar race in *Betrothed.* In "Edo and Enam" an actual dream is at stake where the *levana* is a character and the writer (via the narrator) is implicated in this scene of blurred gender distinctions. Indeed, it seems as if this fluidity between male and female roles is a prerequisite for writing.

To go back to Goitein, let me suggest that despite Agnon's ironic stance, he couldn't but have been fascinated by his friend's speculation that the composer of the Song was a great female poet who imprinted her own tale within the Song. Goitein's admiration for the Shulamite and his tracing of a poet's sensibility in her Song must have struck a special chord for Agnon, who was drawn to the beloved's song from the very beginning of his literary career, when he chose to name himself "Agnon," identifying with the Shulamite-like *agunah*. No wonder that the narrator's heart beats fast upon hearing the Greifenbachs speak of the Enamite hymns, like a lover who has heard the name of his beloved evoked all of a sudden. And perhaps it is no coincidence that in "Edo and Enam" it is the narrator who assumes something of Goitein's role in tracing a woman's song in the cadences of the Enamite hymns, discovering what scholars failed to notice.

THE ENDING: THE SONG OF GROFIT

The tale does not end with the tragic death of Gemulah and Ginat. It concludes with the narrator's note on the inexplicable ways in which the Enamite hymns keep circulating after Ginat's death—acquiring ever-growing recognition among readers round the world—despite the latter's attempt to prevent their future publication. In the stubborn vitality of the hymns and the unexpected light that emanates from them, one can glimpse a less bleak potentiality of life and love in Jerusalem. But the foregrounding of the fate of the manuscript is, above all, a final reminder of Agnon's ever-present passion to reflect on the unexpected twists and turns in the lives of authors and texts.[62]

The discarded texts of Ginat bear some resemblance to the Geniza manuscripts, documents that were meant to be buried but were brought back to the cultural stage unexpectedly. They may also call to mind the Mosaic text in *Moses and Monotheism*, returning from the realm of the repressed with greater force, reminding Freud of Schiller's poem: "All that is to live in endless song / Must in life-time first be drown'd."[63] But, above all, the ghostly quality of the Enamite hymns—capable of springing back to life even though their ethnographer or author sought to get rid of them—leads us back to "And Solomon's Wisdom Excelled" (a piece published during the same year as "Edo and Enam," 1950). Agnon's King Solomon, as we have seen, tries to hide his love songs.[64] He goes to the various sites of the ancient biblical love poem in search of a burial space, but all seem far too exposed to unwanted intruders. When he finally buries them in the well-guarded vineyard of Ba'al Hammon, he discovers that despite his efforts, the songs "arose from the ground and were heard between the vines," arousing the young maidens who were dancing there. Solomon does not lose hope and conjures the maidens with the Shulamite's words: "I charge you, O, daughters of Jerusalem. . . . Do not stir up nor awaken love." On hearing his admonition, the maidens "hid their songs in their hearts." And yet they too cannot quite set limits to the songs. The love songs that were supposedly "forgotten" in their hearts are depicted via the verses of the Song of Songs and thus seem to be part and parcel of the known collection of Solomon's poetry. Or else the Song of Songs as we know it is but a remnant of the lost amorous corpus and as such serves as a fragmentary clue to the songs Solomon and the maidens tried to conceal.

The Enamite hymns are reprinted in increasing numbers, but what about the Song of Grofit? Is it the hidden aspect of the Enamite songs, both akin to them and unattainable? In many ways, it is indeed a peculiar version of Solomon's esoteric corpus. Gamzu depicts the Song of Grofit in an overflowing, winding, highly poetic sentence: "The songs of the springs cling to the songs of the high mountains and the high mountains cling to the birds of the sky, and among those birds there is one whose name is Grofit. When Grofit's hour comes to leave the world, it hangs its head in the clouds and trills its voice; and when the bird finishes its song, it departs from the world. And all those songs are linked to Gemulah's tongue. And if she were to utter the song of Grofit, her soul would depart and she would die."[65] The Song of Grofit is a poem of mythical proportions that encompasses the entire world in a grand chain that links the earth and the heaven with nothing less than Gemulah's tongue and trilling voice. It is a mode of poetic expression that is so absolute that it loses touch with content and is closer to music than to the realm of words.[66] To sing it means to fly up onto the alluring, though ominous, realms of heaven, where the clouds are both the epitome of poetic inspiration and an executioner's rope. To utter it means death. It is an exhilarating combination of a whole array of legendary songs—the Siren's song and a swan song—and a series of legendary birds, from the eagle of Psalm 103, allegedly capable (like the Phoenix) of renewing its youth, to Grafit, the inscrutable bird on Solomon's throne in the esoteric midrash "King Solomon's Throne and Hippodrome"[67] In its unparalleled totality, the Song of Grofit calls to mind another sequence in Zohar Shemot, *Terumah* (also quoted in *Book, Writer, and Story*): "Solomon uttered the praise of this song, which is totality of the whole Torah, totality of the whole work of Creation, totality of mystery of the patriarchs . . . totality of Israel's exile among the nations and their redemption. . . . Whatever was, whatever is, and whatever will eventually be . . . is all in Song of Songs."[68]

The Enamite hymns bear resemblance to this ultimate Song: they are defined as the splendid primary "link in a chain that bound the beginnings of recorded history to the ages before," and they too are tied to Gemulah's singing. And yet with all their monumental beauty, they are apparently only a trace of the primeval cadences of Grofit.

In his banquet speech on receiving the Nobel Prize, Agnon, as one recalls, recounts a dream:

> In a dream, in a vision of the night, I saw myself standing with my brother-Levites in the Holy Temple, singing with them the songs of David, King of Israel, melodies such as no ear has heard since the day our city was destroyed and its people went into exile. I suspect that the angels in charge of the Shrine of Music, fearful lest I sing in wakefulness what I had sung in dream, made me forget by day what I had sung at night.

Agnon could have just as well said (had it been in keeping with the decorum of the occasion): "In a dream, in a vision of the night I saw myself standing with Solomon, singing with him songs of love . . . melodies such as no ear has heard since the day our city was destroyed. . . . I suspect that the angels in charge of the Shrine of Music, fearful lest I sing in wakefulness what I had sung in dream, made me forget by day what I have sung at night."

"Edo and Enam" is a tale about the aesthetic irresistibility of the Song of Songs, its capacity to emerge, in all contexts, sacred or secular, stirring the hearts of its listeners, defying any attempt to hide it. But it is also a tale about the obstacles that stand in the way of those who search for aesthetic models in the biblical text with the assumption that this archaic literary past is wholly revealed or accessible.[69] In Agnon's meditation on epitome, any attempt to retrieve the originary Song of Songs or the originary setting of its composition—be it by German biblical ethnographers or their Zionist followers—is doomed to be partial, if not deadly. Modern times, with their advanced technology (the train in the narrator's dream) and advanced science, may have created an illusion of hermeneutic progress but by no means made the ancient love poem any more graspable or intelligible.

When the narrator rebukes Gamzu for endangering his somnambulist wife in leaving the door unlocked at night, the bookseller smiles slyly and says:

> Even if I hung seven locks upon the door, and locked every one with seven keys, and threw each key into one of the seven seas of the Land of Israel, my wife would find them all and open the door. (164)

His response sounds like an amusing inversion of Saadia Gaon's commentary on the ancient poem, where he likens the Song of Songs to a lock whose key had been lost. To pin down the Song to a sole interpretation would be, as far as Agnon is concerned, as futile as trying to stop the moon. Even if one were to try to lock the Song with what may seem as the ultimate exegetical key, like Gemulah it would find a way to escape into the moonlit night.

Epilogue: Forevermore

AFTER twenty years of painstaking research, Adiel Amzeh, the protagonist of "Forevermore" ("Ad olam"), yet another fascinating character in Agnon's gallery of scholars, completes his book on the history of the great city of Gumlidata and even finds a worthy publisher: Gebhard Goldenthal. But just as he sets out from his house to submit the manuscript, the elderly nurse Adah Eden suddenly appears and asks whether he has old journals, no longer of use, for the lepers she treats. Although Amzeh is in a rush, he ends up collecting the journals for her and, while doing so, asks about the books that the lepers have been reading. Among the books Adah Eden mentions, is a well-worn parchment, antique and tearstained. It turns out to be a chronicle of none other than Gumlidata. Amzeh stammers with excitement, and instead of going to Goldenthal he follows Adah Eden to the leper hospital in an insatiable quest for unknown details about the fall of Gumlidata. The book, he discovers, "had been infected by the hands of many untouchables, and it seemed almost as if it were not written on parchment, but on a skin of a leper, and not ink but pus had been used to inscribe the words" (245). The degraded condition of the contagious book by no means deters Amzeh from studying it with utmost devotion—forevermore—at the leper hospital, among the "Trees of Eden" (named so in honor of Adah Eden).

> He sat there studying the text, joining letter to letter and word to word until he could read whole passages without trouble. And if he discovered something unusual he would read the passage aloud to the patients in the great hall. "My friends and brothers," he would say, "listen while I read to you." And he would read to them about the people of the great city of Gumlidata, who had been a mighty nation, full of greatness and grandeur, proud-eyed

> and joyous, until the Gothic hordes conquered them and reduced the city to dust and ashes. He would tell them about Gomesh and Gush and Gutz and Guach and Guz, the gods of Gumlidata. . . . He would also tell them about the *Galmudi* and the *Golanae*, which were the dogs and the temple prostitutes, affectionately called *Golshani* and *Golshanae*. And sometimes Adiel Amzeh would tell them about his new theories.
>
> . . . And since there were many things and learning is endless and there is much to discover and investigate and understand, he did not put his work aside and did not leave his place and he remained there forevermore. (248–49)

The book of parchment with its tale of the glory and destruction of an ancient people invites a comparison with the Bible. But it is a bizarre Bible in which the sins of the Jerusalem-like Gumlidata are depicted in loving detail. One of the biblical texts whose terms are borrowed here is the prohibition on cult prostitution in Deuteronomy: "No Israelite woman shall be a cult prostitute, nor shall any Israelite man be a cult prostitute. You shall not bring the fee of a whore or the pay of a dog into the House of the Lord your God in fulfillment of any vow, for both are abhorrent to the Lord your God" (23:18–19, New JPS translation). Temple prostitutes of both sexes (note that "dog" is the biblical designation for a male prostitute) figure prominently in Amzeh's studies of the sexual promiscuities of Gumlidata. But whereas in Deuteronomy and in the prophetic texts such practices are condemned with much contempt, Amzeh relishes the details of Gumlidata's idolatry so much so that he has intimate knowledge of their terms of endearment for cultic dogs: *Golshani* and *Golshanae* (this is yet another tale in which Agnon provides a signature via an excessive use of the letters *gimel* and *ayin*).

Kurzweil speaks of Agnon as a writer obsessed with the rupture between the modern book of secular culture and the Book of Books. Whenever Agnon treats the question of books in modernity, he cannot but touch on the Book of Books—either as a missing book, "eaten by rats" in forlorn libraries, or as an archaic text whose displacement in modern culture creates demonic havoc. Incapable of fully returning to the realm of tradition or of accepting the precepts of secular culture, Agnon, for Kurzweil, remains torn between the two worlds.[1]

Let me suggest that by setting odd scriptural texts on center stage—be it Balak's inscription, Rechnitz's seaweed, the Enamite magical leaves, or the Book of Gumlidata—Agnon strives indeed to capture the estrangement of this ancient text in modern contexts, where it is handled by scholars and readers who are haunted by ghosts of which they are unaware.

"Forevermore" offers a rich final note for our consideration of modern biblicism as a whole and of Israeli biblicism in particular. Written at the peak of Ben-Gurion's Bible cult, in 1954, only a year after Ben-Gurion wrote his famous letter about the Bible "shining in its own light," "Forevermore" offers a distinct comment on this exegetical scene. Adi Zemach notes the Ben-Gurionian connection in an essay on "Edo and Enam" and "Forevermore"—the only, however brief, discussion of Israeli biblicism in Agnon criticism.[2] Zemach notes that the meaning of the name "Adiel Amzeh" is "God's-Ornament This-People" and suggests that the specific "people" who are ridiculed in this tale are the Zionists who see themselves as a clear-cut "biological continuation" of the ancient Israelites and as such adopt the Bible as their cherished, founding epos. Against Ben-Gurion's literalism, Zemach contends, Agnon shows that there is nothing sacred about the text itself with its extensive representations of a corrupt, perverse Jerusalem/Gumlidata. Rather, the sanctity of the Bible derives from the tears shed upon it by the lepers, from the meanings it acquired during the many years of its circulation among pariah Jews in the Diaspora. By rejecting diasporic Judaism and its vast exegetical traditions, cherishing instead the sense of locality provided by Canaanite traditions (most palpably exemplified in the Canaanite movement), Zionism was in the absurd position of overlooking the true spiritual power of the biblical text.[3]

Zemach vividly conveys Agnon's critique of Ben-Gurion's Bible cult but overlooks the multiple perspectives that Agnon juggles and the broader aesthetic-exegetical project at stake. For Agnon, as I have been arguing, Zionist exegetes are, despite themselves, a peculiar chapter in an intriguingly complex history of biblical reception. While they aspire to break with the culture of the yeshiva and ignore the exegetical traditions of their predecessors, in their obsessive immersion in the Bible, in their insistence on devoting their lives to this ancient text and to its study *ad olam*, they turn out to be—if antithetically and heretically—part of the chain.

THE BOOK OF HERESIES: ELDAG AND THE WILD ASS

If I chose "Forevermore" as my closing note it is also because here the heretical line of modern Bibles is far more elaborate. Benjamin Lazier calls attention to the preoccupation of leading Jewish-German thinkers with the question of heresy in interwar Europe. "The interwar era," he writes, "witnessed a resurgence of interest in the heretic as both object and inspiration."[4] Their response to a world made derelict by God's absence and the "interruption of his call" was to resurrect the two most powerful challenges to monotheism: gnosticism and pantheism. "There was at least one man so convinced of God's absence, yet so desperate for his presence, and so suspicious of indulging just that want . . . that he could imagine only one way out. God, this man reasoned, must be nowhere and everywhere, nothing and everything—and all at once! That man was Gershom Scholem . . . and in his person is exemplified a generation."[5] The Book of Gumlidata seems to be the product of precisely such insistence to renounce God's presence and to desperately seek it in a world that is the very antithesis of monotheism.

In *Only Yesterday*, the Zionist Bible is associated with the wicked king of Moab, Balak, and a pagan sorcerer, Balaam; in *Betrothed*, a heretical undercurrent is implicated in Rechnitz's determination to seek the "lower worlds" of marine biology via classical models as well as in the lunar dance of the maidens by the sea; in "Edo and Enam," the magical world of ancient Enam is polytheistic, not to mention Gemulah's affinity with Ishtar; but in "Forevermore," heresy is at the very core of Gumlidata, a city that is not only pagan but also perverse in a way that is reminiscent of the sexual promiscuity of the Sabbatians and perhaps even of the more extreme Frankists.

In Scholem's "Redemption through Sin" (*mitzvah ba'a be'avera*), his renowned, early study of the heretical legacy of Sabbatai Zevi, the great apostate messiah of the seventeenth century, he provides an account of the ways in which the Sabbatians redefined the kabbalistic distinction between "Torah of *beriah*" (Torah of Creation) and "Torah of *atzilut*" (Torah of Emanation).[6] The meaning of the terms in the later additions to the Zoharic corpus (*Tikkunei ha-Zohar* and *Ra'ya Mehemna*), Scholem explains, is somewhat nebulous, but for the Kabbalists of the School of Safed, they refer to two faces of one essential Torah: the Torah in the lower World of *beriah* and the Torah in the supernal World of *atzilut*.

> What the Sabbatian now did was to seize this idea and expound it in the light of the theory of cosmic aeons. The Torah of *beriah*, they argued . . . is the Torah of the unredeemed world of exile, whose purpose it was to serve as a garment for the Shekhinah . . . in her state of distress. The Torah of *atzilut*, on the other hand, is the "true" Torah which, like "the mystery of the Godhead" it makes manifest, has been in a state of concealment for the entire period of the exile. Now that the redemption has commenced it is about to be revealed,

> and although in essence it is identical with the Torah of *beriah*, its way of being read will be different, thus, all the commandments and prohibitions of the Torah of *beriah* will now be reinterpreted by the light of the World of *atzilut*, in which . . . as is stated in several Kabbalistic sources, there is no such thing as forbidden sexual practices.[7]

The Book of Gumlidata exhibits something of the interplay between the hidden and revealed Torahs of Sabbatianism: it is hidden in the leper hospital, but even there it is only partially revealed, partially deciphered, fragment by fragment, *ad infinitum*. Above all, the Book of Gumlidata comes close to a mock, heretical Torah of *atzilut* in its excessive endorsement of the violation of every imaginable commandment. The idolatrous dogs and prostitutes are but one abomination. Homosexuality and even bestiality, or the unsettling collapse of the distinction between humans and animals, are other notable violations of biblical law.

Eldag, the untamed Hun seductress, whose name contains the word *dag* (fish) and means "on-fish," a mermaid of sorts, is a key figure in Gumlidata's heresies.[8] Kept by the Count as a captive concubine in his court, she shows him "hidden and daring ways of love he had known with no other lad or woman" (246) in an attempt to win his trust and advance schemes that would lead to the fall of Gumlidata by the Goths. Eldag's true affection is bestowed upon her peculiar pet: a wild ass, one of the many animals in the garden that had the privilege of suckling at the breast of a woman, better still, a noble woman (246). On playing with him in the garden one day, with striking intimacy, she wraps her mantle around his neck and makes him bow, as if in thanks (247). Just then, on noticing the mantle's strange design of bands of calves' eyes (*gimoniyot shel eyney egel*), woven in the shape of the Valley of Cranes (Gumlidata's counterpart to the idolatrous Valley of Hinnom), Eldag's heart begins "to beat wildly." She suddenly realizes that her pet could serve as the perfect messenger. And, indeed, once the Goths catch sight of the ass with the mantle, they recognize the encrypted message of Eldag and set out to search for the weak spot in the wall by the Valley of the Cranes. She is their Rahab, with a touch of the more apocryphal Judith.

That Eldag's mantle is designated at one point as an *efod* (the term for the garment of the high priest in the Temple) and displays images of calves' eyes (a provocative multiplication of the Golden Calf) augments the sacrilegious bent of her gesture.[9] Why eyes? Surely, an Agnonian wink that adds flare to the flaunting of the letter *ayin*—Agnon's signature throughout the tale—in this case, with the added pun of the double meaning of the term *ayin* as "letter" and "eye," not to mention the fact that the term *egel*, "calf," also begins with an *ayin*. But there is more. The expression *eyney egel*, "calves eyes," refers in the Mishnah to a deformity that renders a man unfit for priesthood and in Modern Hebrew it stands for a dumb or perplexed gaze.[10] Here, in its aggrandized multiplication, this expression acquires a heretical touch via the echoes of the designation of the Angel of Death and Lilith as "full of eyes" as well as the antithetical designation of the true Zoharic mystic as one fully awake, "full of eyes," full of supernal insight, capable of opening the eyes embedded in the Torah or in sublime splendor.[11] Embodying the perplexed look of the calf, the lures of Lilith, Satan, and the mystical eyes of the Zohar, Eldag's *efod* is a miniature, visual replica of the enigmatic, heterodox text of the fall of Gumlidata.

What makes this episode seem as a tongue-in-cheek reference to Sabbatian heresies in particular is the fact that Eldag's favorite pet is an ass, the animal upon which the Messiah will allegedly ride when entering the redeemed city of Jerusalem, as Zechariah proclaims: "Rejoice greatly, O daughter of Zion, shout, O daughter of Jerusalem; behold, thy king cometh unto thee, he is triumphant, and victorious, lowly, and riding upon an ass, even upon a colt the foal of an ass" (Zechariah 9:9). In "Forevermore," the ass is a wild ass and the daughter of Zion is the wayward unredeemed, prophetic figuration of Zion or Jerusalem. Accordingly, we get a wild, inverted tale of a messianic impulse that leads to the redemption of none other than the enemy.[12]

THE MESSIANIC SUBTEXT OF THE LEPER HOUSE

Agnon surely shares Scholem's fascination with heresy, but he also shares something of his friend's apprehension vis-à-vis Zionism's flirtation with messianic delusions. In a lecture delivered in 1974, Scholem spells out some of the dangers he had intuited in his 1926 letter to Rosenzweig. "Zionism is not to be regarded as a species of messianism," he declared. "I consider it the pride of Zionism that it is not a messianic movement. It is a great error, therefore—for which Zionism may have to pay dearly—if the movement attributes to itself messianic significance. Zionism is rather a movement within the mundane, immanent process of history; Zionism does not seek the end of history, but takes responsibility within the history of an *unredeemed* and *unmessianic* world."[13] Scholem was, as Lazier puts it, ultimately committed to "present and future Jewish worldliness."[14]

Within the Agnonian corpus, there are no essays on Zionism and messianism (or on any other topic of current events for that matter), but in his tales, as we have seen, the question reverberates via the somber notes of the arousal of national love and its aftermath. "Forevermore" offers an intriguing variation in this connection not only in the embedded tale of the mock messianic fall of Gumlidata but also in the frame story of Amzeh's quest. Within an allegorical framework where Amzeh is the embodiment of "This-People," his choice to join the leper house may be construed as an eschatological, messianic move: historical time is suspended and the responsibility for historical processes is relinquished. On following Adah Eden to the leper house, Amzeh declares: "No I'm not late for my appointment. . . . In fact, this is only the beginning of my appointment" (243). The final line—*adraba zohi tehilat hamo'ed*—is charged with messianic innuendoes and may also mean: "this is only the beginning of time."[15] Amzeh may be mimicking the Messiah of Tractate Sanhedrin 98a, who, out of great compassion for the outcasts, sits among the lepers by the Gate of Rome, changing his bandages one at a time (instead of all at once), as he is always alert for the imminent cue for redemption. And yet Amzeh is not quite an agent who can rescue the outcasts and lead them out of their marginal position on the outskirts of the city.[16] He is trapped, with the lepers, in a regressive move away from worldliness.

Instead of founding a liberating national home in an earthly Eden, where the Bible may shine in a new light, instead of taking on historical responsibility, Zionism runs the danger, Agnon intimates, of having founded a house of lepers, isolation being its incurable fixation.

But perhaps Amzeh's move to the leper house is not only a reminder of the perils of delusional messianic aspirations but also an acknowledgment of the absurdity and limits of such dreams in modern contexts. Benjamin's Hasidic tale in his Kafka essay, a tale he evokes in speaking of the complication of redemption in Kafkaesque worlds, is relevant to Agnon as well.

> In a Hasidic village, so the story goes, Jews were sitting together in a shabby inn one Sabbath evening. They were all local people, with the exception of one person no one knew, a very poor, ragged man who was squatting in a dark corner at the back of the room. All sorts of things were discussed, and then it was suggested that everyone should tell what wish he would make if one were granted him. One man wanted money; another wished for a son-in-law; a third dreamed of a new carpenter's bench; and so everyone spoke in turn. After they had finished, only the beggar in his dark corner was left. Reluctantly and hesitantly he answered the question. "I wish I were a power-

ful king reigning over a big country. Then, some night while I was asleep in my palace, an enemy would invade my country, and by dawn his horsemen would penetrate my castle and meet with no resistance. Roused from my sleep, I wouldn't have time even to dress and I would have to flee in my shirt. Rushing over hill and dale and through forests day and night, I would finally arrive safely right here at the bench in this corner. This is my wish." The others exchanged uncomprehending glances. "And what good would this wish have done you?" someone asked. "I'd have a shirt," was the answer.[17]

Benjamin presents the tale as Hasidic, but as Freddie Rokem points out, it is a modernized Hasidic tale whose source is unidentifiable.[18] The dark humor of the tale points to the futility of all wishes, the futility that leads the beggar to exchange, in Benjamin's terms, "the wish for its fulfillment."[19] Having a shirt turns out to be the absurd fulfillment of an absurd wish. Yearning for a "lost messianic kingdom," as Rokem (elaborating on Scholem's observation) suggests, is the subtext of this grave joke.[20] And yet, the very fact that the beggar, despite his initial reluctance, ventures to make a wish or, rather, to tell a tale, holds a dim hope for a redeeming moment in the future.

Benjamin's Hasidic tale resembles Agnon's biting, modern renditions of messianic lore in "A Whole Loaf" (Pat Shlema) and other tales of "The Book of Deeds" (Sefer HaMa'asim). In fact, it almost sounds like an Agnonian tale from this collection. But it is also relevant to "Forevermore," where one can discern a line of reasoning that is akin to that of the beggar. Amzeh's greatest wish is to live among lepers and decipher infected, ragged parchments. It is the kind of absurd wish that may find fulfillment in a world replete with diseases and catastrophes. But here too the very act of wishing is not without significance. It calls for a distinction between the destructive ramifications of messianic dreams and the vitality inherent in seeking redemption (however limited it may be) in any imagining of a better future.

Drawing a brief comparison between Kafka and Agnon in the *Jüdische Rundschau* in 1928, Scholem comments that both "drew an apocalyptic sense of reality," but whereas redemption is nowhere to be found in Kafka's writings, Agnon conveys its potentiality.[21] Scholem somewhat mitigates the traces of redemptive longings in Kafka and the forcefulness of Agnon's deep suspicion of messianic visions, but his distinction is nonetheless insightful. What makes Agnon less bleak than Kafka, I think, is the thickness of the allusive network: the unending, obsessive, juggling of sources and commentaries—be it the Bible, the Talmud, the Zohar, or Hasidic lore. If in Kafka's tales, as Benjamin puts it, the students of Holy Writ are students of a lost text, in Agnon's oeuvre, lost books and manuscripts have a stubborn vitality, an uncanny power to return from the realm of the repressed.[22] Solomon's hidden songs surface between the vines, the hymns of Enam are printed despite Ginat's request to refrain from further publication, and the Book of Gumlidata is rescued from oblivion through the fervent study of Amzeh at the leper house. This may not be a "lost messianic kingdom," but Agnon's students of Holy Writ have the privilege of grappling with the magic of a textual treasure that springs back to life, however partial or altered in form.

STUDYING TORAH FOR ITS OWN SAKE: ARS POETIC REFLECTIONS

In keeping with Agnon's excessive interweaving of multiple exegetical possibilities, "Forevermore" is also a comment on modern scholarship and, more implicitly, on the practices of biblical criticism. Amzeh, like Rechnitz and Ginat, is a biblical scholar of sorts whose inquiries ironically call to mind traditional modes of study.[23] In a passage that parodies philology as a whole and biblical philology in particular, Amzeh explains: "[T]he plural of crane in the language of Gumlidata is *aphardat*; the word does not mean ravens or chestnut trees or overshoes as is claimed by Professor Alpha, Professor Beta, or . . . Professor Gamma, whose pictures you may have seen in the magazines when they were given honorary medals. . . . In point of fact, 'raven' in the language of Gumlidata is *eldag* and the plural *elgadata*, since when the letters 'd' and 'g' come together in the plural they reverse their order" (240).[24] His fanciful transition from one term to the next as he supposedly reveals the hidden meaning of minor details is a modern counterpart of Talmudic *pilpul*. More importantly, in his rejection of the glittering world of academic celebrities and preference of the leper hospital, he seems to be an advocate of *Torah lishma*, of the study of Torah for its own sake.[25] But if the scriptural text for which he renounces the world is that of Gumlidata and its sins, what is the value of his total devotion?

Scholarly questions intersect with aesthetic ones. Amzeh's colored maps of Gumlidata follow no cartographic convention but bear the enchanting mark of artistic license. One of the maps provides a "general view of the city," another a "view of its temples," a third a representation of each of its gods, "not to mention the temple prostitutes . . . and the dogs—for each and every one a different color, to denote position and function, harlot's pay, or price" (233).

Rather than offer a standard representation of major sites, these imaginary maps denote the different participants in Gumlidata's idolatrous practices and present bizarre details such as the figures of the "harlot's pay, or price," details that Amzeh supposedly finds in his excursions, on interviewing the city's infamous dogs.

Immersed in the world he reconstructs, Amzeh is also something of a writer, all the more so after he discovers the manuscript in the leper house. It is never quite clear whether he deciphers new passages in the parchment or invents them. Thinking of the chronicler of Gumlidata as he reads the final pages of the parchment, he ruminates, "How great is the true writer . . . who does not abandon his work even when the sword of death hangs over his neck, who writes with his very blood, in his soul's own script, what his eyes have seen!" (248). Yet Amzeh too is implicated in this scene of "true" writing, given his willingness to risk his health in joining the leper house and dedicating himself to the diseased book of Gumlidata.[26] Before Amzeh handles the untouchable book for the first time, "they tied him in an antiseptic apron which reached from his neck to his feet. They took the book out of the chest where it was stored in, and gave it to him with a warning not to touch it. Amzeh stared at it until his eyes seemed to occupy half his face. He looked at it for a long time, then jumped up quickly to open it"(244). And although they force Amzeh to wear gloves (Agnon uses an archaic expression: *batey yadayim*, literally "houses of hands"), he doesn't always adhere to these cautionary instructions, eager as he is to plunge into the world of the ancient city.

To the extent that a self-reflexive dimension is at stake, Agnon seems to reflect on his own semi-heretical mingling of literature, exegesis, and scholarship; he seems to wonder about the risks a writer needs to take in laying bare the script inscribed in his blood, soul, and eyes; he seems to wonder about his own commitment to and compassion for the outcasts, he seems to share with Amzeh, the urgent passion to rescue lost texts against all odds, the need to insist on cultural preservation and humanistic values—all the more so at times of catastrophe, when the muses are too easily relegated to the margins. He seems to crave, with Amzeh, for the unique power of the biblical scribes to get under the skin, to fashion texts of utmost relevance to their readers—so binding that they are inscribed on the body while absorbing their readers' tears and pus. And yet such ultimate writing can be fully approached only in dreams and is as partial in modern times as is the singing of the Levites in the Temple to which Agnon refers in his banquet speech.

AMZEH'S SONG: EXEGETICAL INCONGRUITIES

The Song of Songs is not a pivotal text in "Forevermore," but its echoes may be traced at different points. Perhaps even the fact that the Book of Gumlidata is defined as a contaminating text that requires special handling discloses a certain affinity with the Song. When the canonicity of the Song was disputed, the question at stake was whether or not it "defiles the hands" (*metame 'et ha-yadayim*). According to rabbinic enactment, hands that come into contact with a biblical book contract uncleanness in the second degree. Indeed, such impurity needs to be removed by means of a ritual washing of the hands. It may seem paradoxical, but the underlying logic of this halakhic rule has to do with the attempt to define the use and circulation of sacred texts in different terms. We do not know what was the content of the rabbinic argument regarding the ancient love poem, but Rabbi Akiva is the one who rescues the text by declaring: "Heaven forbid that any man in Israel ever disputed that the Song of Songs renders the hands unclean, for that the whole world is not worth the day on which the Song of Songs was given to Israel, for all the Writings are holy, and the Song of Songs is the Holy of Holies" (Mishnah Yadayim 3:5).[27]

Other, more pronounced echoes of the Song are evident in Amzeh's addresses to Adah Eden as "my sister." If "sister" in the Song means "beloved," in "Forevermore" Agnon plays on the triple meanings of *ahot*: sister, beloved, nurse.[28] The elderly nurse Adah Eden is a mock romantic Shulamite, but she nonetheless has something of the lure of Shoshana and Gemulah insofar as she leads Amzeh to a paradisiacal world—her last name is "Eden"—which verges on death.[29]

Amzeh follows "his sister" to the leper house, but his true love (or some kind of imaginary extension of Adah Eden) turns out to be Wisdom, who seductively whispers in the closing lines of the tale: "Sit, my love, sit and do not leave me" (249). A combination of the Wisdom of Proverbs, Hokhma, the kabbalistic configuration of the Shekhinah as sister, and the classical Sophia, she might even be, writes Robert Alter, "enslaving the discoverer of truth to his own ruin."[30] However ambiguous, the amorous bond between Amzeh and Wisdom is yet another evocation of traditional allegories of the Song (both Jewish and Christian), where the Beloved stands for some kind of abstract ideality.

But what makes "Forevermore" particularly vital to understanding the Song's reception is its flaunting of exegetical incongruities, in this case, the discrepancy between the sexual promiscuity and daunting animality of Gumlidata and its consecration by Amzeh and the lepers. I quoted Amzeh's words "I am as lustful for knowledge and curious as a psychoanalyst" (*sakran te'ev da'at, mamash ke-psychoanalytikan*) in my opening remarks. Within the context of "Forevermore," they appear in the sequence in which Amzeh urges Adah Eden to reveal any possible detail about Gumlidata. His evocation of psychoanalysis—which is uncharacteristic of his scholarly vocabulary—calls attention to the relevance of psychoanalytic tools to understanding the contradiction between Amzeh's monastic life and his unstinting devotion to the abominations of Gumlidata and craving to touch the untouchable parchment. In fact, his "lust" for knowledge seems to disclose a certain fascination with Gumlidata precisely because of its blatant sexuality. The one missing detail for which Amzeh pines—"[f]rom which side Geditons brigades entered the city" (240)—is, after all, a riddle inextricably connected to the schemes of the seductive Eldag.

"I don't know through which gate [Amzeh] entered [the lepers' hospital] or how much time it took before he was granted admittance" (244), remarks the narrator of "Forevermore," as he whimsically conflates the enigma of Gumlidata's conquest with Amzeh's story, as if losing, with his protagonist, the capacity to distinguish between imaginary and real worlds. On entering his leprous Eden, Amzeh succeeds in deciphering a few hidden "calves eyes" in the worn-out parchment, but he remains as blind as Norbert Hanold in *Gradiva* to the delusional aspects of his total immersion in a quest for traces of an alluring female figure in the ruins of the past.

The Song represents a love that is far from the perverse, sinful practices of Gumlidata, but its bold eroticism has definitely posed a challenge to readers throughout its circuitous exegetical history. Consider the rabbis reading of the verse "Thy two breasts are like two fawns that are twins of a gazelle" (Song 7:4) in Song of Songs Rabbah:

> "Your two breasts are like two fawns."
> This refers to Moses and Aaron.
> Just as a woman's breasts are her glory and her ornament,
> so Moses and Aaron are the glory and the ornament of Israel.
> Just as a woman's breasts are her charm,
> so Moses and Aaron are the charm of Israel. . . .
> Just as a woman's breasts are full with milk,
> so Moses and Aaron are full of Torah.[31]

When the rabbis read the two breasts of the beloved as Moses and Aaron, they yoke the particular features of the female body to the representation of national figures and canonical history. To modern eyes, they seem surprisingly detached from the literal context of the Song. In "Agunot" ("Forsaken Wives"), Agnon evokes this midrash in his ironic rendition of the discrepancy between Ben-Uri's pious ruminations regarding the ark he had fashioned and his repressed erotic longings for Dinah. "To what might the ark have been compared at that moment? To a woman who extends her palms in prayer, while her breasts—the Tables of the Covenant—are lifted with her heart, beseeching her Father in heaven."[32]

Exegetical incongruities, as far as Agnon is concerned, are inescapable—be they traditional or modern. In fact, they are part of what makes the meditation on exegetical imagination so riveting. If the exegetes of Song of Songs Rabbah were somewhat oblivious to the literal dimension of the text, the Zionists were only semi-aware of the allegories that they themselves were spinning around the ancient love poem and of their own contribution to the forging of a new mode of consecration. What is more, in the end of the day, even the Zionists, much like Agnon's modern scholarly characters, cannot quite face the intensities of earthly eros and love. Among the numerous musical adaptations of verses of the Song in Israeli culture, there is no rendition of "Thy two breasts are like two fawns that are twins of a gazelle." It is not the kind of verse that would be celebrated in the ceremonial events of the kibbutzim during Passover or in evenings of folk dancing.

THE SONG'S RECEPTION BEYOND THE 1950S: A SKETCH

What happened to the Song in Israeli culture since the 1950s? Like the Bible as a whole it gradually lost something of its position as a founding national text. For a nation no longer in the making, the need to fashion a national epos via the Bible was no longer paramount. But despite these changes, the Bible by no means has ceased to play a central part in all realms of Israeli culture.[33] This is especially true of the Song of Songs. It continues to be a key text in modern Israeli poetry—from Haviva Pedaya's *From a Sealed Ark* (1996) to Yehuda Amichai's "The Bible and You, the Bible and You, and Other Midrashim" (1998); it continues, if less so, to have resonance in prose as well, all the more so in recent years: Haim Be'er's *In That Place* (2007) ends with an evocation of the Shulamite, and the protagonist of David Grossman's *To the End of the Land* (2008) chooses to call her son "Ofer" in light of the Song's young hart; it continues to be (even more than before) an indispensable part of wedding ceremonies—both secular and religious; and it still thrives in popular music.

I will map out, however briefly, some of the fascinating developments in the musical realm, which until today remains the most prominent exegetical scene of the Israeli Song of Songs. The history of the reception of the ancient love poem is already long enough for parodic versions to crop up, as in Arik Einstein's "Shir mispar shemoneh" ("Song Number Eight"; 1971), better known as "Yonati, tamati" ("My Dove, My Perfect One"), a tongue-in-cheek variation on Yemenite adaptations of the Song in the 1940s. It is seldom a Song of group singing and folk dances (though the classics remain) but rather tends to be personal and more attuned to the painful qualities of love. Idan Raichel's "Hinakh yafa" ("Behold, Thou Art Fair, My Love"—Song 1:15; 2002), one of the greatest contemporary hits, is exemplary, underscoring as it does the nocturnal scene of Song 3. In this case, there is yet another intriguing twist: Raichel replaces the tradition of Yemenite women singers and Yemenite tunes with Ethiopian women singers and Ethiopian melodies—the new exotic sphere of the last decade.

The most dramatic change, however, is evident in Mizrahi music—a realm that became, from the mid-1980s on, a major component of popular Israeli music.[34] There are numerous secular Mizrahi adaptations of the Song—from "Hanale hitbalbela" ("Hanale was Rattled"; 1970s) of Tzliley ha-'ud (Sounds of the Oud), with its evocation of "He hath brought me to the banqueting house" (Song 2:4), to Sarit Hadad's more recent "Holat ahava" ("Lovesick"; 2011).[35] But alongside this secular trend, one finds a remarkable renewal of traditional *piyyutim*, among them poems of the great medieval poets Shlomo Ibn Gabirol and Yehuda Halevi, where the Song is evoked in depictions of divine love.[36] Curiously enough, this trend has had a sweeping impact beyond the traditional corpus, so much so that Sara Levi-Tanai's "El ginat egoz" has been recently rearranged as a Mizrahi *piyyut* by Ravid Kahalani of Yemen Blues (first performed at the Piyyut Festival of 2010). Levi-Tanai herself, however, paved the road to such a move in her 1982 production *The Song of Songs* where she insisted on combining the literal and the allegorical. In fact, the piece begins with a voice-over of Levi-Tanai's dramatic reading of Rabbi Akiva's renowned endorsement of the sanctity of the Song.[37]

This turn back to traditional allegories in the exegetical history of the Song in Israeli culture is, I believe, something that Agnon had already anticipated in the 1940s and 1950s, when he set out to uncover the lingering traces of religious paradigms in Zionist biblical culture, complicating normative conceptions of Zionist secularism.

CODA

Imagine our five moonstruck lovers—Shoshana, Rechnitz, Gemulah, Ginat, and Gamzu—on the roof of the leper house of "Forevermore" on a moonlit night (the building that served as inspiration for Agnon, the Hansen Hospital, still stands there across from the Jerusalem Theater). I don't know through which gate we need to enter, but there they are, the lovers, with the Shulamite's Song inscribed on their skin: *'ani yeshena ve-libbi 'er*, "I sleep, but my heart waketh." Like the singing, somnambulist Shulamite, they seek love but cannot quite find it; they can neither cope with the maddening intensities of earthly love nor handle the maladies of the Love for Zion; they can neither follow these loves nor relinquish them; they are at risk of falling off the roof, unaware of the abysses that lurk below.

But as these somnambulist lovers stand there on the roof, amid the moonlit trees, the *levana* races above them and reminds us that the Song is unbound, that it is ultimately owned by no culture and can travel from one corner of the globe to another. It reminds us that the ancient love poem is a spectacular aesthetic touchstone that leads to imaginary, magical worlds, where Rechnitz's wondrous weeds and the inscrutable Enamite leaves may intersect, where letters, colors, and forms are forever shifting; it reminds us that modernity has invented no decisive exegetical key; it urges us, nonetheless, to continue the somnambulist chase after a Song that is in a state of perpetual flight—forevermore.

Appendix

Musical Adaptations of the Song of Songs 1930s–1950s

Selected Songs*

NO	TITLE	TRANSLITERATION	COMPOSER	WRITER/SOURCE	YEAR	SINGER
1	"What Is Thy Beloved More than Another Beloved"	"Ma Dodekh Mi'dod"	Admon, Yedidya	Song of Songs	1943 (composed); 1953 (recorded)	Damari, Shoshana; Hillel and Aviva
2	"The Pomegranate Tree"	"Ets ha-rimon"	Admon, Yedidya; Folk music	Orland, Yaakov	1937–8 (written) 1944 (composed)	Aharoni, Chana; Hillel and Aviva; Raz, Ruchama; Haza, Ofra; and others
3	"For She Will Be Pleasant"	"Ki Tin'am"	Aldema, Gil	Kashtan, Michael	1953	Yarkoni; Yaffa, Emanuel Zamir Group
4	"Look Not upon Me"	"Al Tir'uni"	Amiran, Emanuel	Song of Songs		Aharoni, Chana
5	"Little Foxes"	"Shu'alim Ketanim"	Amiran, Emanuel	Song of Songs	1938 (composed)	
6	"The Song of the Signalman"	"Shir Ha-atat"	Amiran, Emanuel	Bartora (Bergman), Avraham		Ben Shachar, Leah
7	"The Light of Lilies"	"Or Havatslot"	Folk music	Levi-Tanai, Sara	1946	Gvirtz, Shimon and Ilana
8	"O My Dove, That Art in the Clefts of the Rock"	"Yonati Be-Hagvei Ha-Sela"	Biderman, Shlomo	Song of Songs		Kashi, Aliza
9	"My Beloved to Me"	"Dodi Li"	Chen, Nira	Song of Songs	1948 (composed)	Zur, Naomi; Zakai, Mira; Avni, Fran; and others
10	"With Me from Lebanon"	"Iti Mi-Levanon"	Chen, Nira	Song of Songs	1948 (composed)	Zur, Naomi; Rave, Hillel and Aviva
11	"By the Spring"	"Al Yad Ha-Ein"	Chen, Zalman	Chen, Zalman		
12	"I Am the Lily of Sharon"	"Ani Havatselet Ha-Sharon"	Cohen Melamed, Nisim	Song of Songs		Aharoni, Chana
13	"Ho Mother"	"Hoi Ima"	Eukranian folk music	Ukranian folk lyrics		Mishmarot Choir Veter-ans; Alon, Azaria
14	"A Yearning Dove"	"Yona Homyia"	Folk music	HaLevi Latris, Meir		
15	"There Foxes Dwell"	"Sham Shu'alim Yesh"	Folk music	Silman, Kaddish-Yehuda		
16	"The Song of the Shepherd"	"Shir Ha-Ro'e"	Folk music	Emanuel Harusi	1933 (written)	
17	"Put Your Hand"	"Simi Yadekh"	Folk music	Folk lyrics	1958 (recorder); various versions in the 1940s	Yarkoni, Yaffa (and others)

* Recordings of many of these songs are available in Zemereshet

18	"The Guard's Son"	"Ben Ha-Shomer"	Folk music/ Bieck, Moshe	Shimoni, David	before the 1930s	
19	"And David with His Beautiful Eyes"	"Ve-David Yefe Einayim"	Gamliel, Eliyahu; Shelem, Matityahu	Book of Samuel	1943–1944 (written and composed); 1955 (recorded)	Yarkoni, Yaffa
20	"The Dream of Shulamite"	"Halom Shulamit"	Goldfaden, Abraham	Mohar, Yehiel		
21	"An Evening of Roses"	"Erev Shel Shoshanim"	Hadar, Yosef	Dor, Moshe	1957 (released)	
22	"Graceful Apple"	"Tapuah Hinani"	Hadar, Yosef	Dor, Moshe		Ha-Dudaim
23	"The Shepherds' Song"	"Shir Ha-Nokdim"	Hadar, Yosef	Dor, Moshe		Ha-Dudaim
24	"Twosomes Dance"	"Rikud Tsmadim"	Hadar, Yosef	Gilad, Zerubavel		Renanim Group
25	"I Am My Beloved's"	"Ani le-dodi"	Hadar, Yosef	Song of Songs		Ran and Na'ama
26	"As a Rose among Thorns"	"Ke-Shoshan Bein Ha-Hohim"	Hadar, Yosef	Song of Songs		Carmon Band
27	"A Day to the Dryland"	"Yom La'Yabasha"	Hassidic folk music	Halevi, Yehuda		Ha-Givatron
28	"Answer Me"	"Ane"	Havatselet, Ze'ev	Havatselet, Ze'ev		Hendel, Nechama
29	"Our Dance Is for Two"	"Meholenu hu Bi'Shna'im"	Heiman, Nahum	Havatzelet Ze'ev		Yadin, Yossi; The Shnei-Sharim Duo
30	"Flower Buds Have Appeared in the Land"	"Nitsanim Nir'u Ba-'arets"	Heiman, Nahum	Song of Songs	1951	Ha-Givatron
31	"The Flowers"	"Ha-Nitsanim"	Kirsch, Haim	Song of Songs	1955	Sansonov, Rama
32	"The Train"	"Ha-Rakevet"	Kling, Berta	Rolnick, Yosef	1907 (written)	Havkin, Drora
33	"Come My Beloved"	"Bo'a Dodi"	Lavry, Mark	Eliaz, Rephael		Aharoni, Chana; Zakai, Mira (1990)
34	"Hark! My beloved!"	"Kol Dodi"	Levi-Tanai, Sara	Song of Songs	1944	Damari, Shoshana
35	"Into the Garden of Nuts"	"El Ginat Egoz"	Levi-Tanai, Sara	Song of Songs	1944	Aharoni, Chana and the Emanuel Zamir Group
36	"The Daughter of the Rocks"	"Bat Tsurim"	Levi-Tanai, Sara	Levi-Tanai, Sara		Carmon Group
37	"Come, My Beloved"	"Lekha Dodi"	Levi-Tanai, Sara	Elkabetz, Rabbai Shlomo		Nahum-Abas, Reuma
38	"For, Lo, the Winter Is Past"	"Hine Ha-Stav Avar"	Levi-Tanai, Sara	Song of Songs		
39	"Hark! My Beloved!"	"Kol Dodi"	Levi-Tanai, Sara	Song of Songs	1944	
40	"I Am My Beloved's and My Beloved Is Mine"	"Ani Le-Dodi Ve-Dodi Li"	Levi-Tanai, Sara	Song of Songs	1944	

41	"Thou Has Ravished My Heart, My Sister, My Bride"	"Libavtini"	Levi-Tanai, Sara	Song of Songs	1944	
42	"Thou That Dwellest in the Gardens"	"Ha-Yoshevet Ba'Ganim"	Levi-Tanai, Sara	Song of Songs	1944	
43	"I Am a Lily of Sharon"	"Ani Havatselet Ha-Sharon"	Levi-Tanai, Sara	Song of Songs	1944	
44	"I Am Black, but Comely"	"Shehora Ani Ve'Naava"	Levi-Tanai, Sara	Song of Songs	1944	
45	"Into the Garden of Nuts"	"El Ginat Egoz"	Levi-Tanai, Sara	Song of Songs	1944	
46	"Who Is This That Cometh up out of the Wilderness"	"Mi Zot Ola Min Ha-Midbar"	Levi-Tanai, Sara	Song of Songs	1944	
47	"Turn Away Thine Eyes from Me"	"Hasevi Eina'ikh Mi'negdi"	Levi-Tanai, Sara	Song of Songs	1944	
48	"The Beauteous Land"	Be-Eretz Ha-Tsvi	Lithuanian folk music	Maironis (Hebrew version: Yaffe, Avraham Leib)		
49	"Between the River Prat"	"Bein Nehar Prat"	Mideastern folk music	Bialik, Haim Nahman	1905 (written); 1928 (recorded)	Zefira, Bracha; Hendel, Nechama
50	"Shepherds' Debka"	"Debkat Ro'im"	Mideastern folk music	Zamir, Emanuel		Gamliel, Eliyahu; Emanuel Zamir Group
51	"The Dance of the Vineyard"	"Mehol Ha-Kerem"	Mohar, Yehiel	Cohen, Avshalom		
52	"Avinoam"	"Avinoam"		Unknown		Ha-Dudaim
53	"Three Bukharan Folk Songs"	"Shlosha Shirei Am Bukharim"	Nardi, Nahum		between 1937–1950	Zefira, Bracha
54	"A Wedding Song"	"Shir Hatuna"	Nardi, Nahum		between 1937–1950	Zefira, Bracha
55	"Out of Depths"	"Mi-Ma'amakim"	Nardi, Nahum	Admon, Yedidya	between 1937–1950	Zefira, Bracha
56	"To My Beloved I Am Terrible"	"Ani Le'Dodi Ayuma"	Nardi, Nahum	A Jewish liturgical poem (Piyyut) from the 10th century	between 1937–1950	Zefira, Bracha
57	"Awake O North"	"Uri Tsafon"	Nardi, Nahum	Song of Songs		
58	"Open to Me, My Sister, My Love"	"Pithi-Li Ahoti Ra'Ayati"	Nardi, Nahum	Song of Songs	1940s (recorded)	Aharoni, Chana
59	"To Greet Shabbat"	"Likrat Shabat"	Nardi, Nahum	Kipnis, Levin	before 1960	
60	"Do Not Say Goodbye to Me"	"Al Na Tagidi Li Shalom"	Nardi Nahum	Avishar, Oded		Gamlilait, Esther; Goren, Edna

61	"We Will Go Out and Live Tranquil"	"Netse'a, Nagura Sha'ananim"	Nardi, Nahum	Tchernichovsky, Shaul	1893-written; composed before 1966	Zadok, Ahuva
62	"Yemen's Rose"	"Shoshanat Teiman"	Nardi, Nahum; Folk music	Alterman, Nathan	1939	Yarkoni, Yaffa
63	"The Dance of the Guards"	"Mehol Ha-Shomrim"	Nardi, Nahum; Folk music	Halevi, Assaf		Zefira, Bracha
64	"I Have a Garden"	"Yesh Li Gan"	Nardi, Nahum; Syrian Folk Music	Bialik, Haim Nahman	1907 (written)	Zefira, Bracha; Hendel, Nehama
65	"The Taste of the Manna"	"Ta'am Ha-Man"	Navon, Yitzchak Eliyahu	Navon, Yitzchak Eliyahu	before 1953	Aharon, Sharona; Eliran, Ran
66	"The Comeliest of the Daughters"	"Ha-Naava Ba-Banot"	Ne'eman, Amitai	Ne'eman, Amitai		Damari, Shoshana; Eliran, Ran
67	"Behold, Thou Art Fair"	"Hinakh Yafa Ra'ayati"	Ne'eman, Amitai	Song of Songs	1955	Tsur, Naomi
68	"My Precious"	"Hemdati"	Ne'eman, Amitai	Song of Songs		Ha-Dudaim
69	"To the Vineyards"	"El Hakramim"	Ne'eman, Amitai	Unknown	1952 (recorded)	Livnat, Shulamit
70	"For, Lo, the Winter Is Past"	"Hine Ha-Stav Avar"	Nisimov, Nisim	Song of Songs		
71	"Hephtsi-bah"	"Hephtsi-bah"	Oleri-Nuzik, Mordechai	Orland, Yaakov		Yarkoni, Yaffa
72	"Sleepless Night"	"Laila Lo Nim"	Persian folk music	Eliaz, Rephael	1947 (recorded)	Zefira, Bracha
73	"Black One"	"Sheharhoret"	Raviv, Tuli	Raviv, Tuli	1949 (recorded); 1948 (first performance)	Yarkoni, Yaffa; Hishatron Group (military singing group)
74	"Spring"	"Aviv"	Scottish folk music	Scottish folk music (Hebrew version: Broshi, Avraham)		Avigal, Miriam
75	"Behind the Gate"	"Me'ahorei Ha-Sha'ar"	Sephardic folk music; Melamed, Nissan Cohen	Bialik, Haim Nahman		
76	"The Song of the Veteran"	"Shir Ha-Vatik"	Shelem, Matityahu	Shelem, Matityahu		
77	"They Made Me Keeper	"Samuni Notera"	Shelem, Matityahu	Song of Songs		
78	"For, Lo, the Winter Is Past"	"Hine Ha-Stav Avar"	Shelem, Matityahu	Song of Songs	1945–1947 (composed)	
79	"The Rain Is Over and Gone"	"Pana Ha-Geshem"	Shelem, Matityahu	Shelem, Matityahu	1943	Shemer, Naomi; Paley, Cindy; Sulkin, Ether
80	"Watchman, What of the Night?"	"Shomer Ma Mi'Leil"	Shelem, Matityahu	Shelem, Matityahu	1940 (written and composed); 1967 (recorded)	Rave, Hillel (Ilka); Raz, Tamar
81	"O You Are the Land"	"Hoi At Eretz"	Shelem, Matityahu	Shelem, Matityahu		Gluska, Ofira

82	"Go Thy Way Forth,My Sister, My Bride"	"Kumi Tse'i A'hoti Kala"	Shemer Naomi	Bialik, Haim Nahman	In the 1970s (composed)	Gaon, Yehoram
83	"With Thousands of Hands"	"Be'Alfei Yada'im"	Shlonsky Vardina	Alterman, Nathan; Goldberg, Leah; Shlonsky, Avraham		Ha-Givatron
84	"A Mountain and a Meadow Have Turned Green"	"Har Ve-Kar Horiku"	Tataric folk music	Achai, Yosef	1944	Nave, Hillel and Aviva
85	"Flower Buds"	"Nitsanim"	Ukrainian folklor music	Levi-Tanai, Sara		Hadasim Group
86	"I Haven't Slept All night"	"Kol Ha-Laila Lo Yashanti"	Unknowm	Unknown	1947	Gamliel, Eliyahu
87	"Those Going Down to the Vineyards"	"Ve-Ha-yordot El Bein Ha-Kramim"	Unknown	Unknown		Har'el, Menashe
88	"There in a Peaceful Valley I Strolled"	"Sham Be-Gai Shalev Tyialti"	Unknown (classic)	Unknown		
89	"Miriam Bat Nissim"	"Miriam Bat Nissim"	Vilenski, Moshe	Alterman, Nathan	1947	Damari, Shoshana
90	"Shulamite"	"Shulamit"	Vilenski, Moshe	Alterman, Nathan	1946	Damari, Shoshana
91	"My Beloved Is Gone Down into His Garden"	"Dodi Yarad Le-Gano"	Vilenski, Moshe	Song of Songs	1950	Damari, Shoshana; Zefira, Bracha
92	"Will You Remember?"	"Ha-Tizkor?"	Vilenski, Moshe	Emanuel Harusi	1959 (recorded)	Damari, Shoshana
93	"We Are the Shepherds"	"Anahnu Ha-Ro'im"	Vilenski, Moshe	Mohar, Yehiel		Damari, Shoshana
94	"To Whom a Good Stone"	"Lemi Even Tova"	Vilenski, Moshe	Bialik, Haim Nahman		Tal, Michal
95	"In Yemen's Vineyard"	"Be-Kerem Teiman"	Vilensky, Moshe; Zeira, Mordechai	Alterman, Nathan	1937	Atari, Yona and Banai, Yossi; Gmalielit, Esther and Gaon, Yehoram; Zohar, Rivka and Zilber-man, Menachem
96	"Come in Peace, Dew"	"Bo Be-Shalom, Tal"	Yaron, Re'uven	Unknown		
97	"The Song of the Yemenites"	"Shir Ha-Teimanyiot"	Yemenite folk music	Alterman, Nathan	1934	Tochner, Mina
98	"At Dawn"	"Im Ha-Shahar"	Yemenite folk music	Levi-Tanai, Sara		Ha-Dudaim; Zitner, Ora
99	"A Pomegranate Split Open"	"Le-Pelach Ha-Rimon"	Yemenite folk music	Moshe the Author from Rome		
100	"Precious Fruits"	"Megadim"	Zamir, Emanuel	Zamir, Emanuel	1951(recorded)	Yarkoni, Yaffa; Emanue Zamir Group; Gamliel, Eliyahu

101	"A Caravan from Yemen"	"Orha Mi-Teiman"	Zamir, Emanuel	Zamir, Emanuel		Mishmarot Choir Veterans
102	"Debka Abayia"	"Debka Abayia"	Zamir, Emanuel	Rajuan, Naim		Haza, Ofra
103	"The Vineyards' Daughter"	"Bat Ha-Kramim"	Zehavi, David	Halfi, Shimon	before 1961	
104	"Two Roses"	"Shtei Shoshanim"	Zeira, Mordechai	Orland, Yaakov	written and composed before 1960	Zefira, Bracha; Damari, Shoshana; Ravitz, Yehudit; and many others
105	"The Rose"	"Ha-Shoshana"	Zunser, Eliakum	Zunser, Eliakum	1860 (written); 1917 (recorded) and later in the 1970s	The Kibbutz Ha-Meuchad Choir; Benot Ha-Zemer Choir- Ma'agan Michael; Alberstein, Chava
106	"Terrible in the Mountain of Mor"	"Ayuma Be-Har Mor"		Shabbazi, Shalom Ben Yosef		Zefira, Bracha
107	"Terrible the Silk"	"Ayuma Ha-Mshi"		Shabbazi, Shalom Ben Yosef		Zefira, Bracha
108	"The Song of Songs"	"Shir Ha-Shirim"		Song of Songs		Zefira, Bracha
109	"The Minister in Charge"	"Sar Ha-Memune"		Shabbazi, Shalom Ben Yosef		Zefira, Bracha
110	"I Sleep"	"Ani Yeshena"		Song of Songs		Berzak, Nika

Musical Adaptations of the Song of Songs from the 1960s to the present

Selected Songs

NO	TITLE	TRANSLITERATION	COMPOSER	WRITER	YEAR	SINGER
1	"Many, Many Waters"	"Mayim Rabim, Rabim"	Alberstein, Chava	Alberstein, Chava	1988	Alberstein, Chava
2	"Of All the Myrrh Flowers in the Garden"	"Mi-kol Pirhei Mor Ba-Gan"	Aldema, Gil	Tchernichovsky, Shaul	1977	Shlishyat Gesher Ha-Yarkon
3	"The Dance of the Mistresses"	"Mehol Ha-Pilagshim"	Aloni, Bezalel		1978	Haza, Ofra
4	"For Love Is Strong as Death"	"Aza Ka-Mavet A'hava"	Aloni, Bezalel	Song of Songs	1978	Haza, Ofra
5	"My Beloved Is White and Ruddy"	"Dodi Tsah Ve-Adom"	Amiran, Emanuel	Song of Songs		Hendel, Nehama
6	"This Is My Beloved More than Another Beloved"	"Ze Dodi Mi-Dod"	Argov, Sasha	Alterman, Nathan		Gluska, Ofira
7	"The Midrash of My Dove"	"Midrash Yonati"	Ariel, Meir	Ariel, Meir	1988	Ariel, Meir
8	"A Stolen Song"	"Shir Ganuv"	Ariel, Meir	Song of Songs	1988	Ariel, Meir
9	"Because of an Apple"	"Be-shel Tapu'ah"	Artzi, Shlomo	Bialik, Haim Nahman	1973	Artzi, Shlomo
10	"I Sleep, but My Heart Waketh"	"Ani Yeshena Ve-Libi Er"	Avimeir, Yair	Song of Songs	1978	Haza, Ofra
11	"We Have a Little Sister"	"A'hot Lanu Ketana"	Aviv, Micky	Song of Songs	1978	Haza, Ofra
12	"That Feedeth among the Lilies"	"Ha-Roe Ba-Shoshanim"	Azioni, Binyamin	Aloni, Bezalel	1978	Haza, Ofra
13	"A Joyful Song of Songs"	"Shir Ha-Shirim Be-Sha'ashu'im"	Azioni, Binyamin	Aloni, Bezalel	1978	Haza, Ofra
14	"O Thou Fairest among Women"	"Ha-Yafa Ba-Nashim"	Azioni, Binyamin	Song of Songs	1978	Haza, Ofra
15	"By Night on My Bed"	"Al Mishkavi Ba-Leilot"	Azioni, Binyamin	Song of Songs	1978	Atari, Yona
16	"Father"	"Aba"	Banai, Eviatar	Banai, Eviatar	2009	Banai, Eviatar
17	"The Letters of the Law Soar Upward"	"Otiyot Porhot Ba-Avir"	Banai, Eviatar	Banai, Eviatar	2009	Banai, Eviatar
18	"Until Tomorrow"	"Ad Mahar"	Banai, Eviatar	Banai, Eviatar	2009	Banai, Eviatar
19	"My Beloved Is Gone Down into His Garden"	"Dodi Yarad Le-Gano"	Biderman, Shlomo	Song of Songs		Ha-Parvarim
20	"The Fire of My Love"	"Esh A'havati"	Big Fishi	Big Fishi	2000	Big Fishi

21	"Return, O Shulamite"	"Shuvi Ha-Shulamit"	Caspi, Matti	Shemer, Naomi	1988	Caspi, Matti
22	"A Lovely Hind"	"Ayelet A'havim"	Chagidakis, Manos	Shemer, Naomi; Chagidakis, Manos	1964	Einstein, Arik; Haza, Ofra; Gaon, Yehoram
23	"Set Me as a Seal"	"Simeni Ka-Hotam"	Chitman, Uzi	Hazon, Michal	1998	Avidan, Aviva
24	"Set Me as a Seal"	"Simeni Ka-Hotam"	Cohen, Sagiv	Song of Songs	2007 (album), 2010 (single)	Cohen, Sagiv
25	"Many Waters"	"Mayim Rabim"	Cohen, Yaron	Cohen, Yaron	2004	Peretz, Kobi
26	"Love-Sick"	"Holat A'hava"	Dori, Tamir and Dikla	Dikla	2010	Dikla
27	"A Ballad to the King"	"Balada La-Melekh"	Einav, Baruch	Aloni, Bezalel	1978	Haza, Ofra
28	"Exploding Because of You"	"Mitpotsets Biglalekh"	Elimelech, Doron	Lev, Rami	2011	Golan, Eyal
29	"The Time of Love, O Bride"	"Et Dodim, Kala"	Folk music	Ben Sahal, Rabbi Chaim	1980	Argov, Zohar; Zohar, Geula; Sharif
30	"Open the Gate, My Beloved"	"Sha'ar Petah Dodi"	Folk music	Ibn Gabirol, Shlomo	2009	Sakharof, Berry and Mociach, Re'a
31	"Pleasures of Love"	"A'hava Be-Ta'anugim"	Freilich, Amir	Song of Songs	1978	Haza, Ofra
32	"Song Number Eight"	"Shir Mispar Shemone"	Gavrielov, Miki	Rotblit, Yaakov	1971	Einstein, Arik
33	"Maybe Tomorrow"	"Ulai Mahar"	German, Yael	Goldberg, Leah	1976	Galron, Nurit
34	"The Time of Love, O Bride"	"Et Dodim, Kala"	Giladi, Moti	Ben Sahal, Rabbi Hayim	1976	Haza, Ofra
35	"The Song of Songs"	"Shir Ha-Shirim"	Glikman, Omri	Glikman, Omri	2009	Hatikvah 6
36	"A Lovely Hind"	"A'yeley A'havim"	Hadar, Yosef	Dor, Moshe		Rave, Ilka
37	"Return to Me"	"Shuvi Elai"	Haimov, Yoram	Haimov, Uri	1984	Moshe, Haim
38	"Love-Sick"	"Holat A'hava"	Henree	Henree	2011	Hadad, Sarit
39	"Go Thy Way Forth"	"Kumi U-ts'ei"	Henree	Henree	2011	Hadad, Sarit
40	"The Scent of the Apple and Scarlet's Red"	"Re'ah Tapuah Ve-odem Shani"	Heiman, Nahum	Teharlev, Yehoram	1966	Ha-Givatron; Ha-Dudaim; Haza, Ofra; Gaon, Yehoram; Cohen, Izhar; Shlishyat Gesher Ha-Yarkon
41	"I Wrote You a Song"	"Katavti Lakh Shir"	Hollander, Yaakov	Rosen, Shmuel		Ha-Irusim
42	"Here I Swear to You"	"Nishba Lakh Kan"	Kandevi, Ariel and Cohen, Yonatan	Cohen, Yonatan	2010	Golan, Eyal

43	"From Me to You"	"Mimeni Elaikh"	Leon, Adi	Gispan, Yossi	2011	Levi, Yishai
44	"Where Shall I turn"	"Ana Efne"	Lev-Ari, Erez	Lev-Ari, Erez	2007	Lev-Ari, Erez
45	"Thou Hast Ravished My Heart"	"Libavtini"	Lev-Ari, Erez and Ha-Yetsira, Refael	Lev-Ari, Erez	2007	Lev-Ari, Erez
46	"Shulamite"	"Shulamit"	Levi, Shem Tov	Alterman, Nathan	1984	
47	"Jama'a in the Desert"	"Jama'a Ba-Midbar"	Lieber, Gilli	Lieber, Gilli and Zioni, Ayelet	1999	Gaya Band and Aviv, Din-Din
48	"The Love of My Heart"	"Ahuvat Levavi"	Machdon, Shlomo	Machdon, Shlomo	1997	Daklon
49	"The Sheikh's Son"	"Ben Ha-Sheh"	Manor, Ehud	Abdel Wahab, Mohammed	1989	Arazi, Yardena
50	"I Love Your Beauty"	"Ani Ohev et Yofyekh"	Melichi, Avichai	Melichi, Avichai	1998	Yitzchak, Yoav
51	"Go Thy Way Forth"	"Tse'i Lakh"	Nardi, Nahum	Song of Songs	1965 (published in writing)	Zadok, Ahuva
52	"The Song of Songs"	"Shir Ha-Shirim"	Nehama, Ze'ev	Nehama, Ze'ev		
53	"Bride, O Bride"	"Kala Kala"	Nehama, Ze'ev; Kliski, Tamir and Alon, Gil	Nehama, Ze'ev	1992	Etnix
54	"A Wedding Song"	"Shir Klulot"	Nisim, Aloni	Lerer, Oded	1973	Levi, Shayke; Bashan, Igal
55	"I Am Black, but Comely"	"Shehora Ani Ve-Nava"	Nissim, Meir	Song of Songs	1976	Tavori, Shimi
56	"The Song of Songs"	"Shir Ha-Shirim"	Ozeri, Ahuva	Ozeri, Ahuva		Ozeri, Ahuva
57	"Day and Night"	"Yomam Va-Laila"	Paiss, Amir and Ben-Ari, Mosh	Paiss, Amir; Ben-Ari, Mosh and Ron-Shama, Gil	1999	Sheva Band
58	"I Will Give the Night to You"	"Eten Lakh Et Ha-Laila"	Philosof, Tsuf	Philosof, Tsuf	1992	Bassan, Danni
59	"Behold, Thou Art Fair"	"Hinakh Yafa"	Raichel, Idan	Raichel, Idan	2002	The Idan Raichel Project
60	"Segula"	"Segula"	Rand, Shuli	Rand, Shuli	2008	Rand, Shuli
61	"You Are Light to Me"	"At Li Or"	Ro'e, Yoni	Ro'e, Yoni	1991	Levi, Ofer and Lupatin, Leah
62	"I Do Not Forget"	"Lo Shokhe'ah"	Sakharof, Berry and Mociach, Re'a	Sakharof, Berry	2005	Sakharof, Berry and Mociach, Re'a
63	"Graceful Doe"	"A'yelet Ha-hen"	Shacher, Nathan	Betzer, Oded	1965	Haza, Ofra
64	"The Song of Songs"	"Shir Ha-Shirim"	Sharabi, Boaz	Song of Songs	1978	Haza, Ofra
65	"My Sister Ruhama"	"A'hoti Ruhama"	Shemer, Naomi	Shemer, Naomi	1983	Ha-Gashash Ha-Hiver; Gaon, Yeoram

66	"Go Thy Way Forth, My Sister, My Bride"	"Kumi Ts'ei A'hoti Kala"	Shemer, Naomi	Bialik, Haim Nahman	In the 1970s (recorded)	Gaon, Yehoram; Cohen, Izhar (composed)
67	"I Am Not Giving Up"	"Ani Lo Merim Yadayim"	Tal, Avraham	Tal, Avraham	2010	Tal, Avraham
68	"Touching the Light"	"Laga'at Ba-Or"	Tsur, Tamir	Cohen, Yonatan		Shar-el
69	"Mercy"	"Rahamim"	Vilenski, Moshe	Mohar, Yehiel	1985 (recorded, the song was written during the 1950s)	Haza, Ofra
70	"Hello to You, My Beloved"	"Shalom Lekha Dodi"	Wahabi, Mohammad	Ibn Gabirol, Shlomo	2009	Sakharof, Berry and Mociach, Re'a
71	Medley: "Tsur Menati" / "Go Dove" / "Do Tell Me Undefiled"	Mahrozet: "Tsur Manti" / "Tse'i Yona" / "Sapri Tama"	Yemenite folk music	Shabbazi, Rabbi Shalom, and Ben-Amram, Saadia	1984	Banai, Meir
72	"Graceful Doe"	"A'yelet Ha-hen"	Yemenite folk music	Shabbazi, Rabbi Shalom	1984	
73	"Love-Sick"	"Holat A'hava"	Zafri, Shirley	Zohar, Ikka	2003	Zafri, Shirley
74	"Come, My Beloved"	"Lekha Dodi"	Zeira, Mordechai	Elkabetz, Rabbai Shlomo	1979	
75	"The Song of Songs"	"Shir Ha-Shirim"	Zilber, Ariel	Song of Songs	2001	Zilber, Ariel

Notes

1. INTRODUCTION: UPON THE HANDLES OF THE LOCK

1 Gershom Scholem, "Reflections on S. Y. Agnon," *Commentary*, December 1967, 59–66. A lecture in English delivered at University College, London, May 30, 1967, it was first published in German as "S. J. Agnon—der letzte hebräische Klassiker?," Literatur und Kunst, *Neue Zürcher Zeitung*, October 15, 1967.

2 Scholem, "Reflections on S. Y. Agnon," 60.

3 Gershom Scholem, letter to Franz Rosenzweig, December 26, 1926, reprinted in *Die Gabe: For Franz Rosenzweig on His 40th Birthday*, ed. Martin Goldner (New York: Leo Baeck Institute, 1987), 48–49. For more on this letter, see Stéphane Mosès, *The Angel of History: Rosenzweig, Benjamin, Scholem*, trans. Barbara Harshav (Stanford, Calif.: Stanford University Press, 2009), 168–82; Robert Alter, *Necessary Angels: Tradition and Modernity in Kafka, Benjamin, and Scholem* (Cambridge, Mass.: Harvard University Press, 1991), 35–38; Jacques Derrida, "The Eyes of Language: The Abyss and the Volcano," in *Acts of Religion*, ed. Gil Anidjar (New York: Routledge, 2002), 189–227; Galili Shahar, *She'erit ha-hitgalut: Ha-hok, ha-guf ve-she'elat ha-sifrut* [The Remnants of Revelation: The Law, the Body and Literature] (Jerusalem: Bialik Institute, 2011), 92–97. Note that Agnon was among the contributors to Rosenzweig's volume. The piece he chose for this collection was from "In the Heart of the Seas" (Bilvav yamim). For more on Agnon's homage to Rosenzweig in this connection, see Anne Golomb Hoffman, *Between Exile and Return: S. Y. Agnon and the Drama of Writing* (New York: State University of New York Press, 1991), 177–79.

4 Scholem, "Reflections on S. Y. Agnon," 60.

5 Ibid., 59.

6 The Second Aliyah was a highly influential wave of immigration between 1904 and 1914, during which approximately forty thousand Jews, primarily from Eastern Europe, arrived in Palestine.

7 For more on Agnon's biography, see Arnold Band, *Nostalgia and Nightmare: A Study in the Fiction of S. Y. Agnon* (Berkeley: University of California Press, 1968); Harold Fisch, *S. Y. Agnon* (New York: F. Ungar Publishing, 1975); Dan Laor, *Hayey Agnon: Biyografyah* [S. Y. Agnon: A Biography] (Jerusalem and Tel Aviv: Schocken, 1998); Benjamin Harshav, "The Only Yesterday of *Only Yesterday*," introduction to *Only Yes-*

terday, by S. Y. Agnon, trans. Barbara Harshav (Princeton, N.J.: Princeton University Press, 2000), vii–xxix; and Alan L. Mintz and Anne Golomb Hoffman, introduction to *A Book That Was Lost: Thirty-Five Stories*, by S. Y. Agnon, ed. Alan L. Mintz and Anne Golomb Hoffman (New Milford, Conn.: Toby Press, 2008), 9–34.

8 Scholem, "Reflections on S. Y. Agnon," 60.

9 I provide an extensive consideration of Melville and American biblicism in *Melville's Bibles* (Berkeley: University of California Press, 2008).

10 A note on terminology: I alternate between referring to this biblical culture as "Zionist" and "Israeli." In using the former I want to highlight the historical trajectory at stake, and in using the latter I point to the unmistakable peak of this exegetical trend. From the very beginning of the Zionist movement, the return to Zion was construed as inseparable from the return to the biblical text. And yet the Bible acquired a central position as a founding national text only in the decade preceding the foundation of the State of Israel and in the decade that followed, that is, in the 1940s and 1950s.

11 Adi Zemach, "Al ha-tefisa ha-historiosofit bi-shnayim mi-sipurav ha-me'uharim shel Agnon" [On the Historical Conception in Two of Agnon's Stories], *Ha-Sifrut* 1, no. 2 (1968): 378–85.

12 Meshulam Tochner, *Pesher Agnon* [Readings of Agnon] (Ramat Gan: Masada, 1968); Baruch Kurzweil, *Masot 'al sipurey Shai Agnon* [Essays on S. Y. Agnon] (Jerusalem and Tel Aviv: Schocken, 1970); Dov Sadan, *'Al Shai Agnon: Kerekh masot u-ma'amarim* [On S. Y. Agnon: Essays and Articles] (Tel Aviv: Hakibbutz Hameuchad, 1978); Gershon Shaked, *Shmuel Yosef Agnon: A Revolutionary Traditionalist* (New York: New York University Press, 1989).

13 Hoffman, *Between Exile and Return*; Yaniv Hagbi, *Language, Absence, Play: Judaism and Superstructuralism in the Poetics of S. Y. Agnon* (Syracuse, N.Y.: Syracuse University Press, 2009).

14 Robert Alter, *After the Tradition: Essays on Modern Jewish Writing* (New York: E. P. Dutton, 1969), 131–32.

15 For more on Agnon as anthologist, see Scholem, "Reflections on S. Y. Agnon"; and Hagbi, *Language, Absence, Play*, chap. 1. Of his various anthologies, *Days of Awe* has been the most popular (relatively speaking), serving as a sourcebook in some synagogues during the holidays. Note that Agnon did not only compile anthologies but was also involved in the preservation of Jewish lore. Alan L. Mintz and Anne Golomb Hoffman point out that he was "an important figure in Mekitze Nirdamim (Those Who Awaken the Sleeping), a group devoted to the retrieval, preservation, and dissemination of old Jewish manuscripts." Mintz and Hoffman, introduction to *A Book That Was Lost*, 18.

16 Agnon, "Prakim shel sefer ha-medina" [Chapters in the Book of the State], in *Samukh ve-nir'eh* [Near and Apparent], of *Kol sipurav shel Shmuel Yosef Agnon* [The Complete Works of Shmuel Yosef Agnon] (Jerusalem and Tel Aviv: Schocken, 1998), 211. For more on Agnon's stylistic innovation, see Robert Alter, *The Invention of Hebrew Prose: Modern Fiction and the Language of Realism* (Seattle: University of Washington Press, 1988), 13, 73–75.

17 Anita Shapira, "The Bible and Israeli Identity," *AJS Review* 28, no. 1 (2004): 11–42.

18 Ibid., 17.

19 Ibid., 24–25. See also Anita Shapira, "Ben-Gurion and the Bible: The Forging of a Historical Narrative?," *Middle Eastern Studies* 33, no. 4 (1997): 645–74. For more on Ben-Gurion and Bible scholars, see Michael Keren, *Ben-Gurion and the Intellectuals: Power, Knowledge, and Charisma* (DeKalb: Northern Illinois University Press, 1983), 100–117.

20 The letter, titled "Ha-tanakh zore'ah be-'or 'atsmo" [The Bible Shines in Its Own Light], is reprinted in David Ben-Gurion, *Iyunim ba-mikra* [Bible Studies] (Tel Aviv: Am Oved, 1969), 41–49. For more on Israeli biblicism, see Zali Gurevitch, *'Al ha-makom* [On Space and Place] (Tel Aviv: Am Oved, 2007).

21 Ben-Gurion, "Ha-tanakh zore'ah be-'or 'atsmo," in *Iyunim ba-mikra*, 48.

22 Quoted in Shapira, "The Bible and Israeli Identity," 31.

23 Jonathan Sheehan, *The Enlightenment Bible: Translation, Scholarship, Culture* (Princeton, N.J.: Princeton University Press, 2005), ix–xi.

24 Ibid., book jacket. For a recent reassessment of secularism in Israeli culture, see Christoph Schmidt and Eli Schonfeld, eds., *HaElohim lo ye'alem dom: Hamoderna ha-yehudit ve-hate'ologia ha-politit* [God Will Not Stand Still: Jewish Modernity and Political Theology] (Jerusalem: Van Leer / Hakibbutz Hameuchad, 2009).

25 The exchange of letters appears in *Kurzweil-Agnon-Azag: Hilufey 'igrot* [Kurzweil, Agnon, Azag: Correspondence], ed. Lillian Debbi-Guri (Ramat Gan: Bar-Ilan University Press, 1987), 19–20. Baruch Kurzweil, "'Al Balak, ha-kelev ha-demoni" [On Balak, the Demonic Dog], in *Masot 'al sipurey Shai Agnon*, 104–15.

26 On the midrash and the question of consistency, see James Kugel, "Two Introductions to Midrash," in *Midrash and Literature*, ed. Geoffrey Hartman and Sanford Budick (New Haven, Conn.: Yale University Press, 1986), 77–103.

27 Stéphane Mosès's formulation of Benjamin's approach. See Mosès, *The Angel of History: Rosenzweig, Benjamin, Scholem*, 99.

28 Walter Benjamin, *The Origin of German Tragic Drama*, trans. John Osborne (London: NLB, 1977). For more on the problems of signification and representation posed by allegory, see Stephen J. Greenblatt's introduction to *Allegory and Representation*, ed. Greenblatt (Baltimore: Johns Hopkins University Press, 1981). I am indebted to Anat Danziger's Ph.D. proposal, "Between Pain and Writing: The Allegorical Body in Kafka and Agnon," for sharpening my understanding of the relevance of Benjamin's perception of allegory to Agnon's work.

29 For a semiotic reading of Balak and his inscription, see Shira Hadad, *Mi she-'ose siman* [The Sign Maker] (Jerusalem: Bialik Institute, 2011).

30 Band, *Nostalgia and Nightmare*, 414–47; Dan Miron, "Bein shtey neshamot: Ha-analogia ha-Faustit bi-Tmol shilshom le-Shai Agnon" [Between Two Souls: On the Faustian Analogy in S. Y. Agnon's *Tmol shilshom*], in *Mi-Vilna li-Yerushalyim: Mehkarim be-toldoteihem u-vetarbutam shel yehudei mizrah eropa mugashim le-profesor Shmuel Werses* [Studies in East European Jewish History and Culture in Honor of Professor Shmuel Werses], ed. David Assaf, Israel Bartal, Shmuel Feiner, Yehuda Friedlander, Avner Holtzman, and Chava Turniansky (Jerusalem: Magnes Press,

2002), 539–608. On the Kafkaesque connection, see Hillel Barzel, *Bein Agnon le-Kafka: Mehkar mashveh* [Between Agnon and Kafka: A Comparative Study] (Ramat Gan: Bar-Ilan University Press, 1972).

31 Aharon Bar-Adon, *Shai Agnon u-tehiyat ha-safa ha-ʿivrit* [S. Y. Agnon and the Revival of the Hebrew Language] (Jerusalem: Bialik Institute, 1977); Todd Hasak-Lowy, "A Mad Dog's Attack on Secularized Hebrew: Rethinking Agnon's *Tmol shilshom*," *Prooftexts* 24, no. 2 (2004): 167–98. See also Hoffman, *Between Exile and Return*, 125–48.

32 I offer an extensive examination of this episode in Numbers in *The Biography of Ancient Israel: National Narratives in the Bible* (Berkeley: University of California Press, 2000), chap. 6.

33 Sidra DeKoven Ezrahi, "Sentient Dogs, Liberated Rams, and Talking Asses: Agnon's Biblical Zoo—or Rereading *Tmol shilshom*," *AJS Review* 28, no. 1 (2004): 105–36.

34 *Only Yesterday* [Tmol shilshom], trans. Barbara Harshav (Princeton, N.J.: Princeton University Press, 2000), 485. Subsequent citations are given in parentheses in the text.

35 The number thirty-six is not without significance. It calls to mind the thirty-six righteous men: *lamed vav zaddikim*.

36 On Schimmelmann as a "moldy man," see Amos Oz, *The Silence of Heaven: Agnon's Fear of God* (Princeton, N.J.: Princeton University Press, 2000), 126–27.

37 Leah Goldberg, "Motivim bi-yetsirato" [Motifs in His Work], in *Shai Agnon ba-bikoret ha-ʿivrit-sikumim ve-haʾarkhot ʿal yetsirato* [S. Y. Agnon: Critical Essays of His Writings], ed. Avinoam Barshai (Jerusalem and Tel Aviv: Schocken, 1991), 1:184; my translation.

38 For more on Agnon's irony, see Ariel Hirschfeld, *Likro et Shai Agnon* [Reading S. Y. Agnon] (Tel Aviv: Ahuzat bayit, 2011), 45–62.

39 When the canonicity of the Song was disputed, the question at stake was whether or not it "defiles the hands" (*metame ʾet ha-yadayim*). According to rabbinic enactment, hands that come into contact with a sacred book contract uncleanness in the second degree.

40 Following the contours of Agnon's exegetical world, I mentioned exemplary allegories within Jewish tradition. There is, to be sure, a vast corpus of Christian allegories as well. For a survey of the different allegorical readings of the Song, see Marvin H. Pope, *The Song of Songs*, The Anchor Bible (Garden City, N.Y.: Doubleday, 1977). For more on the history of traditional Jewish allegories of the Song, see David Stern, "Ancient Jewish Interpretation of the Song of Songs in a Comparative Context," in *Jewish Biblical Interpretation and Cultural Exchange: Comparative Exegesis in Context*, ed. Natalie B. Dohrmann and David Stern (Philadelphia: University of Pennsylvania Press, 2008), 87–107; and Michael Fishbane, *The Kiss of God: Spiritual and Mystical Death in Judaism* (Seattle: University of Washington Press, 1994).

41 Uriel Simon provides an illuminating consideration of Zionist "midrash" but does not consider the intricacies of Zionist allegories of the Song. See Simon, "The Place of the Bible in Israeli Society: From National *Midrash* to Existential *Peshat*," *Modern Judaism* 19 (1999): 217–39.

42 Kurzweil, *Masot 'al sipurey Shai Agnon*, 103.

43 Whether or not Agnon had Reuven Rubin's *First Fruits* (*Ha-perot ha-rishonim*; 1923) in mind, Isaac's ruminations call to mind this renowned triptych with its visual rendition of the erotic, Orientalized construction of local fruits in early Zionist art. Note that the cover of the Harshav translation of *Only Yesterday* most appropriately shows a detail of Rubin's painting. For more on Rubin's *First Fruits*, see Gideon Ofrat, *Al ha-'aretz: Ha-omanut ha-'eretz-yisraelit; Pirkey 'avot* [On the Ground: Early Eretz-Israeli Art; Founding Fathers] (Jerusalem: Yaron Golan, 1993), 2:531–48.

44 Agnon, "And Solomon's Wisdom Excelled," trans. Mordechai Beck, *Ariel—Israel Review of Arts and Letters* 92 (1993): 277–82; Hebrew text: "Vaterev hokhmat shlomo," in *Ad hena* [Thus Far], of *Kol sipurav shel Shmuel Yosef Agnon*, 233–37. Subsequent references are provided in the text. Before citing these medieval exegetes, Agnon refers to a midrash from Song of Songs Rabbah (1:11): "Some of our rabbis . . . maintain that Solomon himself spoke three thousand proverbs on every verse, and to every proverb gave one thousand and five meanings" (277).

45 Moshe Idel, *Kabbalah and Eros* (New Haven, Conn.: Yale University Press, 2005), 142–43.

46 This commentary goes as follows: "Now, you might ask, 'Why isn't a *thousand* mentioned here?' Surely, that *thousand* was concealed and remains concealed until the Wife [Shekhinah] unites with her Husband [*Yesod*, the divine phallus]. Therefore, Solomon endeavored to bring that *thousand* to the Bride in the secrecy of the seal of supernal Wisdom." Translated by Daniel C. Matt, *The Zohar*, vol. 5, Pritzker Edition (Stanford, Calif.: Stanford University Press, 2004–9), *Terumah* 2:145b, 327. For a helpful elucidation of this passage, see Matt's notes. For more on the question of concealment and revelation in the Zohar, see Yehuda Liebes, "Ha-mashiah shel ha-Zohar: Lidmuto shel rabbi Shimon bar Yohai" [The Messiah of the Zohar: The Messianic Character of R. Shimon bar Yohai], in *Ha-Ra'yon ha-meshihi be-Yisrael: Simposion leregel mlot shmonim shana le-Gershom Scholem* [The Messianic Idea in Israel: A Symposium in Honor of Gerschom Scholem] (Jerusalem: Israel Academy of Sciences and Humanities, 1982), 87–236, esp. 138–51; Moshe Halbertal, *Concealment and Revelation: Esotericism in Jewish Thought and Its Philosophical Implications* (Princeton, N.J.: Princeton University Press, 2007); and Melila Hellner-Eshed, *A River Flows from Eden: The Language of Mystical Experience in the Zohar*, trans. Nathan Wolski (Stanford, Calif.: Stanford University Press, 2009), 157–83.

47 Agnon's poetics bears some resemblance to the pseudo-epigraphic character of the Zohar. Whereas the Zohar is written in a quasi-archaic, midrashic genre but is in fact a mode of medieval, mystical exegesis, Agnon's tales take the form of midrash (though not always extensively) but are set within an entirely different framework.

48 See Isaiah 27:2–5, where the nation is likened to God's vineyard. Allegorical readings of the Beloved as Zion often rely, indeed, on the use of metaphors prevalent in the ancient love poem—such as the vineyard or the rose—in prophetic configurations of the nation as woman.

49 Franz Rosenzweig, *The Star of Redemption*, trans. William W. Hallo (Boston: Beacon Press, 1964), 199.

50 For more on Rosenzweig's reading of the Song, see Samuel Moyn, "Divine and Human Love: Franz Rosenzweig's History of the Song of Songs," *Jewish Studies Quarterly* 12 (2005): 194–212; and Paul Mendes-Flohr, "Between Sensual and Heavenly Love: Franz Rosenzweig's Reading of the Song of Songs," in *Scriptural Exegesis: The Shapes of Culture and the Religious Imagination; Essays in Honour of Michael Fishbane*, ed. Deborah A. Green and Laura S. Lieber (Oxford: Oxford University Press, 2009). For a broader discussion on Rosenzweig's aesthetic-hermeneutic project, see Leora Batnitzky, *Idolatry and Representation: The Philosophy of Franz Rosenzweig Reconsidered* (Princeton, N.J.: Princeton University Press, 2000).

51 I am indebted to Márton Farkas for calling my attention to the ambiguous position of the songs between the oral and the written. The fact that in Hebrew *shir* is both "song" and "poem" only adds to the confusion.

52 On "Agunot" and the Song, see Gershon Shaked, "Midrash and Narrative: Agnon's 'Agunot,'" in Hartman and Budick, *Midrash and Literature*, 285–306; and Ariel Hirschfeld, "Between Story and Folktale: On Two of S. Y. Agnon's Stories" [Bein sippur le-sippur-'am bi-shnei sippurim shel Agnon], *Mirkamim le-Galit Hasan-Rokem, Mehkarei Yerushalayim be-sifrut ivrit* 2 (2013):531–50.

53 On the echoes of the Song in one of the most renowned stories of *Upon the Handles of the Lock* ("In the Prime of Her Life" [*bidmi yameh*]), see Ruth Ginsburg, "Bidmi yameh meta Tirza or 'yafa at ra'ayati ke-Tirzah nava ki-Yerushalyim ayuma ka-nidgalot" [Tirza Died in the Prime of Her Life: Thou Art Beautiful, O My Love, as Tirzah, Comely as Jerusalem, Terrible as an Army with Banners], *Dapim Le'Mekhkar Be'sifrut* 8 (1992): 285–300. On the Song and "Bilvav yamim," see Shmuel Werses, *Shai Agnon ki-fshuto: Keri'a bi-khtavav* [S. Y. Agnon Literally: Studies of His Writings] (Jerusalem: Bialik Institute, 2000), 160–62; and Sidra DeKoven Ezrahi, *Booking Passage: Exile and Homecoming in the Modern Jewish Imagination* (Berkeley: University of California Press, 2000). See the different responses to Agnon's "The Sense of Smell" by Naomi Sokoloff, David G. Roskies, and Alan L. Mintz in *Reading Hebrew Literature: Critical Discussions of Six Modern Texts*, ed. Alan L. Mintz (Waltham, Mass.: Brandeis University Press; Hanover, N.H.: University Press of New England, 2003), 109–34.

54 *Days of Awe* [Yamim nora'im] (Jerusalem and Tel Aviv: Schocken, 1998), 347.

55 Both *Betrothed* and "Edo and Enam" are included in the volume *Thus Far* (*Ad hena*). Interestingly enough, they appear together on their own in Walter Lever's English translation, titled *Two Tales*, published by Schocken in 1966, the year in which Agnon received the Nobel Prize for Literature. This translation, in fact, turned out to be instrumental in introducing the Nobel laureate to American readers. Note that Lever uses the name "Susan" as an English substitute for "Shoshana," but given the great resonance of the Hebrew name (*shoshana* means "rose") in the novella, I will use it throughout the book in my own discussion as well as in the quotations from *Two Tales*.

56 I use the translation of Walter Lever, *Two Tales* (New York: Schocken Books, 1966), 165–66. All future references to *Betrothed* and "Edo and Enam" are to this edition and appear in parentheses in the text unless otherwise indicated.

57 Lever uses another spelling: "Ginath." Here as elsewhere, I follow the more common transliteration of this name: "Ginat."

58 Hebrew text: Agnon, *Tmol shilshom* (Jerusalem and Tel Aviv: Schocken, 1998), 89.

59 Agnon is outright obsessed with the question of the affinity between his own work and scholarly investigation. Manfred Herbst, the protagonist of *Shira*—a lecturer in Byzantine history who aspires to write a tragedy—is undoubtedly the most elaborate example in this connection (*Shira* also provides the most detailed account of academic life at the Hebrew University in its early days). But given that hermeneutic questions and biblical exegesis are not pivotal to *Shira*, I will refer to it only occasionally. For more on the representation of scholarship in *Shira*, see Robert Alter, "Agnon's Last Word," *Commentary* 51 (1971): 77; Alan L. Mintz, *Translating Israel: Contemporary Hebrew Literature and Its Reception in America* (Syracuse, N.Y.: Syracuse University Press, 2001), chap. 4; Nitza Ben-Dov, *Ve-hi tehilatekha: Iyyunim bi-yetsirot Shai Agnon, A. B. Yehoshua ve-Amos Oz* [Studies in the Works of S. Y. Agnon, A. B. Yehoshua, and Amos Oz] (Jerusalem and Tel Aviv: Schocken, 2006), pt. 1, chap. 4.

60 Scholem, "Reflections on S. Y. Agnon," 62.

61 Gershom Scholem, "Agnon in Germany: Recollections," trans. Werner J. Dannhauser, in *On Jews and Judaism in Crisis: Selected Essays*, ed. Werner J. Dannhauser (New York: Schocken Books, 1976), 117–18. Scholem's address was a speech in Hebrew delivered at the house of the president of Israel, November 16, 1966, in celebration of Agnon's receiving the Nobel Prize.

62 Nitza Ben-Dov, *Agnon's Art of Indirection: Uncovering Latent Content in the Fiction of S. Y. Agnon* (Leiden: Brill, 1993), 12–13. I provide an extensive consideration of Agnon's dialogue with Freud in Chapter 3.

63 My translation from Agnon's "Forevermore" [Ad olam], trans. Joel Blocker, in *Modern Hebrew Literature*, ed. Robert Alter (New York: Behrman House, 1975). Subsequent references are given in parentheses in the text. The reference in the Hebrew text is Agnon, *Ha'esh ve-ha-'etzim* [The Fire and the Wood] (Jerusalem and Tel Aviv: Schocken, 1998), 262.

64 Arnold Band, "Agnon megale peney Freud" [Agnon Discovers Freud's Face], in *She'elot nikhbadot* [Profound Questions], Masa Kritit (Be'er-Sheva: Dvir, Heksherim, Ben-Gurion University, 2007), 208–9.

65 Sigmund Freud, "Delusions and Dreams in Jensen's *Gradiva*" (1907), in *The Standard Edition of the Complete Psychological Works of Sigmund Freud*, trans. and ed. James Strachey (London: Hogarth Press, 1973), 9:51.

66 Sigmund Freud, *Moses and Monotheism* (1939), trans. Katherine Jones (New York: Vintage Books, 1967), 52.

67 I use the Old Jewish Publication Society (OJPS) translation (1917) because it is closer to the archaic character of Agnon's writing. See the captivating new translation by Chana Bloch and Ariel Bloch, *The Song of Songs* (New York: Modern Library, 2006, 1995).

68 Following the King James Version (KJV), I use "lock" rather than the OJPS translation "bar" for *man'ul*. "Bar" does not capture the poetic power and implicit metaphoricity of the verse to the same extent.

69 On the question of sexuality and its mitigation in the Song, see Gershon D. Cohen, "The Song of Songs and the Jewish Religious Mentality," in *The Samuel Friedland Lectures, 1960–1966* (New York: Jewish Theological Seminary of America, 1966), 1–21. See also Julia Kristeva, *Tales of Love*, trans. Leon S. Roudiez (New York: Columbia University Press, 1987), 97.

70 Kristeva, *Tales of Love*, 100.

71 Much has been written about Agnon's choice of pen name as representative of his exilic positioning of himself as a writer but with no attention to the gender reversal at stake. Note that *agunah* is a halakhic term designating a woman who is not free to marry because her husband disappeared without divorcing her.

72 On gender fluidity in Agnon in the context of *Shira*, see Hoffman, *Between Exile and Return*, chap. 8.

73 On Agnon's ongoing preoccupation with "unhappy loves," see Nitza Ben-Dov, *Ahavot lo me'uashrot: Tiskul eroti, omanut u-mavet bi-yetsirat Agnon* [Unhappy Loves: Erotic Frustration, Art, and Death in the Works of Agnon] (Tel Aviv: Am Oved, 1997).

74 Joseph Kafah, ed. and trans., *The Five Scrolls with Various Commentaries* (Jerusalem: ha-Aguda le-hatsalat Ginze Teman, 1962), 26.

2. THE SONG OF SONGS AS CULTURAL TEXT

1 For a recent consideration of the cultural role of "The Binding of Isaac," see Yael Feldman, *Glory and Agony: Isaac's Sacrifice and National Narrative* (Stanford, Calif.: Stanford University Press, 2010). For an account of the Book of Joshua in Israeli culture, see Rachel Havrelock, *River Jordan: The Mythology of a Dividing Line* (Chicago: University of Chicago Press, 2011).

2 Johann Gottfried Herder, *Lieder der Liebe: Die ältesten und schönsten aus Morgenlande* (Leipzig, 1778); repr. J. G. Müller, ed., *Werke* (Stuttgart and Tübingen, 1827), vol. 4; 5:1318 (Munich: Hanser, n.d.).

3 Quoted in Moyn, "Divine and Human Love," 200.

4 Ibid.

5 Herder develops his notion of the Bible's Oriental aesthetics in his monumental *The Spirit of Hebrew Poetry*, trans. James Marsh (1782–83; Burlington, Vt.: E. Smith, 1833).

6 Hans W. Frei, *The Eclipse of Biblical Narrative: A Study in Eighteenth- and Nineteenth-Century Hermeneutics* (New Haven, Conn.: Yale University Press, 1974), 185.

7 Quoted in ibid.

8 Quoted in John D. Baildam, *Paradisal Love: Johann Gottfried Herder and the Song of Songs* (Sheffield: Sheffield Academic Press, 1999), 82–83.

9 Ibid., 84.

10 Johann Gottfried Herder, "On the German-Oriental Poets," in *Selected Early Works, 1764–1767: Addresses, Essays, and Drafts; Fragments on Recent German Literature*, ed. Ernest A. Menze and Karl Menges, trans. Ernest A. Menze and Michael Palma (University Park: Pennsylvania State University Press, 1992), 178.

11 Moyn, "Divine and Human Love," 201.

12 Quoted in Baildam, *Paradisal Love*, 189.

13 Quoted in Moyn, "Divine and Human Love," 203. Goethe's interest in the Song, as Moyn suggests, is evident in *Faust* as well, primarily in Faust's poetic address to Gretchen.

14 Richard I. Cohen, "Urban Visibility and Biblical Visions: Jewish Culture in Western and Central Europe in the Modern Age," in *Cultures of the Jews*, ed. David Biale (New York: Schocken Books, 2002), 762–86. For more on the Jewish Enlightenment, see Shmuel Feiner, *The Jewish Enlightenment*, trans. Chaya Naor (Philadelphia: University of Pennsylvania Press, 2002). David Biale provides a reconsideration of the pre-Enlightenment Jewish precursors of Zionist biblicists, among them Shlomo Ibn Gabirol and Baruch Spinoza, in his recent book *Not in the Heavens: The Tradition of Jewish Secular Thought* (Princeton, N.J.: Princeton University Press, 2011).

15 Levisohn was also inspired by J. F. / T. C. Jacobi's reading of triangular dramas in the Song, as Marvin H. Pope points out in *Song of Songs*, 111–12.

16 Tova Cohen, *Melitsat yeshurun li-Shlomo Levisohn: Ha-yetsira ve-yotsra* [*Melitzat Yeshurun* by Shlomo Levisohn: The Work and Its Author] (Ramat Gan: Bar-Ilan University Press, 1988), 219.

17 Ibid., 205.

18 On the Orient in Levisohn's work, see Amir Banbaji, "The Orient in the Literature of the Haskalah: A Levantine Reading of Euchel, Löwisohn, and Mapu", *Journal of Levantine Studies* 1 (2011): 95–130.

19 Cohen, *Melitsat yeshurun li-Shlomo Levisohn*, 224–25. For more on Levisohn, see Yosef Klausner, "Shlomo Levisohn (1789–1821)," in *Historia shel ha-sifrut ha-'ivrit ha-hadasha* [The History of Modern Hebrew Literature] (Jerusalem: Ahiasaf, 1952), 1:261–74; and Tova Cohen's introduction to *Melitsat yeshurun li-Shlomo Levisohn*.

20 On Mapu's use of *melitsah*, see Dan Miron, *Bein hazon le-'emet: Nitsaney ha-roman ha-'ivri ve-hayiddi ba-me'a ha-tesha 'esre* [From Romance to the Novel: Studies in the Emergence of the Hebrew and Yiddish Novel in the Nineteenth Century] (Jerusalem: Mosad Bialik, 1979), 15–51.

21 Abraham Mapu, *The Love of Zion*, trans. Joseph Marymount (New Milford, Conn.: Toby Press, 2006), chap. 4, 38–40. In addition to the many evocations of the Song in the plot, almost every chapter opens with an epigraph from the ancient love poem. (These epigraphs do not appear in the English translation.)

22 For more on Mapu's reconstruction of the Land of Israel's geographies via the biblical text and contemporary sources, above all, Levisohn's *Mehkaey eretz*, see Tova Cohen, *Me-halom limtsi'ut: Eretz Yisrael be-sifrut ha-haskala* [From Dream to Reality: Descriptions of Eretz Yisrael in Haskalah Literature] (Ramat Gan: Bar-Ilan University Press, 1982), 93–133. For a consideration of the novel as the founding text of the Zionist space, see Yigal Schwartz, *Ha-yada'ata 'et ha-eretz sham ha-limon poreah: Handasa enoshit ve-hashivat ha-merhav ba-sifrut ha-'ivrit* [Do You Know the Land Where the Lemon Blooms? Human Engineering and Landscape Conceptualization in Hebrew Literature] (Or Yehuda: Kinneret Zmora-Bitan, 2007), 29–82.

23 KJV's translation.

24 For more on the special case of Judaism in the context of Orientalism, see Paul Mendes-Flohr, "Fin-de-siècle Orientalism, the *Ostjuden*, and the Aesthetics of Jewish Self-Affirmation," in *Studies in Contemporary Jewry*, ed. Jonathan Frankel (Bloomington: Indiana University Press, 1984), 1:96–139; and Ivan Davidson Kalmar and Derek J. Penslar, eds., *Orientalism and the Jews* (Waltham, Mass.: Brandeis University Press; Hanover, N.H.: University Press of New England, 2005).

25 Quoted in Shapira, "The Bible and Israeli Identity," 12.

26 Cohen, "Urban Visibility and Biblical Visions," 781–82. See also Richard I. Cohen, *Jewish Icons: Art and Society in Modern Europe* (Berkeley: University of California Press, 1998).

27 On Lilien, Herzl, and Moses, see Milly Heyd, "Lilien: Between Herzl and Ahasver," in *Theodor Herzl: Visionary of the Jewish State*, ed. Gideon Shimoni and Robert S. Wistrich (Jerusalem: Magnes Press, 1999), 265–93.

28 The lilies entail something of a personal signature as well, given that the name "Lilien" means "lilies" in German. In Herzl's letter to Lilien on January 30, 1902, he addresses the artist as his "lilies of the field" (quoted in Ofrat, *Al ha-aretz*, 1:16). On the history of the Star of David, see Gershom Scholem, *Magen-David: Toldotav shel semel* [The Star of David: History of a Symbol], ed. Galit Hasan-Rokem (Ein-Harod: Mishkan le-omanut, 2008), 25–55. Lilien's Bible includes other illustrations of the Song as well, among them, an image of Solomon and a highly erotic embrace of the two lovers. A note on the translation of the Song's flora. The KJV and the OJPS regard the *havatselet* as "rose" and the *shoshana* as "lily". Following the common perception of these flowers in Israeli culture, I adhere to the opposite translation and render *havatselet* as "lily" and *shoshana* as "rose". See note 19 on p.152.

29 For more on Lilien and the Rose of Jericho, see Tamar Manor-Friedman, "The Rose of Jericho: A Dormant Parable," in *Larry Abramson: The Rose of Jericho* (Jerusalem: Jerusalem Print Shop, 2004), xii–xv. Within the realm of Zionist literature, the two notable texts on the Rose of Jericho are Moses Hess, *Rome and Jerusalem*, and Baruch Chizik, *Tsimchiel: Agadot ve-sihot ʿal tsimhey ertz-yisrael* [Legends and Conversations on the Plants of the Land of Israel] (Tel Aviv, 1930).

30 The Society for the Promotion of Travel in the Holy Land was sponsored by the Jewish National Fund.

31 For more on Ze'ev Raban, see Batsheva Goldman Ida, *Ze'ev Raban: A Hebrew Symbolist* (Tel Aviv: Tel Aviv Museum of Art; Jerusalem: Yad Yzhak Ben-Zvi, 2001); Dalia Manor, "Biblical Zionism in Bezalel Art," *Israel Studies* 6, no. 1 (2001): 55–75; and Ofrat, *Al ha-aretz*, 1:297–343.

32 On the Haggadot of the kibbutzim, see Hanna Herzog, "HaHaggadah ha-kibbutzit" [The Kibbutz Haggadah], *Ha-Kibbutz*, nos. 3–4 (1977): 237–46; Muki Zur and Yuval Danieli, *Yots'im be-hodesh ha-aviv: Pesach Eretz—Yisraeli be-hagadot ha-kibbutzim* [The Kibbutz Haggadah: Israeli Pesach in the Kibbutz] (Jerusalem: Yad Ben-Zvi, Makhon Ben-Gurion, Yad Tabenkin, and Yad Ya'ari, 2004).

33 The term *spring* appears in the designation of the month (*hodesh aviv*) of the Exodus (see Exodus 13:4).

34 Robert Alter, *The Art of Biblical Poetry* (New York: Basic Books, 1985), 203.

35 See Yair Zakovitch, *Shir ha-shirim: Mikra le-Yisrael* [The Song of Songs: Introduction and Commentary] (Jerusalem: Magnes Press; Tel Aviv: Am Oved, 1992), 66–67.

36 For the full list of kibbutz composers whose songs were included in Haggadot, see Zur and Danieli, *Yots'im be-hodesh ha-aviv*, 49–53.

37 Matityahu Shelem, "Al shir ha-shirim" [On the Song of Songs], *Niv ha-kevutsa* 16 (1967): 136–43.

38 Heiman, interview by Yoav Yefet, January 27, 2011, available on YouTube, http://www.youtube.com/watch?v=qT6ivtbZL08.

39 "Sheharhoret" was originally a well-known Ladino song, but upon its translation into Hebrew, the lyrics were endowed with echoes of the Song and became part of its musical exegetical scene. I am indebted to Edwin Seroussi for calling my attention to the special trajectory of this piece.

40 I am greatly indebted to Ruth HaCohen and to Nathan Shachar for their insightful comments on this musical scene and their help in finding the data. The Zemereshet website (www. zemereshet.co.il) provides invaluable online information and recordings of many of these adaptations.

41 My account of Levi-Tanai's biography and work is indebted to Giora Manor, *The Choreography of Sara Levi-Tanai* (Tel Aviv: Inbal Dance Theater and the Ethnic Multicultural Center Inbal, 2001); and Gila Tolidanu, *Sippura shel lehaka: Sara Levi-Tanai ve-te'atron ha-mahol Inbal* [A Story of a Company: Sara Levi-Tanai and the Inbal Dance Theater] (Tel Aviv: Resling, 2005). Bracha Zefira—another famous Yemenite singer/composer—was also at Shfeya during this period. Zefira was part of this Song of Songs scene as well. She was, among other things, the composer and singer of "Kumi lakh ra'ayati" ("Rise Up, My Love").

42 The more familiar melody of "Kol dodi" is a folk song arranged by Levi-Tanai. She did, however, use it as the opening theme of a longer piece, under the same title. Other songs of the Song that Levi-Tanai composed for the 1944 Seder in Ramat HaKovesh were "Shir ha-shirim asher li-Shlomo" (1:1); "Libavtini" (4:9); "Ani le-dodi ve-dodi li" (6:3); "Ha-yoshevet ba-ganim" (8:13); "Ani havatzelet ha-Sharon" (2:1); "Hagida li she-'ahava nafshi" (1:7); "Shehora ani ve-nava" (1:5); "Ana halakh dodekh" (6:1); and "Mi zot 'ola min ha-midbar" (3:10). Later, she also composed tunes for "Or havazalot" and "Ma yafu pe'amayikh." I am very grateful to Nathan Shachar for his inquiries regarding Levi-Tanai's Song of Songs project.

43 Shortly after, this production of the Song was performed in the Assembly of Choirs (*kinus arzi shel makhelot*) in Kfar Yehezkel and Ein Harod and, in modified form, at the Daliah Dance Festival.

44 Robbins and Sokolow, but mostly the latter, actually worked with the dancers of Inbal and paved their way into the international scene. See Manor, *The Choreography of Sara Levi-Tanai*, 30–48.

45 Ibid., 58.

46 Quoted in Judith Brin Ingber, ed., *Seeing Israeli and Jewish Dance* (Detroit: Wayne State University Press, 2011), 26.

47 In 1982, Levi-Tanai created a new piece titled "Song of Songs." By 1982, however, she was determined to rely on traditional exegesis of the Song as well and create a blend

of a literal-allegorical work, relying on midrashim and *piyyutim*. I return to this piece in my Epilogue.

48 Daniel Boyarin, *Unheroic Conduct: The Rise of Heterosexuality and the Invention of the Jewish Man* (Berkeley: University of California Press, 1997), 274–76. For more on the Zionist body within the context of modern Hebrew literature, see Michael Gluzman, *Ha-guf ha-zioni: Le'umiyut, migdar u-miniyut ba-sifrut ha-'ivrit ha-hadasha* [The Zionist Body: Nationalism, Gender, and Sexuality in Modern Hebrew Literature] (Tel Aviv: Hakibbutz Hameuchad, 2007).

49 James Joyce, *Ulysses* (1914; New York: Vintage Books, 1961), 477.

50 David Biale, *Eros and the Jews: From Biblical Israel to Contemporary America* (New York: Basic Books, 1992), 177.

51 See Chana Kronfeld's reading of the network of allusions to the Song in Fogel's "Bintot ha-yom," in *On the Margins of Modernism: Decentering Literary Dynamics* (Berkeley: University of California Press, 1996), 92–103.

52 Nathan Alterman, who wrote the lyrics of "Shulamit" (1946) and "Shoshanat Teiman" ("Rose of Yemen"; 1939), is another case in point.

53 Both Hareuveni and Goitein were not members of the Bible Department at the Hebrew University. The only Bible professor who engaged in a scholarly pursuit of the Song in the early days of the Bible Department was Moshe Zvi Segal. In his *Introduction to the Bible*, Segal devotes a chapter to a survey of the literalist approaches to the ancient love poem but does not quite offer a new reading of his own. Segal, *Introduction to the Bible* [Mavo ha-mikra] (Jerusalem: Kiryat Sefer, 1967), 668–84.

54 Brit Shalom (literally Covenant of Peace) was a group of Jewish intellectuals in Palestine, founded in 1925. The original Brit Shalom sought a peaceful coexistence between Arabs and Jews, endorsing an alternative vision of Zionism in Palestine as a center for Jewish cultural life (in keeping with Ahad Ha'am's vision).

55 Sheehan, *The Enlightenment Bible*, 191–211.

56 Ariel Hirschfeld, "Botanical Epiphany," in *The Botanist's Brush: Shmuel Charuvi's Drawings for the Hareuveni "Floral Treasury of the Land of Israel,"* ed. Tamar Manor-Friedman (Jerusalem: Israel Museum, 2006), 112.

57 Tamar Manor-Friedman, "The Song of Plants," in *The Botanist's Brush*, 117. Immanuel's Löw's *Die Flora der Juden* was one of his inspirations. See Hareuveni's article on Löw in *Hateva ve-ha'aretz* 2, no. 10 (1934): 491–97.

58 For more on the couple's mission and excursions, see Noga Hareuveni, *Teva ve-nof be-moreshet yisrael* [Nature and Landscape in Israel's Heritage] (Neot Kedumim: Neot Kedumim, 1980), 9.

59 For an extensive consideration of Hareuvenis' relations with the Hebrew University, see Yair Paz, "Ha-gan ha-botani ve-gan ha-nevi'im: Al shnei proyektim le-hakamat ganim limudiyim ba-oniversita ha-'ivrit" [The Botanical Garden and the Garden of the Prophets: Two Projects for the Establishment of Educational Gardens at the Hebrew University], in *The History of the Hebrew University: A Period of Consolidation and Growth*, edited by Hagit Lavsky (Jerusalem: Magnes Press, 2005), 2:443–72.

60 Ephraim Hareuveni and Hannah Hareuveni, "Gan ha-nevi'im ve-hakhmey ha-

talmud" [The Garden of the Prophets and Sages], *Hatoren* 40, nos. 1–3 (1924): 65–79.

61 Ibid., 68.

62 Ibid., 69. On the intricacies of the Zionist reconstruction of the biblical past, see Yael Zerubavel, *Recovered Roots* (Chicago: University of Chicago Press, 1995), chap. 2.

63 Hareuveni and Hareuveni, "Gan ha-nevi'im ve-hakhmey ha-talmud," 70.

64 Ambivalence prevailed among Jewish Studies scholars as well. While Otto Warburg tried to convince the Institute of Jewish Studies to accept Hareuveni, Josef Klausner considered the latter's studies far more relevant to the exploration of local botany. The only good word Klausner had for Hareuveni was that his excursions to Arab villages and interviews with their inhabitants were exceptionally courageous.

65 Paz, "Botanical Garden," 443–54. See also the issue of *Hateva ve-ha'aretz* devoted to the memory of Alexander Eig (vol. 5, no. 9 [November 1938]: 412–31).

66 Interestingly enough, Zohary published a book on biblical botany in a later stage of his career. See Michael Zohary, *Plants of the Bible* (Cambridge: Cambridge University Press, 1982).

67 In addition to Bialik, the Hareuvenis received letters of support from prominent public figures such as Moshe Harlap and Chief Rabbi Avraham Yitzhak Ha-Cohen Kook.

68 English translation of Bialik's letter by Batnadiv HaKarmi-Weinberg. The image of Bialik's letter is reproduced from Manor-Friedman, *The Botanist's Brush*, 31. See Hirschfeld's comments on this letter, in ibid., 30–33.

69 Quoted in Manor-Friedman, "The Song of Plants," 117.

70 Ibid., 116.

71 Hareuveni and Hareuveni, "Gan ha-nevi'im ve-hakhmey ha-talmud," 68.

72 In 1965, Noga Hareuveni founded Neot Kedumim, the Biblical Landscape Reserve in Israel. He realized what his parents failed to see: that such a botanical-exegetical project would be far more appealing to the public at large than to academics. Ben-Gurion provided his unstinting encouragement, and soon Neot Kedumim became a popular site that drew—and continues to draw—thousands of visitors. In many ways, Noga Hareuveni's project was even greater than the original plan—not merely a garden but rather a resort of many acres where visitors could actually embark on the kind of excursions Ephraim and Hannah Hareuveni were so fond of. And yet this new "biblical landscape" lacked one significant element of the initial enterprise: the commitment to a Jewish-Arab coexistence via plant lore. Arab plant lore was relegated to the margins with the names of the Arab villages on whose grounds Neot Kedumim was founded. On the effaced Palestinian landscapes of Neot Kedumim, see W. J. T. Mitchell, "Holy Landscape: Israel, Palestine, and the American Wilderness," *Critical Inquiry* 26, no. 2 (2000): 204.

73 The impulse to provide a botanical account of the flora and fauna of the Song of Songs is evident in a later book by Yehuda Felix, first published in 1974, devoted entirely to the study of the Song: *Shir ha-shirim: Teva, 'alila ve-'alegorya* [*The Song of Songs: Nature, Plot, and Allegory*] (Jerusalem: Ha-hevra le-heker ha-mikra, 1974). Felix's book is a curious specimen in which the detailed literalist analyses of the plants at stake are accompanied by quotations of Rashi's allegorical readings.

74 Boris Schatz, *Yerushalyim habenuyah: Halom behakits* [Rebuilt Jerusalem: A Daydream] (Jerusalem: Bezalel, 1924), 24. See also his utopian description of Jerusalem as a garden of the Song of Songs in a later section in his novel (165–66).

75 On Goitein's biography, see Mark R. Cohen's "Eulogy: Shelomo Dov Goitein," in *American Philosophical Society Year Book* (Philadelphia: American Philosophical Society, 1987); and Jacob Lassner's foreword to *A Mediterranean Society: An Abridgment in One Volume*, by Shlomo Dov Goitein (Berkeley: University of California Press, 1999), xi–xxii. I am indebted to conversations with Mark R. Cohen and Ayala Gordon in this connection.

76 Shlomo Dov Goitein, "Research among the Yemenites," in *Studies in Jewish Folklore: Proceedings of a Regional Conference of the Association for Jewish Studies* (Cambridge, Mass.: Association for Jewish Studies, 1980), 123.

77 Ibid., 125. Goitein's books on the Yemenites—among them, *Travels in Yemen: An Account of Joseph Halevi's Journey to Najran* (1941) *and From the Land of Sheba: Tales of the Jews of Yemen* (1947)—exhibit his great interest in the literary dimension of his work. "No questionnaire," he claimed in his depiction of how he collected the tales that were to become part of *From the Land of Sheba*, "could have elicited more significant ethnological material than that provided by the narrator" (ibid., 128).

78 Amitav Ghosh, *In an Antique Land: History in the Guise of a Traveler's Tale* (New York: Vintage Books, 1994); Adina Hoffman and Peter Cole, *Sacred Trash: The Lost and Found World of the Cairo Geniza* (New York: Schocken Books, 2011). The Hebrew term *geniza* designates a repository of discarded writings. According to Jewish belief, texts bearing the name of God should be put aside in a special room to await burial in a cemetery, just as the human body should be buried to await resurrection. Thanks to this custom, a vast treasure of variegated medieval documents had been preserved in a synagogue in Fustat, or, as it is called today, Old Cairo.

79 Shlomo Dov Goitein, *Omanut ha-sipur ba-mikra* (Jerusalem: Ha-Sokhnut Hayehudit le-Eretz Yisrael, 1956); *Hora'at ha-tanakh* (Tel Aviv: Javneh, 1957); and *Iyunim bamikra* (Tel Aviv: Javneh, 1957).

80 Goitein, *Hora'at ha-tanakh*, 55. This chapter, "Al ha-yesodot ha-iyuniyim shel hora'at ha-tanakh be-vet ha-sefer ha-'ivri" (On the Teaching of the Bible in Hebrew Schools), was published in 1939 in a collection titled *Al ha-hinukh ha-tikhoni ha-'ivri be-eretz yisrael* (On High School Education in the Land of Israel).

81 Goitein, *Hora'at ha-tanakh*, 55; my translation.

82 Ibid., 65.

83 Interestingly, Goitein's contribution to Rosenzweig's collection (he too was among the contributors) was a piece on the problematic exclusion of rabbinic Judaism and the Talmud from the new curriculum in Palestine. See Hoffman, *Between Exile and Return*, 179.

84 Each of Goitein's chapters was translated separately. The first, "Women as Creators of Biblical Genres," translated by Michael Carasik, appeared in *Prooftexts* 8, no. 1 (1988): 1–33. Excerpts of the second appear in Athalya Brenner, ed., *A Feminist*

Companion to the Song of Songs (Sheffield: JSOT Press, 1993).

85 Goitein, "Women as Creators of Biblical Genres," 1.

86 Goitein's questionnaires at the time include questions such as "Are you familiar with women singers and songs composed by women?" These questionnaires are reprinted in Shlomo Dov Goitein, *HaTeymanim: Historia, sidrey hevra, hayei ruah* [The Yemenites: History, Society, and Spiritual Life], ed. Menachem Ben-Sasson (Jerusalem: Makhon Ben Zvi, 1983), 350.

87 Excerpted in Brenner, *A Feminist Companion to the Song of Songs*, 65–66.

88 Goitein even anticipates, if briefly, Phyllis Trible's reading of the Song as a revision of the curse in the Garden of Eden in its egalitarian perception of the relationship between the sexes. See Trible, *God and the Rhetoric of Sexuality* (Philadelphia: Fortress Press, 1978).

89 Pope, *Song of Songs*, 145–53.

90 The writings of Umberto Cassuto on the interrelations of the Bible and the mythologies of the ancient Near East may have had some impact as well.

91 J. G. Wetzstein, "Die syrische Dreschtafel," *Zeitschrift für Ethnologie* 5 (1873): 270–301.

92 G. H. Dalman, *Palaestinischer Diwan* (Leipzig, 1901); S. H. Stephan, "Modern Palestinian Parallels to the Song of Songs," *JPOS* 2 (1922): 1–80.

93 Sheehan, *The Enlightenment Bible*, 209–10. Abraham Z. Idelsohn's folkloric study on the biblical echoes of Yemenite songs is also of relevance. See Idelsohn, *Jewish Music in Its Musical Historical Development* (New York: Schocken Books, 1967). See Edwin Seroussi's essay on Idelsohn, "Yesod ehad lahen: Giluy ha-mizrah ve-ahdutan shel mesorot ha-musika ha-yehudiyot be-mishnat Avram Zvi Idelsohn" [The Discovery of the East and the Affinity between Musical Traditions in the Writings of Abraham Zvi Idelsohn], *Pe'amim* 100 (2004): 125–46.

94 Galit Hasan-Rokem, "Textualizing the Tales of the People of the Book: Folk Narrative Anthologies and National Identity in Modern Israel," *Prooftexts* 19, no. 1 (1999): 72.

95 Later, in Goitein's introductory comments to an anthology of essays on the Yemenites, he speaks of his encounter with the Yemenites as entailing a "precious personal dimension": the feeling that something his forefathers had "lost" in their long exile in northern countries has been returned to him (Goitein, *HaTeymanim*, 3). On Goitein's "creative symbiosis," see Steven M. Wasserstrom, *Between Muslim and Jew: The Problem of Symbiosis under Early Islam* (Princeton, N.J.: Princeton University Press, 1995). See also Miriam Frenkel, "Ketivat ha-historia shel yehudei 'artsot ha-Islam bi-ymei ha-beinayim" [The Historiography of Jews of Islamic Cultures in the Middle Ages], *Pe'amim* 92 (2002): 23–61.

96 For a discussion on how Bible scholars at the Hebrew University took part in the formation of a "national midrash" despite their professed objectivity, see Simon, "The Place of the Bible in Israeli Society," 224–25.

97 Rosenzweig, *The Star of Redemption*, 201.

3. RECHNITZ'S BOTANY OF LOVE

1 Agnon, *Shevu'at emunim*, in *Ad hena*, 168; my translation. On Agnon's Jaffa, see Barbara E. Mann, *A Place in History: Modernism, Tel Aviv, and the Creation of Jewish Urban Space* (Stanford, Calif.: Stanford University Press, 2006), 186–93.

2 The expression "my vineyard" (*karmi sheli*) appears in Song 1:6 and 8:12. The expression "my orchard" (*pardesi sheli*) does not appear as such in the Song, but the Shulamite is likened to an orchard in 4:12–13.

3 *Shevu'at emunim* literally means an "oath of faith." A more accurate translation is that of Band, who renders the title as "The Betrothal Oath." Band, *Nostalgia and Nightmare*, 367.

4 Arnold Band, "Me-Hemdat le-doktor Rechnitz" [From Hemdat to Dr. Rechnitz], in *Kovets Agnon* [Essays on Agnon], ed. Emunah Yaron, Rafael Weiser, Dan Laor, and Reuven Mirkin (Jerusalem: Magnes Press, 1994), 286–94.

5 Anne Golomb Hoffman offers another interesting link in pointing to the affinity between Rechnitz and Otto Weininger. In his book *Sex and Character* (which is mentioned in passing in the novella), Weininger, Hoffman writes, "refers to beautiful sketches of processes of fertilization in Mediterranean seaweed that illustrate natural forces of attraction." Hoffman, "A Streetcar Named Desire: A Note on Otto Weininger in *Shevu'at emunim*," in *Essays on Hebrew Literature in Honor of Avraham Holtz*, ed. Zvia Ben-Yosef Ginor (New York: Jewish Theological Seminary of America, 2003), 54.

6 Israel Asael, "Midrash 'atzot" [A Midrash of Seaweeds], *Keshet*, Fall 1966, 22.

7 Ibid., 25.

8 Ephraim Hareuveni to Agnon, December 5, 1946, folder ARC, 4, 1270 05 0280, Agnon Archive, the National Library, Jerusalem.

9 *Shevua't emunim*, 212 (Hebrew text).

10 A similar critique of academic pretensions at the Hebrew University appears in Agnon's *Shira*.

11 Quoted in David Myers, *Re-inventing the Jewish Past* (New York: Oxford University Press, 1995), 40.

12 Ibid., 41. Myers calls attention to the intricate oscillation of scholars at the Institute of Jewish Studies in the early years of the Hebrew University, between a commitment to the founding principles of *Wissenschaft*, with its standards of scientific validation and critical distance, and a quest, however idiosyncratic at times, to break with some of its presuppositions—whether because of changing perceptions of what counts as Jewish Studies or because of a growing need to contribute to the burgeoning national project of Zionism and its sense of mission.

13 In tracing the Jewish line behind the classical one, I am indebted to Dov Sadan's reading in *'Al Shai Agnon*, 88–107.

14 My translation, *Shevu'at emunim*, 170 (Hebrew text).

15 Band briefly refers to the profusion of echoes from the Song in the gardens of *Betrothed* in *Nostalgia and Nightmare*, 381.

16 *Shevu'at emunim*, 193 (Hebrew text).

17 My translation, *Shevu'at emunim*, 194 (Hebrew text).

18 See Sadan, *'Al Shai Agnon*, 96; Band, *Nostalgia and Nightmare*, 377. Note that some of the Hebrew translations of the Grimms' tale follow the German model and use "Shoshana bein ha-hohim" as a title rather than "Ha-yefeifiya ha-nirdemet" (sleeping beauty). Agnon plays with both titles. In Agnon's "Hill of Sand" ("Givat ha-hol"), another Jaffa story, there is a similar somewhat morbid revision of "Sleeping Beauty" and the Song, though in reference to a male protagonist. Hemdat (the young artist) defines himself, in a confessional moment, as a *ben-melekh nirdam* (a sleeping prince): "I'm a sleeping prince whose true love puts him back to sleep. I'm love's beggar walking around with love in a torn old bag." Agnon, "Hill of Sand," trans. Anne Golomb Hoffman, in *A Book That Was Lost*, 113.

19 The identification of these flowers varies from one translation to another. Given that in his use of *shoshana* Agnon has a rose in mind and given that this is the common usage in modern Hebrew, I'll be using the term "rose" as translation for *shoshana*—instead of the OJPS's (and KJV's) "lily." To preserve floral variation, I will use "lily" for *havatselet*.

20 See Alter, *The Art of Biblical Poetry*, 200–203. For more on the metaphorical network of the Song, see Francis Landy, *Paradoxes of Paradise: Identity and Difference in the Song of Songs* (Sheffield: Almond Press, 1983).

21 Blochs' translation, *The Song of Songs*, 85.

22 *Shevu'at emunim*, 190 (Hebrew text).

23 My translation, *Shevu'at emunim*, 190 (Hebrew text).

24 See Band, "Me-Hemdat le-doctor Rechnitz," 289.

25 For a historical account of the early years of psychoanalysis in the Zionist context with a brief discussion of Agnon, see Eran J. Rolnik, *Osey ha-nefashot: 'Im Freud le-Eretz Yisrael 1918–1948* [Freud in Zion: History of Psychoanalysis in Jewish Palestine/Israel, 1918–1948] (Tel Aviv: Am Oved, 2007), 270–77.

26 Freud acknowledges the death instinct only in "Beyond the Pleasure Principle."

27 See Shaked, *Shmuel Yosef Agnon: A Revolutionary Traditionalist*, 170–87; and Gershon Shaked, "Portrait of the Immigrant as a Young Neurotic," *Prooftexts* 7, no. 1 (1987): 441–52.

28 Adhering to the Hebrew text, I use the name "Arzaf" rather than "Ilyushin" (in Lever's translation). For more on Agnon and Bezalel, see Shmuel Werses, "Agnon be-'olamo shel Bezalel" [Agnon in the World of Bezalel], in *Shai Agnon ki-fshuto*, 287–90. In *Only Yesterday*, Agnon provides a more detailed account of Arzaf. His zoological inquiries of Jewish sources are mentioned along with his solitary, semi-mad, or even demonic, embalming of animals. Like Hareuveni, Aharoni was a fervent explorer of the natural realities of the Bible and Talmud in the Land of Israel. In *Memories of a Hebrew Zoologist* (*Zikhronot zoolog 'ivri*), he depicts in detail his dialogue with Gustaf Dalman, the founder of the Jerusalem Research Institute of the Holy Land who conducted a whole array of studies of local customs, botany, and zoology. Although the renowned Dalman was familiar with variegated Jewish sources (unlike other Christian zoologists and botanists who ignored postbiblical materials), Aharoni presents himself as far more familiar with these ancient texts

and far more aware of their relevance to the study of zoological life in Palestine. For more on Dalman, see Yehoshua Ben-Aryeh, "Orhot hayim u-minhagim shel ha-'ukhlusiya ha-mekomit ha-Eretz Yisraelit kefi she-nilmedu ba-me'a ha-19 ve-'ad 1948" [Modes of Life and Customs of Local Communities in Eretz Yisrael from the 19th Century until 1948], in *Ve-Zot l-Yehuda: Mehkarim be-toldot Eretz Israel vi-yeshuva* [Studies in the History of the Land of Israel: Presented to Yehuda Ben-Porat], ed. Yehoshua Ben-Aryeh and Elhanan Reiner (Jerusalem: Yad ben Zvi, 2003), 477–80.

29 Agnon, "Al ha-sheina" [On Sleep], in *Me'atsmi le-atsmi* [From Myself to Myself] (Jerusalem and Tel Aviv: Schocken, 2000), 442.

30 Band, "Me-Hemdat le-doctor Rechnitz," 292–93.

31 Virgil, *The Aeneid*, trans. Robert Fitzgerald (New York: Vintage, 1983), 206. Freud provides the quotation in Latin: *Flectere si nequeo superos, Acheronta movebo* (see the title page of *The Interpretation of Dreams* [1899], Standard Edition, 4:9). I am indebted to Ruth Ginsburg for calling my attention to the relevance of the epigraph of *The Interpretation of Dreams*. What adds a heretical touch to this descent downward is Rechnitz's use of the terms *elyonim* and *tahtonim* on speaking of upper and lower worlds. These terms are charged with mystical resonance—all the more so given that the tree is a major trope in depictions of the upper spheres in the Zohar. Rather than seek supernal knowledge up high in sefirotic plants, Rechnitz ironically searches for the hidden truths of the lower rungs of seaweeds. And perhaps this is a playful evocation of the inverted character of the tree of *sefirot*, imagined as a cosmic tree growing downward from its roots above.

32 Brown provides a detailed consideration of Agnon's debt to Freud's "Delusions and Dreams in Jensen's *Gradiva*" in "A Pompeiian Fancy under Jaffa's Sea: Agnon's *Betrothed* and Jensen's *Gradiva*," *Prooftexts* 16, no. 3 (1996): 245–70.

33 Freud, "Delusions and Dreams in Jensen's *Gradiva*," 34.

34 Freud, *The Interpretation of Dreams*, 5:525.

35 Interestingly, Freud, as one recalls, primarily relied on classical models in his theories until his very last book, *Moses and Monotheism*.

36 Avraham Kariv, "Min ha-hol 'el ha-kodesh" [From the Profane to the Holy], *Gevilin*, September 1960, 12–13.

37 Sadan, *'Al Shai Agnon*, 103.

38 Hannan Hever, *El ha-hof ha-mekuve: Ha-yam ba-tarbut ha'ivrit u-vasifrut ha'ivrit ha-modernit* [Toward the Longed-for Shore: The Sea in Hebrew Culture and Modern Hebrew Literature] (Tel Aviv: Van Leer Institute and Hakibbutz Hameuchad, 2007), 89–99.

39 Dina Stern offers an elaborate discussion concerning the allegorical aspects of *Betrothed* and devotes a chapter to traditional allegories of the Song. Nonetheless, she does not take into account its reception in Zionist culture. Stern, *Ha-begidah ve-likcha: Shevu'at emunim me'et Shai Agnon* [Betrayal and Its Moral: S. Y. Agnon's *Betrothed*] (Jerusalem and Tel Aviv: Schocken, 1989).

40 Benjamin, *Origin of German Tragic Drama*, 166.

41 The relevance of Benjamin's renowned essay on allegory to this tale is noted by

Hever, *El ha-hof ha-mekuve*, 92.

42 Matt, *The Zohar*, 1:1. Note that these are the very opening lines of the introduction to the Zohar (Haqdamat Sefer ha-Zohar).

43 In another renowned Zoharic passage on the Rose, the Beloved is first imagined as a "lily of Sharon" who yearns to be watered by the deepest of all rivers. Once she is kissed by the King "whose lips are as roses" (Song 5:13), she becomes the "rose of the valleys," changing colors from green to deep red with white hues (Zohar 1:221a–b). The Zohar thus plays with the parallelism of Song 2:1. Attuned to the intensification that often accompanies the move from the first verset to the second in biblical parallelisms (see Alter, *The Art of Biblical Poetry*, chap. 3), the Zoharic exegetes envision the moist rose of the valleys as more intense and sublime than the lily of Sharon. Melila Hellner-Eshed provides an extensive reading of this passage and of the role of the Rose in the Zohar in *A River Flows from Eden*, 341–48.

44 In "Shalosh ha-shevu'ot" ("Three Oaths"), Agnon offers an explicit commentary on this allegorical tradition. Aviezer Ravitzky provides a detailed account of the impact of the three oaths in *Messianism, Zionism, and Jewish Religious Radicalism*, trans. Michael Swirsky and Jonathan Chipman (Chicago: University of Chicago Press, 1993), 211–34.

45 Freud, *Moses and Monotheism*, 148–56. For more on *Moses and Monotheism* and the return of the repressed, see Ruth Ginsburg and Ilana Pardes, eds., *New Perspectives on Freud's "Moses and Monotheism"* (Tübingen: Niemeyer, 2006).

46 My translation, *Shevu'at emunim*, 210 (Hebrew text).

47 Agnon, "The Tale of the Scribe," trans. Isaac Franck, in *A Book That Was Lost: Thirty-Five Stories*, 186. It is noteworthy that another allegory of the Song is at stake, revolving around the first part of the same verse (6:2): *dodi yarad le-gano* ("my beloved is gone down into his garden"). To give but two examples, in Talmud Yerushalmi, Tractate Berakhot 2:8 and Shir Ha-Shirim Rabbah 6:2, it designates God's descent to the garden of Israel to take away (*lesalek*) true zaddikim, bringing upon them an untimely death. Rafael, as it were, positions himself in the role of God and his wife in the role of the zaddik.

48 Hoffman, *Between Exile and Return*, 34.

49 Asael, "Midrash Atsot," 21.

50 My translation, *Shevu'at emunim*, 220 (Hebrew text).

51 My translation, based in part on Lever's, 128–29.

52 In addition to the Song, there are distinct echoes of Genesis 1:2 in this passage. The spirit of God is replaced in this case with the *levana* and a haunted moon-dominated world that stands in contrast to the biblical one. I am grateful to Robert Alter for calling my attention to this point.

53 Rosenzweig, *The Star of Redemption*, 202.

54 Note that Rosenzweig relies on the Song itself in his attempt to capture its unique qualities ("like a gazelle or a young stag upon the mountains") much as Agnon uses the Song's metaphors in the aesthetic allegories of "And Solomon's Wisdom Excelled."

55 Robert Alter, "Agnon's Mediterranean Fable," in *Defenses of the Imagination: Jewish Writers and Modern Historical Crisis* (Philadelphia: Jewish Publication Society of America, 1977), 196.

56 I provide a more substantive consideration of the moon as a symbol of the Shekhinah in the next chapter.

57 Kurzweil, *Masot 'al sipurey Shai Agnon*, 121.

58 Agnon's dialogue with Bialik is more nuanced. Bialik was a complex advocate of Hebrew renaissance, who definitely had qualms about its prospects, most evident in the great *poema* "The Dead of the Desert." And yet he did not hesitate to be one of its most flowery advocates, as his letter to the Hareuvenis indicates (see Chapter 2).

59 Agnon's speech at the Nobel banquet at the city hall in Stockholm, December 10, 1966, http://www.nobelprize.org/nobel_prizes/literature/laureates/1966/agnon-speech.html.

60 Agnon's evocation of David's songs (Psalms) is accompanied by an implicit allusion to the Zohar's rendition of Solomon's Song as even more sublime. Whereas in David's times the Temple had not yet been built, Solomon's Song emerged after its construction. As such, Solomon's Song could unite the upper and the lower worlds, sung, as it was, by both the Levitical musicians and singers in the Temple below and by their corresponding heavenly choir above. The Zoharic commentary goes as follows: "King David uttered *A song of ascents* (Psalms 125:1). King Solomon opened with *Song of Songs*, a song of those musicians. What is the difference between them, for it seems that all is one? Well, surely all is one, but in the days of David all those musicians were not arranged in their places to play fittingly and the Temple had not been built. Consequently, they were not arranged above in their places; for just as there are watches arranged on earth, so too in heaven, standing corresponding to one another." Matt, *The Zohar*, vol. 5, *Terumah* 2:143b, 310–11 (quoted in Agnon's *Book, Writer and Story*, 71). For more on the privileged position of the Song of Songs in relation to David's Songs of Ascents, see Yehuda Liebes, *Torat ha-Yetsirah shel Sefer Yetsirah* [Ars Poetica in Sefer Yetsirah] (Jerusalem and Tel Aviv: Schocken, 2000), 123–26. For an extensive consideration of the ways in which the singing of Levites in the Temple is construed as an earthly counterpart of the Song of Songs that is sung in the Temple of the upper worlds, see Shifra Asulin, "Ha-parshanut ha-mistit le-shir ha-shirim be-sefer ha-Zohar ve-rik'ah" [The Mystical Exegesis of the Song of Songs in the Zohar] (Ph.D. diss., Hebrew University, 2006), 36–43.

61 Haim Nahman Bialik, "Revealment and Concealment in Language," in *Revealment and Concealment: Five Essays—Haim Nahman Bialik* (Jerusalem: Ibis Editions, 2000).

62 G. W. F. Hegel, *Aesthetics: Lectures on Fine Art*, 2 vols., trans. T. M. Knox (Oxford: Clarendon, 1975), 1:149–50.

63 Bialik too, to be sure, was intrigued by the interdependence of poetry and prose. On his intricate experiments in this connection, see Na'ama Rokem, *Prosaic Conditions: Heinrich Heine and the Spaces of Zionist Literature* (Evanston, Ill.: Northwestern University Press, 2013).

64 The craving for renewal through love and poetry (in the broad sense of the term)

is the major topic of *Shira*, whose title designates both the name of the sought-for woman and "poetry." See Alter's comments on *Shira* in "Agnon's Last Word," 77. See also Dan Miron, "Ashkenaz: Ha-havaya ha-yehudit-germanit be-kitvey Agnon" [Ashkenaz: The Jewish-German Experience in Agnon's Writings], in *Ha-rofe ha-medumeh: Iyunim ba-siporet ha-yehudit ha-classit* [La Médecin Imaginaire: Studies in Classical Jewish Fiction] (Tel Aviv: Hakibbutz Hameuchad, 1995), 297–306; and Mintz, *Translating Israel*, 106.

4. THE BIBLICAL ETHNOGRAPHIES OF "EDO AND ENAM" AND THE QUEST FOR THE ULTIMATE SONG

1 Adhering to the Hebrew name, I use the transliteration "Grofit" rather than Lever's "Grofith" here and throughout the chapter.

2 Tochner, *Pesher Agnon*, 106–22.

3 Tzachi Weiss, *Mot ha-Shekhinah bi-yetsirat Agnon: Kri'ah be-arba'ah sipurim* [Death of the Shekhinah: Readings in Four Agnon Stories and in Their Sources] (Ramat Gan: Bar-Ilan University Press, 2009), 117–32.

4 "Gershom Scholem on Agnon," interview by Dan Miron, pts. 1 and 2, *Ariel—Israel Review of Arts and Letters* 52 (1982): 94–106; 53 (1983): 61–75, 63. Scholem's comment on Agnon's relationships with writers is something of an exaggeration. Especially in his first years in Palestine, Agnon had significant friendships with Yosef Haim Brenner and Bialik. See Haim Be'er, *Gam ahavatam gam sina'atam: Bialik, Brenner, Agnon—ma'arakhot yehasim* [Their Love and Their Hate: Bialik, Brenner, Agnon—Relations] (Tel Aviv: Am Oved, 2002).

5 Scholem, "Reflections on S. Y. Agnon," 62.

6 For an English translation of the German version, which includes this reference to "Edo and Enam," see Scholem, *On Jews and Judaism in Crisis*, 103.

7 Agnon goes so far as playing with the pun in the Song between *gan na'ul* (locked garden) and *gal na'ul* (locked spring) when the newspapers mistakenly print the name "Gilat" instead of "Ginat" (227).

8 Freud, "Female Sexuality" (1931), in Standard Edition, 21:226. Freud returns to the question of matriarchy in *Moses and Monotheism* in his study of the rise of monotheism against its predecessors.

9 *Bein Shlomo Dov Goitein ve-Shmuel Yosef Agnon* [Between Shlomo Dov Goitein and Shmuel Yosef Agnon], ed. Ayala Gordon (Jerusalem: private publication, 2008). A copy is available at the National Library at Givat Ram.

10 Dan Laor, review of the collection of letters between Agnon and Goitein, in "Gentlemen and Scholars," *Haaretz*, January 14, 2009.

11 See Ayala Gordon's introduction to *Between Shlomo Dov Goitein and Shmuel Shai Agnon*, 4–11.

12 Quoted in Laor, "Gentlemen and Scholars."

13 As Agnon's American connection, Goitein also informed his friend of the young promising American critic of modern Hebrew literature—Robert Alter. See letter no. 55, in *Between Shlomo Dov Goitein and Shmuel Yosef Agnon*, 88.

14 Goitein, "S.Y. Agnon: Personal Account," in *A Memorial Tribute to Dr. Shmuel Yosef Agnon*, presented by Dropsie University and the Consulate General of Israel, Sunday, March 29, 1970 (Philadelphia: Dropsie University, 1970), 12. Note that in addition to this personal account, Goitein wrote other essays on Agnon's work: "Rabbi Yudil," *Davar*, April 1932, reprinted in *Shai Agnon ba-bikoret ha-'ivrit* [S. Y. Agnon: Critical Essays of His Writings] (Tel Aviv: Open University of Israel and Schocken, 1992), 2:6–11; "Al sippur pashut" [On a Simple Story], *Haaretz*, August 12, 1938; "Al 'Shevu'at emunim'" [On *Betrothed*], *Gazit* 5, nos. 9–10 (1943): 32–34; and "Besh'ah ahat" [Within One Hour] in *leAgnon Shai* [A Homage to Agnon] (Jerusalem, 1959). All are reprinted in the volume edited by Ayala Gordon, *Between Shlomo Dov Goitein and Shmuel Yosef Agnon*.

15 Note that Scholem's first name—Gershom/Gerhard—also begins with a *gimel*, not to mention the fact that Greifenbach's first name is "Gerhard."

16 I am indebted to Nitza Ben-Dov for calling my attention to the relevance of the *tet* and the *nun* as well.

17 Rosenzweig, *The Star of Redemption*, 200–201.

18 David Myers, "Franz Rosenzweig and the Rise of Theological Anti-Historicism," in *Resisting History: Historicism and Its Discontents in German-Jewish Thought* (Princeton, N.J.: Princeton University Press, 2003), 68–105.

19 Moyn, "Divine and Human Love," 210–11. Note that Said devotes a brief section to the projection entailed in the quest for biblical realities through the contemporary Orient in his consideration of Holy Land travel narratives. See Edward Said, *Orientalism* (New York: Random House, 1978), 168.

20 Freud, "Delusions and Dreams in Jensen's *Gradiva*," 17.

21 Ibid., 14.

22 Kurzweil underscores the network of allusions to Ecclesiastes but overlooks the resonance of the Song in the tale. See Kurzweil, *Masot 'al sipurey Shai Agnon*, 141–60.

23 For more on the representation of Jerusalem in "Edo and Enam" and elsewhere in Agnon's writings, see Sidra DeKoven Ezrahi, "S. Y. Agnon's Jerusalem: Before and after 1948," *Jewish Social Studies* (forthcoming).

24 One of the questions in Goitein's questionnaires regarding Yemenite culture is, "Are there Hakhamim in your community? Or authors of books and poems?" Goitein, *HaTeymanim*, 350.

25 On the aesthetic passions Ginat and Gamzu have in common, see Michal Arbel, *Katuv 'al 'oro shel kelev: Al tfisat ha-yetsira etsel Shai Agnon* [Written on the Skin of a Dog: S. Y. Agnon, Concepts of Art and Creativity] (Jerusalem: Keter and Ben-Gurion University, 2006).

26 The other major biblical text at stake is Judges 21:20–23. Other pertinent sources, as Shlomo Zuker observes, are Mishnah Ta'anit 4:8 and a parallel *braita* cited in the Talmud: Ta'anit 31a. See Zuker, "Mekorot be-'itsuv ha-merhav ve-hadmuyot be-Edo ve-Enam le-Shai Agnon" [Sources for the Fashioning of Space and Characters in Agnon's "Edo and Enam"], *Mehkarey Yerushalayim be-sifrut ivrit* 3 (1982): 44. See also Hillel Weis, *Agnon: Agunot, Edo ve-Enam; Mekorot, mivnim u-mashma'uyot*,

vols. 2–3 [Agnon: "Agunot" and "Edo and Enam"; Sources, Structure, and Significance] (Tel Aviv: Open University Press, 1981). Note that in his ethnographic account of another remote village in the East, Gamzu actually refers to the practice of reciting the Song of Songs (193).

27 "Edo ve-Enam, in *Ad hena*, 284 (Hebrew text).

28 Tosefta Sanhedrin 12:10. This commentary appears in the section on the Song of Songs in Agnon, *Sefer, sofer ve-sippur* (*Book, Writer, and Story*) (Jerusalem and Tel Aviv: Schocken, 2000), 71. Ta'anit 4:8 is yet another remnant of an ancient literalist tradition, as Ephraim E. Urbach suggests ("Drashot hazal u-ferushei origenes le-Shir Ha-Shirim ve-ha-vikuah ha-yehudi-notsri," *Tarbiz* 30 [1965]: 148 [a homage to S. D. Goitein on the occasion of his sixtieth birthday]). "Rabban Simeon b. Gamaliel said: There were no happier days for Israel than the 15th of Ab and the Day of Atonement, for on them the daughters of Jerusalem used to go forth in white raiments; and these were borrowed, that none should be abashed which had them not. . . . And the daughters of Jerusalem went forth to dance in the vineyards. And what did they say? 'Young man, lift up thine eyes and see what thou wouldst choose for thyself: set not thine eyes on beauty, but set thine eyes on family" (Mishnah Ta'anit 4:8, Danby translation, 200–201).

29 Shlomo Dov Goitein, "Religion in Everyday Life as Reflected in the Documents of the Cairo Geniza," in *Religion in a Religious Age*, ed. Shlomo Dov Goitein (Cambridge, Mass.: Association for Jewish Studies, 1974), 3–4.

30 Leah Goldberg, "Agnon bi-shlosha kolot" [Agnon in Three Voices], *Al HaMishmar*, October 27, 1950; reprinted in Goldberg, *Ha-Ometz le-hulin* [Courage for the Quotidian] (Tel Aviv: Sifriyat HaPoalim, 1950), 190–95.

31 Goldberg, "Agnon bi-shlosha kolot"; my translation.

32 My translation, "Edo ve-Enam," 304 (Hebrew text).

33 For more on Gemulah's name, see Zuker, "Mekorot be-'itsuv ha-merhav."

34 My understanding of the kabbalistic themes in this tale is indebted to Zuker, "Mekorot be-'itsuv ha-merhav," and to Michal Oron, "Semalim u-motivim kabaliyim ba-sipur 'Edo ve-Enam' le-Shai Agnon" [Symbols and Kabbalistic Motifs in Agnon's "Edo and Enam"], *Baseminar*, 1976, 160–72.

35 Gershom Scholem, *Major Trends in Jewish Mysticism* (New York: Schocken Books, 1961), 27–28.

36 Susan Handelman, *Fragments of Redemption: Jewish Thought and Literary Theory in Benjamin, Scholem, and Levinas* (Bloomington: Indiana University Press, 1991), 106.

37 In a sense, Agnon's mingling of the two approaches to the symbol/allegory debate underscores the points of affinity between Scholem and Benjamin. Despite the dispute between the two, their theories of language, as Steven M. Wasserstrom notes, are quite similar. See Wasserstrom, *Religion after Religion: Gershom Scholem, Mircea Eliade, and Henry Corbin at Eranos* (Princeton, N.J.: Princeton University Press, 1999). Many of the traits of Scholem's symbol may be found in the lost Adamic language Benjamin sketches out in "On Language as Such and on the Language of Man," in *Reflections: Essays, Aphorisms, Autobiographical Writings*, ed. Peter Demetz, trans. Edmund Jephcott (New York: Schocken Books, 1986), 314–32.

38 Idel, *Kabbalah and Eros*, 2. See also Yehuda Liebes, "Eros ve-Zohar" [Eros and the Zohar], *Alpayim*, no. 9 (1994): 67–119.

39 See Arthur Green, "Shekhinah, the Virgin Mary, and the Song of Songs: Reflections on a Kabbalistic Symbol in Its Historical Context," *AJS Review* 26, no. 1 (2002): 1–52; Asulin, "Ha-parshanut ha-mistit le-shir ha-shirim be-sefer ha-Zohar ve-rik'ah."

40 Tochner, *Pesher Agnon*, 111.

41 Matt, *The Zohar*, vol. 5, *Terumah* 2:143a, 309.

42 Ibid., 309n336. On the midrash in Song of Songs Rabbah regarding the singing of the Song during the crossing of the Red Sea, see Daniel Boyarin, "The Song of Songs, Lock or Key: The Holy Song as Mashal," in *Intertextuality and the Reading of Midrash* (Bloomington: Indiana University Press, 1990), chap. 7.

43 As Yair Zakovitch notes, in Song 6:10 the feminine terms for both the sun and the moon are used (*hama*, *levana*) to underscore the Shulamite's feminine beauty. See Zakovitch, *Shir ha-shirim*, 115. Agnon follows the Song in preferring the term *levana* in his depictions of Gemulah.

44 See Moshe Idel, *Kabbalah: New Perspectives* (New Haven, Conn.: Yale University Press, 1988); and Yehuda Liebes, *Studies in Jewish Myth and Messianism*, trans. Batya Stein (Albany: State University of New York Press, 1992). Note that Ginat's name, among other things, evokes the common kabbalistic use of the verse "I went down into the garden of nuts" (*ginat egoz*—Song 6:11) as a code for a mode of hermeneutic speculation that seeks the "innermost kernel." See Gershom Scholem, *On Kabbalah and Its Symbolism* (New York: Schocken Books, 1969), 58.

45 Ariel Hirschfeld, "Locus and Language: Hebrew Culture in Israel, 1890–1990," in Biale, *Cultures of the Jews*, 1053.

46 Kurzweil, *Masot 'al sipurey Shai Agnon*, 141–60. For more on the legends of the wandering Jew, see Galit Hasan-Rokem and Alan Dundes, eds., *The Wandering Jew: Essays in the Interpretation of a Christian Legend* (Bloomington: Indiana University Press, 1986).

47 Robert Alter's paraphrase of Kurzweil's reading, in "Agnon's Symbolic Masterpieces," *Hadassah Magazine* 48, no. 2 (1966): 24.

48 My understanding of Agnon's evocation of the dirges of Tish'a be'Av in this tale is indebted to a seminar paper titled "Agnon's Lament: Song of Songs and Lamentation; Intertextuality in 'Ido and Enam,'" by Batnadiv HaKarmi Weinberg.

49 My understanding of the role of women as dirge singers is indebted to Galit Hasan-Rokem, *Web of Life: Folklore and Midrash in Rabbinic Literature*, trans. Batya Stein (Stanford, Calif.: Stanford University Press, 2000); and Vered Madar, "Text bein kol li-tnu'a: Kinot nashim mi-teiman" [Between Voice and Gesture: Dirges of Yemenite Women], *Mehkarei Yerushalayim be-folklore yehudi* 23 (2005): 89–119.

50 See Oron, "Semalim u-motivim kabaliyim ba-sipur 'Edo ve-Enam,'" 163; Hellner-Eshed, *A River Flows from Eden*, 224–25. For more on the diminution of the moon, see Betty Rojtman, *Selihat ha-levana: 'Al ha-tagiyut ha-mikra'it* [The Forgiveness of the Moon: Essays on Biblical Tragedy] (Jerusalem: Carmel, 2008).

51 For more on the Zohar's configuration of the arousal of the Shekhinah, see Hellner-Eshed, *A River Flows from Eden*, 204–51.

52 Both Gemulah and Shoshana are moonstruck, but each, as Hillel Barzel point out, has her own distinct malady. Whereas Shoshana is a somnambulist whose greatest desire is to sleep, Gemulah is excessively awake. Barzel, *Sipurey ahava shel Shai Agnon* [The Love Stories of S. Y. Agnon] (Ramat Gan: Bar-Ilan University Press, 1975), 89.

53 Cynthia Ozick, "Agnon's Antagonisms," *Commentary* 86 (1988): 45. Note that traces of the golem story are already evident in the opening exchange between the narrator and the Greifenbachs regarding the question of whether or not Ginat has "created a girl for himself" (151).

54 For more on the golem, see Gershom Scholem, *Kabbalah* (Jerusalem: Keter, 1974), 351–55; and Moshe Idel, *Golem: Jewish Magical and Mystical Traditions on the Artificial Anthropoid* (Albany: State University of New York Press, 1990). On the golem in Agnon's oeuvre, see Hagbi, *Language, Absence, Play*; Maya Barzilai, "S. Y. Agnon's German Consecration and the 'Miracle' of Hebrew Prose," *Prooftexts* (forthcoming).

55 The narrator's playful remark regarding *levana* and *lana* does not appear in Lever's translation. In the Hebrew text it may be found in "Edo ve-Enam," 289.

56 To be more precise, Agnon mentions "twenty-two to twenty-seven maidens." The former number is the standard number of the letters of the Hebrew alphabet whereas the latter includes the five final letters (*otiyot sofiyot*).

57 Scholem, *Kabbalah*, 25. *Sefer Yezirah* was found, of all places, in the Cairo Geniza. For more on *Sefer Yetsirah*, see Liebes, *Torat ha-yetsira shel Sefer Yetsirah*. Agnon's compilation *Book, Writer, and Story* (*Sefer, sofer ve-sippur*) includes many passages from *Sefer Yetsirah*. The very title of this compilation, as Liebes points out, is taken from *Sefer Yetsirah* (Liebes, *Torat ha-yetsira shel Sefer Yetsirah*, 273). What is more, there is a whole section in *Sefer, sofer ve-sippur* on the twenty-two letters of the Hebrew alphabet.

58 On the evocation of the revelation at Mount Sinai in this passage, see Tochner, *Pesher Agnon*, 117.

59 The passage from Zohar Shemot, titled "All of Israel Saw the Letters," goes as follows: "The moment these letters came forth, / secretly circling as one . . . and comets shot out in colors like before. / And so on every side . . . Now they came forth, these carved, flaming letters / flashing like gold when it dazzles." *Zohar: The Book of Enlightenment*, trans. Daniel C. Matt (New York: Paulist Press, 1983), 119.

60 For more on the centrality of the narrator, see Band, *Nostalgia and Nightmare*, 394–96.

61 I am indebted to Ruth Weise for this observation.

62 The question of the bleak ending of "Edo and Enam"—and how bleak it is—has troubled many critics. Tochner's account is one of the most intriguing. In contrast to Kurzweil, he claims that on the ideational level the tale is gloomy, but on the aesthetic one it is utterly exhilarating. And the most captivating feature in this aesthetic "castle of marvels" is the rising, bodiless figure of the maiden of the Shekhinah (*ne'arat ha-Shekhinah*)—Gemulah. See Tochner, *Pesher Agnon*, 122.

63 Quoted in Freud, *Moses and Monotheism*, 130. Agnon may also be alluding to the Dead Sea Scrolls which were found between 1946 and 1956. I am indebted to Galit Hasan-Rokem for calling my attention to this possibility.

64 The term for "hide" in "And Solomon's Wisdom Excelled" is *ganaz*, much as it is in the Zohar's commentary on Solomon's hidden corpus.

65 My translation of "Edo ve-Enam," 305 (Hebrew text), based on Lever's translation, 223–24.

66 On the musicality of Agnon, see Ruth HaCohen, "Lishmo'a el ha-rina o el ha-tefila: Leida hadadit shel milim u-lehanim be-hekshrei ha-zemer ha-'ivri" ["To Hear the Singing and Prayer": From Words to Music and from Music to Words in the Israeli Song Culture], *Mehkarei Yerushalayim be-sifrut ivrit* 20 (2006): 14–15.

67 Yaacov Bahat suggests that "Grofit" may also be affiliated with a musical instrument used in the Temple—*magrefa*—an ancient precursor of the organ. Bahat, *Shai Agnon, Haim Hazaz: Iyuney mikra* [S. Y. Agnon, Haim Hazaz: Biblical Studies] (Haifa: Yovel, 1970), 169. For a comparison between the Song of Grofit and Heinrich Heine's "Die Lorelei," see Ozick, "Agnon's Antagonisms." Franz Kafka's "Josephine the Singer" may also be relevant in this connection. In associating music, madness, and death, Agnon engages in a dialogue with German Romanticism. While doing so, he is attuned to Kafka's critique of the Romantic perspective. For more on music and madness in German Romanticism, see John T. Hamilton, *Music, Madness, and the Unknowing of Language* (New York: Columbia University Press, 2008).

68 Matt, *The Zohar*, vol. 5, *Terumah* 2:144a, 314.

69 On Agnon's frustrated quests for a lost perfection, see Kurzweil, *Masot 'al sipurey Shai Agnon*, 283–91.

EPILOGUE: FOREVERMORE

1 Kurzweil, "Ha-yesod ha-dati be-kitvey Agnon" [The Religious Element in Agnon's Writings], in *Masot 'al sipurey Shai Agnon*, 328–52. See Moshe Golchin's account of Kurzweil's reading of Agnon in this connection, in *Baruch Kurzweil ke-farshan tarbut* [Baruch Kurzweil as a Cultural Interpreter] (Ramat Gan: Bar-Ilan University Press, 2008), chap. 4.

2 Zemach, "Al ha-tefisa ha-historiosofit bi-shnayim mi-sipurav ha-me'uharim shel Agnon," 381–85.

3 The Canaanite movement (founded in 1939, reaching its peak in the 1940s) promoted the idea that the Land of Israel was that of ancient Canaan. It sought to continue the traditions of prebiblical cultures in the ancient Near East and accordingly rejected Judaism in favor of a native and rooted Hebrew identity.

4 Benjamin Lazier, *God Interrupted: Heresy and the European Imagination between the World Wars* (Princeton, N.J.: Princeton University Press, 2008), 4.

5 Ibid., 13.

6 Scholem, "Redemption through Sin," in *The Messianic Idea in Judaism, and Other Essays on Jewish Spirituality* (New York: Schocken Books, 1971), 78–141.

7 Ibid., 111–12. For more on the perception of the meaning of the Torah in Jewish mysticism, see Scholem, *On Kabbalah and Its Symbolism*, 32–86; and Moshe Idel, "Torah Hadashah: Messiah and the New Torah in Jewish Mysticism and Modern Scholarship," in *Kabbalah: Journal for the Study of Jewish Mystical Texts* 21 (2010): 57–110.

8 The more accurate transliteration of her name is thus Aldag rather than Eldag.

9 For more on the calves of "Forevermore" and the episode of the Golden Calf in Exodus, see Tochner, *Pesher Agnon*, 144–45. Note that in the biblical text itself the *efod* has, at points, a dubious history. The story of Gideon in Judges 8:27, where the *efod* becomes an idol, is the most pertinent.

10 On calves' eyes as a deformity, see Mishna, Tractate Bekhorot, 7:4.

11 On the many eyes of the Angel of Death, see the Babylonian Talmud, *Avoda Zara*, 20b; on Lilith's scary eyes, see Zohar 1, *Sitrey Torah*, 147–48; on the mystic as one full of eyes, see Hellner-Eshed, *A River Flows from Eden*, 162–63; on the Torah as a maiden without eyes whose sight is restored, as it were, by her exegetes, see Zohar 2:95a; on the eyes within splendor, see Zohar Hadash, Song of Songs, 61:4–62:1. On questions of vision in Jewish mysticism, see Elliot Wolfson, *Through a Speculum That Shines: Vision and Imagination in Medieval Jewish Mysticism* (Princeton N.J.: Princeton University Press, 1994).

12 Tochner provides an extensive consideration of the echoes of the Messiah's ass in "Forevermore"; see *Pesher Agnon*, 146–47. On the question of messianism and sexual transgression from the Bible to the Kabbalah, see Ruth Kara-Ivanov Kaniel, *Kedeshot u-kedoshot: 'Iimahot hamashiah bamitos hayehudi* [Holiness and Transgression: Mothers of the Messiah in Jewish Myth] (Tel Aviv: Hameuchad Hakibbutz, forthcoming). For an extensive consideration of Agnon's critique of Sabbatianism, see Tzahi Weiss, "'Things That Are Better Concealed than Revealed': An Historical-Biographical Study of S. Y. Agnon's Attitude toward the Sabbatian Movement and the Traditional Jewish World," *AJS Review* 36, no. 1 (2012): 103–20.

13 Lazier, *God Interrupted*, 196.

14 Ibid. For more on Scholem's comments on Zionism and messianism, see David Biale, *Gershom Scholem: Kabbalah and Counter-History*, 2nd ed. (Cambridge, Mass.: Harvard University Press, 1982), chap. 5; and Amnon Raz-Karkotzkin, "Bein berit shalom u-veit ha-mikdash: Ha-dialectica shel ge'ula u-meshihiyut be-ikvot Gershom Scholem" [Between Brit Shalom and the Temple: On the Dialectics of Redemption and Messianism of Gershom Scholem], in Schmidt and Schonfeld, *HaElohim lo ye'alem dom*, 293–324.

15 Note in particular the echoes of Psalms 102:14: "Thou wilt arise, and have compassion upon Zion; for it is time to be gracious unto her, for the appointed time is come" (*ki va mo'ed*).

16 I am indebted to Ruth Kara-Ivanov Kaniel for calling my attention to the relevance of Tractate Sanhedrin 98a (Babylonian Talmud) to this tale.

17 Walter Benjamin, *Illuminations: Essays and Reflections*, ed. Hannah Arendt, trans. Harry Zohn (New York: Schocken Books, 1969), 134–35.

18 Freddie Rokem, *Philosophers and Thespians: Thinking Performance* (Stanford, Calif.: Stanford University Press, 2010), 188–90.

19 Benjamin, *Illuminations*, 135.

20 Rokem, *Philosophers and Thespians*, 190.

21 Quoted in Alter, *Necessary Angels*, 13.

22 Walter Benjamin, "Franz Kafka," in *Illuminations*, 139.

23 On Amzeh as an ironic replica of a biblical scholar, see Tochner, *Pesher Agnon*, 130.

24 Agnon's treatment of philology was an inspiration to Joseph Cedar's 2011 film *Footnote*. On Cedar's debt to Agnon, see Michal Shir-El, *Ha-celebs ha-hadashim shetoratam hi pirsumam* [The New Celebrities], *Haaretz*, October 28, 2011. Interestingly, the name "Eldag"/"Aldag," which includes the word "fish," is ironically related philologically to the term for "raven."

25 According to R. Meir: "one who studies Torah for its own sake (*Torah lishma*) . . . the creation of the whole world is worthy of him" (Avot 6:1).

26 In *Shira*, Herbst meets one day a fellow professor, an epidemiologist, who "wanted to study a particularly deadly tropical disease. . . . He exposed his own body to the disease and tried to cure himself with the drug he had invented." The courageous move of the scientist leads him to ask himself: "Would I do anything comparable?" (553). "Forevermore" offers the humanistic counterpart. Amzeh endangers his life in order to rescue a text. It may seem a minor deed, but in Agnon's tales, trying to rescue but one ragged manuscript is analogous to preserving a whole world.

27 The Song is not the only text whose canonicity was disputed in these terms. In Mishnah Yadayim, several other texts are mentioned, such as the Book of Esther, Ezekiel, and Ecclesiastes. Akiva's passionate defense, however, has made the Song the most prominent case.

28 At one point, when Amzeh exclaims, "You are unique, Nurse Eden, you are the only one in the world" (*ahat 'at ba-'olam, ahat 'at ahoti eden*) (237), he evokes not only the many points in the Song in which the beloved is addressed as "sister" but also Song 6:9—"My dove, my undefiled, is but one; she is the only one [*ahat hi*] of her mother; she is the choice one [*ahat hi*] of her that bore her." The nuances of this intertextual nexus are lost in translation. The Hebrew text appears in Agnon, *Ha'esh ve-ha-'etzim*, 259. Note that in *Shira* the beloved is also a nurse and leprosy is a major theme. On the affinities between "Forevermore" and *Shira*, see Hillel Barzel, "Shira ve-Ad olam" [*Shira* and "Ad Olam"], and Gershom Schocken, "Motiv ha-tsara'at be-Shira u-ve-Ad olam" [The Motif of Leprosy in *Shira* and "Ad Olam"], in *Shai Agnon ba-bikoret ha-'ivrit: Sikumim ve-ha'arkhot 'al yetsirato*, 2:373–96.

29 On the ironies of the ending of "Forevermore," see Naomi Sokoloff, "Elements of Plot in Agnon's 'Ad Olam,'" in *Agnon: Texts and Contexts in English Translation*, ed. Leon Yudkin (New York: Markus Wiener Publishers, 1988), 199–234.

30 Robert Alter, introduction to "Forevermore," in Alter, *Modern Hebrew Literature*, 230.

31 Song of Songs Rabbah 4:5.

32 Agnon, "Agunot," trans. Baruch Hochman, in *A Book That Was Lost*, 44.

33 See Yael Zerubavel's study on the role of the Bible in contemporary Israeli culture, "Ha-Tanakh akhshav," *Mirkamim le-Galit Hasan-Rokem, Mehkarei Yerushalayim be-sifrut ivrit* 2 (2013):755–74.

34 For more on the Mizrahi musical scene, see Motti Regev and Edwin Seroussi, *Popular Music and National Culture in Israel* (Berkeley: University of California Press, 2004), 191–235.

35 "Hanale hitbalbela," as Regev and Seroussi point out, was one of the first hits of Mizrahi music. Its history is symptomatic of the strange combinations one can find in

popular Israeli music. Its lyrics are those of the poet Nathan Alterman, although—significantly—the verse from the Song was added by the band. Initially, the music was Eastern European, but it was transformed into a Mizrahi tune, a change that involved a shift in delivery and orchestration. Regev and Seroussi, *Popular Music and National Culture*, 214.

36 Note that the resurgence of traditional allegories of the Song in the realm of *piyyutim* has been accompanied by a similar tendency in the poetry of Mizrahi poets—above all, in the poetry of Haviva Pedaya, one of the leading advocates of the revival of this lost genre. For an extended list of musical adaptations of the Song from the 1960s until the present, see the Appendix.

37 See Tolidanu, *Sippura shel lehaka*, 13–14. Another noteworthy traditional-modernized adaptation of the Song within the Mizrahi world is that of Victoria Hanna. An experimental vocalist, Hanna integrates music, spoken word, and theater, enacting a unique representation of sacred Hebrew texts. In her Song of Songs performance, Hanna oscillates between reciting and singing, relying on a unique blend of Eastern rhythms, whispers of mystical incantations, and contemporary sound effects.

Bibliography

Agnon, Shmuel Yosef. *Ad hena* [Thus Far]. *Kol sipurav shel Shmuel Yosef Agnon* [The Complete Works of Shmuel Yosef Agnon]. Jerusalem and Tel Aviv: Schocken, 1998.

———. "Ad olam" [Forevermore]. In *Ha-esh ve-ha-'etzim* [The Fire and the Wood], 255–69. Jerusalem and Tel Aviv: Schocken, 1998.

———. "Al ha-sheina" [On Sleep]. In *Me'atsmi le-atsmi* [From Myself to Myself]. Jerusalem and Tel Aviv: Schocken, 2000.

———. "And Solomon's Wisdom Excelled" [Vaterev hokhmat shlomo]. Translated by Mordechai Beck. *Ariel—Israel Review of Arts and Letters* 92 (1993): 277–82. Hebrew text in *Ad hena* [Thus Far], of *Kol sipurav shel Shmuel Yosef Agnon* [The Complete Works of Shmuel Yosef Agnon], 233–37. Jerusalem and Tel Aviv: Schocken, 1998.

———. *Bein Shlomo Dov Goitein ve-Shmuel Yosef Agnon* [Between Shlomo Dov Goitein and Shmuel Yosef Agnon]. Edited by Ayala Gordon. Jerusalem: private publication, 2008.

———. *A Book That Was Lost: Thirty-Five Stories*. Edited by Alan L. Mintz and Anne Golomb Hoffman. New Milford, Conn.: Toby Press, 2008.

———. "Edo ve-Enam" [Edo and Enam]. In *Ad hena* [Thus Far], of *Kol sipurav shel Shmuel Yosef Agnon* [The Complete Works of Shmuel Yosef Agnon], 269–309. Jerusalem and Tel Aviv: Schocken, 1998.

———. *Ha-esh ve-ha-'etsim* [The Fire and the Wood]. Jerusalem and Tel Aviv: Schocken, 1998.

———. *Only Yesterday* [*Tmol shilshom*]. Translated by Barbara Harshav. Princeton, N.J.: Princeton University Press, 2000.

———. "Prakim shel sefer ha-medina" [Chapters in the Book of the State]. In *Samukh ve-nir'eh* [Near and Apparent], of *Kol sipurav shel Shmuel Yosef Agnon* [The Complete Works of Shmuel Yosef Agnon], 207–37. Jerusalem and Tel Aviv: Schocken, 1998.

———. *Sefer, sofer ve-sippur* [Book, Writer, and Story]. Jerusalem and Tel Aviv: Schocken, 2000.

———. "Shevu'at emunim" [Betrothed]. In *Ad hena* [Thus Far], 168–232. Jerusalem and Tel Aviv: Schocken, 1998.

———. "The Tale of the Scribe" [Agadat ha-sofer]. Translated by Isaac Franck. In *A Book That Was Lost: Thirty-Five Stories*, edited by Alan L. Mintz and Anne Golomb Hoffman, 177–93. New Milford, Conn.: Toby Press, 2008.

———. *Two Tales*. Translated by Walter Lever. New York: Schocken Books, 1966.

———. *Yamim nora'im* [Days of Awe]. Jerusalem and Tel Aviv: Schocken, 1998.

Alter, Robert. *After the Tradition: Essays on Modern Jewish Writing*. New York: E. P. Dutton, 1969.

———. "Agnon's Last Word." *Commentary* 51 (1971): 74–81.

———. "Agnon's Mediterranean Fable." In *Defenses of the Imagination: Jewish Writers and Modern Historical Crisis*, 169–98. Philadelphia: Jewish Publication Society of America, 1977.

———. "Agnon's Symbolic Masterpieces." *Hadassah Magazine* 48, no. 2 (1966): 19–26.

———. *The Art of Biblical Poetry*. New York: Basic Books, 1985.

———. *The Invention of Hebrew Prose: Modern Fiction and the Language of Realism*. Seattle: University of Washington Press, 1988.

———, ed. *Modern Hebrew Literature*. New York: Behrman House, 1975.

———. *Necessary Angels: Tradition and Modernity in Kafka, Benjamin, and Scholem*. Cambridge, Mass.: Harvard University Press, 1991.

Arbel, Michal. *Katuv 'al 'oro shel kelev: Al tfisat ha-yetsira etsel Shai Agnon* [Written on the Skin of a Dog: S. Y. Agnon, Concepts of Creativity and Art]. Jerusalem: Keter and Ben-Gurion University, 2006.

Asael, Israel. "Midrash 'atzot" [A Midrash of Seaweeds]. *Keshet*, Fall 1966, 22.

Asulin, Shifra. "Ha-parshanut ha-mistit le-shir ha-shirim be-sefer ha-Zohar ve-rik'ah" [The Mystical Exegesis of the Song of Songs in the Zohar]. Ph.D. diss., Hebrew University, 2006.

Bahat, Yaacov. *Shai Agnon, Haim Hazaz: Iyuney mikra* [S. Y. Agnon, Haim Hazaz: Biblical Studies]. Haifa: Yovel, 1970.

Baildam, John D. *Paradisal Love: Johann Gottfried Herder and the Song of Songs*. Sheffield: Sheffield Academic Press, 1999.

Banbaji, Amir. "The Orient in the Literature of the Haskalah: A Levantine Reading of Euchel, Löwisohn, and Mapu." *Journal of Levantine Studies* 1 (2011): 95–130.

Band, Arnold. "Agnon megale peney Freud" [Agnon Discovers Freud's Face]. In *She'elot nikhbadot* [Profound Questions], 207–18. Be'er-Sheva: Dvir, Heksherim, Ben-Gurion University, 2007.

———. "Me-Hemdat le-doktor Rechnitz" [From Hemdat to Dr. Rechnitz]. In *Kovets Agnon* [Essays on Agnon], edited by Emunah Yaron, Rafael Weiser, Dan Laor, and Reuven Mirkin, 286–94. Jerusalem: Magnes Press, 1994.

———. *Nostalgia and Nightmare: A Study in the Fiction of S. Y. Agnon*. Berkeley: University of California Press, 1968.

Bar-Adon, Aharon. *Shai Agnon u-tehiyat ha-safa ha-'ivrit* [S. Y. Agnon and the Revival of the Hebrew Language]. Jerusalem: Bialik Institute, 1977.

Barshai, Avinoam. *Shai Agnon ba-bikoret ha-'ivrit* [S. Y. Agnon: Critical Essays of His Writings]. 2 vols. Tel Aviv: Open University of Israel and Schocken, 1991–92.

Barzel, Hillel. *Bein Agnon le-Kafka: Mehkar mashveh* [Between Agnon and Kafka: A Comparative Study]. Ramat Gan: Bar-Ilan University Press, 1972.

———. *Sipurey ahava shel Shai Agnon* [The Love Stories of S. Y. Agnon]. Ramat Gan: Bar-Ilan University Press, 1975.

Barzilai, Maya. "S. Y. Agnon's German Consecration and the 'Miracle' of Hebrew Prose." *Prooftexts* (forthcoming).

Batnitzky, Leora. *Idolatry and Representation: The Philosophy of Franz Rosenzweig Reconsidered.* Princeton, N.J.: Princeton University Press, 2000.

Be'er, Haim. *Gam ahavatam gam sina'atam: Bialik, Brenner, Agnon—Ma'arakhot yehasim* [Their Love and Their Hate: Bialik, Brenner, Agnon—Relations]. Tel Aviv: Am Oved, 2002.

Ben-Aryeh, Yehoshua. "Orhot hayim u-minhagim shel ha-'ukhlusiya ha-mekomit ha-Eretz Yisraelit kefi she-nilmedu ba-me'a ha-19 ve-'ad 1948" [Modes of Life and Customs of Local Communities in Eretz Yisrael from the 19th Century until 1948]. In *Ve-Zot l-Yehuda: Mehkarim be-toldot Eretz Israel vi-yeshuva* [Studies in the History of the Land of Israel: Presented to Yehuda Ben-Porat], edited by Yehoshua Ben-Aryeh and Elhanan Reiner, 452–93. Jerusalem: Yad ben Zvi, 2003.

Ben-Dov, Nitza. *Agnon's Art of Indirection: Uncovering Latent Content in the Fiction of S. Y. Agnon.* Leiden: Brill, 1993.

———. *Ahavot lo me'uashrot: Tiskul eroti, omanut u-mavet bi-yetsirat Agnon* [Unhappy Loves: Erotic Frustration, Art, and Death in the Works of Agnon]. Tel Aviv: Am Oved, 1997.

———. *Ve-hi tehilatekha: Iyyunim bi-yttsirot Shai Agnon, A. B. Yehoshua ve-Amos Oz* [Studies in the Works of S. Y. Agnon, A. B. Yehoshua, and Amos Oz]. Jerusalem and Tel Aviv: Schocken, 2006.

Ben-Gurion, David. "Ha-tanakh zore'ah be-'or 'atsmo" [The Bible Shines in Its Own Light]. In *Iyunim ba-mikra* [Bible Studies], 41–49. Tel Aviv: Am Oved, 1969.

Benjamin, Walter. *Illuminations: Essays and Reflections.* Edited by Hannah Arendt and translated by Harry Zohn. New York: Schocken Books, 1969.

———. "On Language as Such and on the Language of Man." In *Reflections: Essays, Aphorisms, Autobiographical Writings*, edited by Peter Demetz and translated by Edmund Jephcott, 314–32. New York: Schocken Books, 1986.

———. *The Origin of German Tragic Drama.* Translated by John Osborne. London: NLB, 1977.

Biale, David. *Eros and the Jews: From Biblical Israel to Contemporary America.* New York: Basic Books, 1992.

———. *Gershom Scholem: Kabbalah and Counter-History.* 2nd ed. Cambridge, Mass.: Harvard University Press, 1982.

———. *Not in the Heavens: The Tradition of Jewish Secular Thought.* Princeton, N.J.: Princeton University Press, 2011.

Bialik, Haim Nahman. "Revealment and Concealment in Language." In *Revealment and Concealment: Five Essays—Haim Nahman Bialik.* Jerusalem: Ibis Editions, 2000.

Bloch, Chana, and Ariel Bloch. *The Song of Songs.* Translated with introduction and commentary. New York: Modern Library, 2006.

Boyarin, Daniel. "The Song of Songs, Lock or Key: The Holy Song as Mashal." In *Intertextuality and the Reading of Midrash*, 105–16. Bloomington: Indiana University Press, 1990.

———. *Unheroic Conduct: The Rise of Heterosexuality and the Invention of the Jewish Man.* Berkeley: University of California Press, 1997.

Brown, Erella. "A Pompeiian Fancy under Jaffa's Sea: Agnon's *Betrothed* and Jensen's *Gradiva*." *Prooftexts* 16, no. 3 (1996): 245–70.

Cassuto, Umberto. *A Commentary on the Book of Exodus*. 1941. Translated by Israel Abrahams. Jerusalem: Magnes Press, 1967.

———. *A Commentary on the Book of Genesis*. Pt. 1, *From Adam to Noah*. 1943. Translated by Israel Abrahams. Jerusalem: Magnes Press, 1961.

Cohen, Gershon D. "The Song of Songs and the Jewish Religious Mentality." In *The Samuel Friedland Lectures, 1960–1966*, 1–21. New York: Jewish Theological Seminary of America, 1966.

Cohen, Mark R. "Eulogy: Shelomo Dov Goitein." In *American Philosophical Society Year Book*. Philadelphia: American Philosophical Society, 1987. http://www.princeton.edu/~geniza/goitein.html (accessed October 31, 2012).

Cohen, Richard I. *Jewish Icons: Art and Society in Modern Europe*. Berkeley: University of California Press, 1998.

———. "Urban Visibility and Biblical Visions: Jewish Culture in Western and Central Europe in the Modern Age." In *Cultures of the Jews*, edited by David Biale, 731–96. New York: Schocken Books, 2002.

Cohen, Tova. *Me-halom limtsi'ut: Eretz Yisrael be-sifrut ha-haskala* [From Dream to Reality: Descriptions of Eretz Yisrael in Haskalah Literature]. Ramat Gan: Bar-Ilan University Press, 1982.

———. *Melitsat yeshurun li-Shlomo Levisohn: Ha-yetsira ve-yotsra* [*Melitsat Yeshurun* by Shlomo Levisohn: The Work and Its Author]. Ramat Gan: Bar-Ilan University Press, 1988.

Dalman, G. H. *Palaestinischer Diwan*. Leipzig, 1901.

Derrida, Jacques. "The Eyes of Language: The Abyss and the Volcano." In *Acts of Religion*, edited by Gil Anidjar, 189–227. New York: Routledge, 2002.

Ezrahi, Sidra DeKoven. *Booking Passage: Exile and Homecoming in the Modern Jewish Imagination*. Berkeley: University of California Press, 2000.

———. "S. Y. Agnon's Jerusalem: Before and after 1948." *Jewish Social Studies* (forthcoming).

———. "Sentient Dogs, Liberated Rams, and Talking Asses: Agnon's Biblical Zoo—or Rereading *Tmol shilshom*." *AJS Review* 28, no. 1 (2004): 105–36.

Feiner, Shmuel. *The Jewish Enlightenment*. Translated by Chaya Naor. Philadelphia: University of Pennsylvania Press, 2002.

Feldman, Yael. *Glory and Agony: Isaac's Sacrifice and National Narrative*. Stanford, Calif.: Stanford University Press, 2010.

Fisch, Harold. *S. Y. Agnon*. New York: F. Ungar Publishing, 1975.

Fishbane, Michael. *The Kiss of God: Spiritual and Mystical Death in Judaism*. Seattle: University of Washington Press, 1994.

Frei, Hans W. *The Eclipse of Biblical Narrative: A Study in Eighteenth- and Nineteenth-Century Hermeneutics*. New Haven, Conn.: Yale University Press, 1974.

Frenkel, Miriam. "Ketivat ha-historia shel yehudei 'artsot ha-Islam bi-ymei ha-beinayim" [The Historiography of Jews of Islamic Cultures in the Middle Ages], *Pe'amim* 92 (2002): 23–61.

Freud, Sigmund. "Delusions and Dreams in Jensen's *Gradiva*." 1907. In *The Standard Edition of the Complete Psychological Works of Sigmund Freud*, translated and edited by James Strachey, 9:7–95. London: Hogarth Press, 1973.

———. "Female Sexuality." 1931. In *The Standard Edition of the Complete Psychological Works of Sigmund Freud*, translated and edited by James Strachey, 21:225–43. New York: W. W. Norton, 1960.

———. *Interpretation of Dreams*. 1899. In *The Standard Edition of the Complete Psychological Works of Sigmund Freud*, translated and edited by James Strachey. London: George Allen and Unwin, 1971.

———. *Moses and Monotheism*. Translated by Katherine Jones. New York: Vintage Books, 1939.

Ghosh, Amitav. *In an Antique Land: History in the Guise of a Traveler's Tale*. New York: Vintage Books, 1994.

Ginsburg, Ruth. "Bidmi yameh meta Tirzah or 'yafa at ra'ayati ke-Tirzah nava ki-Yerushalyim ayuma ka-nidgalot" [Tirzah Died in the Prime of Her Life: Thou Art Beautiful, O My Love, as Tirzah, Comely as Jerusalem, Terrible as an Army with Banners]. *Dapim Le'Mekhkar Be'sifrut* 8 (1992): 285–300.

Ginsburg, Ruth, and Ilana Pardes, eds. *New Perspectives on Freud's "Moses and Monotheism."* Tübingen: Niemeyer, 2006.

Gluzman, Michael. *Ha-guf ha-zioni: Le'umiyut, migdar u-miniyut ba-sifrut ha-ivrit ha-hadasha* [The Zionist Body: Nationalism, Gender, and Sexuality in Modern Hebrew Literature]. Tel Aviv: Hakibbutz Hameuchad, 2007.

Goitein, Shlomo Dov. "Al 'Shevu'at emunim'" [On *Betrothed*]. *Gazit* 5, nos. 9–10 (1943): 24–32.

———. "Al sippur pashut" [On a Simple Story]. *Haaretz*, August 12, 1938.

———. *Bein Shlomo Dov Goitein ve-Shmuel Yosef Agnon* [Between Shlomo Dov Goitein and Shmuel Yosef Agnon]. Edited by Ayala Gordon. Jerusalem: private publication, 2008.

———. "Besh'ah ahat" [Within One Hour]. In *leAgnon Shai*. Jerusalem: Ha-va'ad ha-tsiburi le'yovel ha-shiv'im le-Agnon, 1959.

———. *Ha-Teymanim: Historia, sidrey hevra, hayei ruah* [The Yemenites: History, Society, and Spiritual Life], edited by Menachem Ben-Sasson. Jerusalem: Makhon Ben Zvi, 1983.

———. *Hora'at ha-tanakh* [The Teaching of the Bible]. Tel Aviv: Javneh, 1957.

———. *Iyunim bamikra* [Bible Studies]. Tel Aviv: Javneh, 1957.

———. "The Literary Character and Symbolic Interpretation of the Song of Songs." In *A Feminist Companion to the Song of Songs*, edited by Athalya Brenner. Sheffield: JSOT Press, 1993.

———. *Omanut ha-sipur ba-mikra* [The Art of Biblical Narrative]. Jerusalem: Ha-Sokhnut Hayehudit le-Eretz Yisrael, 1956.

———. "Rabbi Yudel." In *Shai Agnon ba-bikoret ha-'ivrit: Parshanut la-romanim* [S. Y. Agnon: Critical Essays of His Writings; Interpretation of His Novels], edited by Avinoam Barshai, 2:6–11. Tel Aviv: Open University of Israel and Schocken, 1992.

———. "Religion in Everyday Life as Reflected in the Documents of the Cairo Geniza." In

Religion in a Religious Age, edited by Shlomo Dov Goitein. Cambridge, Mass.: Association for Jewish Studies, 1974.

———. "S.Y. Agnon: Personal Account." In *A Memorial Tribute to Dr. Shmuel Yosef Agnon*, presented by Dropsie University and the Consulate General of Israel, Sunday, March 29, 1970. Philadelphia: Dropsie University, 1970.

———. "Women as Creators of Biblical Genres." Translated by Michael Carasik. *Prooftexts* 8, no. 1 (1988): 1–33.

Goldberg, Leah. "Agnon bi-shlosha kolot" [Agnon in Three Voices]. *Al HaMishmar*, October 27, 1950. Reprinted in *Ha-Omets le-hulin* [Courage for the Quotidian]. Tel Aviv: Sifriyat HaPoalim, 1950.

———. "Motivim bi-yetsirato" [Motifs in His Work]. In *Shai Agnon ba-bikoret ha-'ivrit: Sikumim ve-ha'arkhot 'al yetsirato* [S. Y. Agnon: Critical Essays of His Writings; Evaluation of His Literary Works], edited by Avinoam Barshai, 1:180–84. Jerusalem and Tel Aviv: Schocken, 1991.

Green, Arthur. "Shekhinah, the Virgin Mary, and the Song of Songs: Reflections on a Kabbalistic Symbol in Its Historical Context." *AJS Review* 26, no. 1 (2002): 1–52.

Greenblatt, Stephen J., ed. *Allegory and Representation*. Baltimore: Johns Hopkins University Press, 1981.

Gurevitch, Zali. *'Al ha-makom* [On Space and Place]. Tel Aviv: Am Oved, 2007.

HaCohen, Ruth. "'Lishmo'a el ha-rina o el ha-tefila': Leida hadadit shel milim u-lehanim be-hekshrei ha-zemer ha-ivri" ["To Hear the Singing and Prayer": From Words to Music and from Music to Words in the Israeli Song Culture]. *Mehkarei Yerushalayim be-sifrut ivrit* 20 (2006): 13–37.

Hadad, Shira. *Mi she-'ose siman* [The Sign Maker]. Jerusalem: Bialik Institute, 2011.

Hagbi, Yaniv. *Language, Absence, Play: Judaism and Superstructuralism in the Poetics of S. Y. Agnon*. Syracuse, N.Y.: Syracuse University Press, 2009.

Halbertal, Moshe. *Concealment and Revelation: Esotericism in Jewish Thought and Its Philosophical Implications*. Princeton, N.J.: Princeton University Press, 2007.

Hamilton, John T. *Music, Madness, and the Unknowing of Language*. New York: Columbia University Press, 2008.

Handelman, Susan. *Fragments of Redemption: Jewish Thought and Literary Theory in Benjamin, Scholem, and Levinas*. Bloomington: Indiana University Press, 1991.

Hareuveni, Ephraim, and Hannah Hareuveni. "Gan ha-nevi'im ve-hakhmey ha-talmud" [The Garden of the Prophets and Sages]. *Hatoren* 40, nos. 1–3 (1924): 65–79.

Hareuveni, Noga. *Teva ve-nof be-moreshet yisrael* [Nature and Landscape in Israel's Heritage]. Neot Kedumim: Neot Kedumim, 1980.

Harshav, Benjamin. Introduction to *Only Yesterday*, by S. Y. Agnon, vii–xxix. Translated by Barbara Harshav. Princeton, N.J.: Princeton University Press, 2000.

Hasak-Lowy, Todd. "A Mad Dog's Attack on Secularized Hebrew: Rethinking Agnon's *Tmol shilshom*." *Prooftexts* 24, no. 2 (2004): 167–98.

Hasan-Rokem, Galit. "Textualizing the Tales of the People of the Book: Folk Narrative Anthologies and National Identity in Modern Israel." *Prooftexts* 19, no. 1 (1999): 71–82.

———. *Web of Life: Folklore and Midrash in Rabbinic Literature*. Translated by Batya Stein.

Stanford, Calif.: Stanford University Press, 2000.

Hasan-Rokem, Galit, and Alan Dundes. *The Wandering Jew: Essays in the Interpretation of a Christian Legend*. Bloomington: Indiana University Press, 1986.

Havrelock, Rachel. *River Jordan: The Mythology of a Dividing Line*. Chicago: University of Chicago Press, 2011.

Hegel, G. W. F. *Aesthetics: Lectures on Fine Art*. 2 vols. Translated by T. M. Knox. Oxford: Clarendon, 1975.

Hellner-Eshed, Melila. *A River Flows from Eden: The Language of Mystical Experience in the Zohar*. Translated by Nathan Wolski. Stanford, Calif.: Stanford University Press, 2009.

Herder, Johann Gottfried. *Lieder der Liebe: Die ältesten und schönsten aus Morgenlande*. In *Werke*, repr. J. G. Müller, ed., 5:1318. Munich: Hanser, 1984–2002.

———. "On the German-Oriental Poets." In *Selected Early Works, 1764–1767: Addresses, Essays, and Drafts; Fragments on Recent German Literature*, edited by Ernest A. Menze and Karl Menges, translated by Ernest A. Menze and Michael Palma, 175–89. University Park: Pennsylvania State University Press, 1992.

———. *The Spirit of Hebrew Poetry*. 1782–83. Translated by James Marsh. Burlington, Vt.: E. Smith, 1833.

Herzog, Hanna. "HaHaggadah ha-kibbutzit" [The Kibbutz Haggadah]. *Ha-Kibbutz*, nos. 3–4 (1977): 237–46.

Hever, Hannan. *El ha-hof ha-mekuve: Ha-yam ba-tarbut ha'ivrit u-vasifrut ha'ivrit ha-modernit* [Toward the Longed-for Shore: The Sea in Hebrew Culture and Modern Hebrew Literature]. Tel Aviv: Van Leer Institute and Hakibbutz Hameuchad, 2007.

Heyd, Milly. "Lilien: Between Herzl and Ahasver." In *Theodor Herzl: Visionary of the Jewish State*, edited by Gideon Shimoni and Robert S. Wistrich, 265–93. Jerusalem: Magnes Press, 1999.

Hirschfeld, Ariel. "Bein sippur le-sippur-'am bi-shnei sippurim shel Agnon" [Between Story and Folktale: On Two of S. Y. Agnon's Stories]. *Mirkamim le-Galit Hasan-Rokem, Mehkarei Yerushalayim be-sifrut ivrit* 2 (2013):531–49.

———. "Botanical Epiphany." In *The Botanist's Brush: Shmuel Charuvi's Drawings for the Hareuveni "Floral Treasury of the Land of Israel,"* edited by Tamar Manor-Friedman, 106–12. Jerusalem: Israel Museum, 2006.

———. *Likro et Shai Agnon* [Reading S. Y. Agnon]. Tel Aviv: Ahuzat bayit, 2011.

———. "Locus and Language: Hebrew Culture in Israel, 1890–1990." In *Cultures of the Jews*, edited by David Biale, 1011–60. New York: Schocken Books, 2002.

Hoffman, Adina, and Peter Cole. *Sacred Trash: The Lost and Found World of the Cairo Geniza*. New York: Schocken Books, 2011.

Hoffman, Anne Golomb. *Between Exile and Return: S. Y. Agnon and the Drama of Writing*. New York: State University of New York Press, 1991.

———. "A Streetcar Named Desire: A Note on Otto Weininger in *Shevu'at emunim*." In *Essays on Hebrew Literature in Honor of Avraham Holtz*, edited by Zvia Ben-Yosef Ginor, 47–59. New York: Jewish Theological Seminary of America, 2003.

Ida, Batsheva Goldman. *Ze'ev Raban: A Hebrew Symbolist*. Tel Aviv: Tel Aviv Museum of Art; Jerusalem: Yad Yzhak Ben-Zvi, 2001.

Idel, Moshe. *Golem: Jewish Magical and Mystical Traditions on the Artificial Anthropoid.* Albany: State University of New York Press, 1990.

———. *Kabbalah: New Perspectives.* New Haven, Conn.: Yale University Press, 1988.

———. *Kabbalah and Eros.* New Haven, Conn.: Yale University Press, 2005.

———. "Torah Hadashah: Messiah and the New Torah in Jewish Mysticism and Modern Scholarship." *Kabbalah: Journal for the Study of Jewish Mystical Texts* 21 (2010): 57–110.

Idelsohn, Abraham Z. *Jewish Music in Its Musical Historical Development.* New York: Schocken Books, 1967.

Ingber, Judith Brin, ed. *Seeing Israeli and Jewish Dance.* Detroit: Wayne State University Press, 2011.

Joyce, James. *Ulysses.* 1914. New York: Vintage Books, 1961.

Kalmar, Ivan Davidson, and Derek J. Penslar, eds. *Orientalism and the Jews.* Waltham, Mass.: Brandeis University Press; Hanover, N.H.: University Press of New England, 2005.

Kara-Ivanov Kaniel, Ruth. *Kedeshot u-kedoshot: 'Iimahot ha-mashiah ba-mitos ha-yehudi* [Holiness and Transgression: Mothers of the Messiah in Jewish Myth]. Tel Aviv: Hakibbutz Hameuchad, forthcoming.

Kariv, Avraham. "Min ha-hol 'el ha-kodesh" [From the Profane to the Holy]. *Gevilin,* September 1960, 12–13.

Keren, Michael. *Ben-Gurion and the Intellectuals: Power, Knowledge, and Charisma.* DeKalb: Northern Illinois University Press, 1983.

Klausner, Josef. "Shlomo Levisohn (1789–1821)." In *Historia shel ha-sifrut ha-'ivrit ha-hadasha* [The History of Modern Hebrew Literature], 1:261–74. Jerusalem: Ahiasaf, 1952.

Kristeva, Julia. *Tales of Love,* translated by Leon S. Roudiez. New York: Columbia University Press, 1987.

Kronfeld, Chana. *On the Margins of Modernism: Decentering Literary Dynamics.* Berkeley: University of California Press, 1996.

Kugel James. "Two Introductions to Midrash." In *Midrash and Literature,* edited by Geoffrey Hartman and Sanford Budick, 77–103. New Haven, Conn.: Yale University Press, 1986.

Kurzweil, Baruch. *Kurzweil-Agnon-Azag: Hilufey 'igrot* [Kurzweil, Agnon, Azag: Correspondence]. Edited by Lillian Debbi-Guri. Ramat Gan: Bar-Ilan University Press, 1987.

———. *Masot 'al sipurey Shai Agnon* [Essays on S. Y. Agnon]. Jerusalem and Tel Aviv: Schocken, 1970.

Landy, Francis. *Paradoxes of Paradise: Identity and Difference in the Song of Songs.* Sheffield: Almond Press, 1983.

Laor, Dan. "Gentlemen and Scholars." *Haaretz,* January 14, 2009.

———. *Hayey Agnon: Biyografyah* [S. Y. Agnon: A Biography]. Jerusalem and Tel Aviv: Schocken, 1998.

Lassner, Jacob. Foreword to *A Mediterranean Society: An Abridgment in One Volume,* by Shlomo Dov Goitein, xi–xxii. Berkeley: University of California Press, 1999.

Lazier, Benjamin. *God Interrupted: Heresy and the European Imagination between the World Wars.* Princeton, N.J.: Princeton University Press, 2008.

Liebes, Yehuda. "Eros ve-Zohar" [Eros and the Zohar]. *Alpayim*, no. 9 (1994): 67–119.

———. "Ha-mashiah shel ha-Zohar: Lidmuto shel rabbi Shimon bar Yohai" [The Messiah of the Zohar: The Messianic Character of R. Shimon bar Yohai]. In *Ha-Ra'yon ha-meshihi be-Yisrael: Simposion leregel mlot shmonim shana le-Gerschom Scholem* [The Messianic Idea in Israel: A Symposium in Honor of Gershom Scholem], 87–236. Jerusalem: Israel Academy of Sciences and Humanities, 1982.

———. *Studies in Jewish Myth and Messianism*. Translated by Batya Stein. Albany: State University of New York Press, 1992.

———. *Torat ha-yetsira shel Sefer Yetsirah* [Ars Poetica in Sefer Yetsirah]. Jerusalem and Tel Aviv: Schocken, 2000.

Madar, Vered. "Text bein kol li-tnu'a: Kinot nashim mi-teiman" [Between Voice and Gesture: Dirges of Yemenite Women]. *Mehkarei Yerushalayim be-folklore yehudi* 23 (2005): 89–119.

Mann, Barbara E. *A Place in History: Modernism, Tel Aviv and the Creation of Jewish Urban Space*. Stanford, Calif.: Stanford University Press, 2006.

Manor, Dalia. "Biblical Zionism in Bezalel Art." *Israel Studies* 6, no. 1 (2001): 55–75.

Manor, Giora. *The Choreography of Sara Levi-Tanai*. Tel Aviv: Inbal Dance Theater and the Ethnic Multicultural Center Inbal, 2001.

Manor-Friedman, Tamar, ed. *The Botanist's Brush: Shmuel Charuvi's Drawings for the Hareuveni "Floral Treasury of the Land of Israel."* Jerusalem: Israel Museum, 2006.

———. "The Rose of Jericho: A Dormant Parable." In *Larry Abramson: The Rose of Jericho*, xii–xv. Jerusalem: Jerusalem Print Shop, 2004.

Mapu, Abraham. *The Love of Zion*. Translated by Joseph Marymount. New Milford, Conn.: Toby Press, 2006.

Matt, Daniel C. *The Zohar*. Pritzker Edition. Stanford, Calif.: Stanford University Press, 2004–9.

Mendes-Flohr, Paul. "Between Sensual and Heavenly Love: Franz Rosenzweig's Reading of the Song of Songs." In *Scriptural Exegesis: The Shapes of Culture and the Religious Imagination; Essays in Honour of Michael Fishbane*, edited by Deborah A. Green and Laura S. Lieber. Oxford: Oxford University Press, 2009.

———. "Fin-de-siècle Orientalism, the *Ostjuden*, and the Aesthetics of Jewish Self-Affirmation." In *Studies in Contemporary Jewry*, edited by Jonathan Frankel, 1:96–139. Bloomington: Indiana University Press, 1984.

Mintz, Alan L., ed. *Reading Hebrew Literature: Critical Discussions of Six Modern Texts*. Waltham, Mass.: Brandeis University Press; Hanover, N.H.: University Press of New England, 2003.

———. *Translating Israel: Contemporary Hebrew Literature and Its Reception in America*. Syracuse, N.Y.: Syracuse University Press, 2001.

Mintz, Alan L., and Anne Golomb Hoffman. Introduction to *A Book That Was Lost: Thirty-Five Stories*, by S. Y. Agnon, edited by Alan L. Mintz and Anne Golomb Hoffman, 9–34. New Milford, Conn.: Toby Press, 1995.

Miron, Dan. "Ashkenaz: Ha-havaya ha-yehudit-germanit be-kitvey Agnon" [Ashkenaz: The Jewish-German Experience in Agnon's Writings]. In *Ha-rofe ha-medumeh: Iyunim ba-siporet ha-yehudit ha-classit* [La Médecin Imaginaire: Studies in Classical Jewish Fiction], 237–307. Tel Aviv: Hakibbutz Hameuchad, 1995.

———. *Bein hazon le-emet: Nitsaney ha-roman ha-'ivri ve-hayiddi ba-me'a ha-tesha 'esre* [From Romance to the Novel: Studies in the Emergence of the Hebrew and Yiddish Novel in the Nineteenth Century]. Jerusalem: Mosad Bialik, 1979.

———. "Bein shtey neshamot: Ha-analogia ha-Faustit bi-Tmol shilshom le-Shai Agnon" [Between Two Souls: On the Faustian Analogy in S. Y. Agnon's *Tmol shilshom*]. In *Mi-Vilna li-Yerushalyim: Mehkarim be-toldotehem u-vetarbutam shel yehudei mizrah eropa mugashim le-profesor Shmuel Werses* [Studies in East European Jewish History and Culture in Honor of Professor Shmuel Werses], edited by David Assaf, Israel Bartal, Shmuel Feiner, Yehuda Friedlander, Avner Holtzman, and Chava Turniansky, 539–608. Jerusalem: Magnes Press, 2002.

———. "Gershom Scholem on Agnon." Interview. Pts. 1 and 2. *Ariel—Israel Review of Arts and Letters* 52 (1982): 94–106; 53 (1983): 61–75.

Mitchell, W. J. T. "Holy Landscape: Israel, Palestine, and the American Wilderness." *Critical Inquiry* 26, no. 2 (2000): 193–223.

Mosès, Stéphane. *The Angel of History: Rosenzweig, Benjamin, Scholem.* Translated by Barbara Harshav. Stanford, Calif.: Stanford University Press, 2009.

Moyn, Samuel. "Divine and Human Love: Franz Rosenzweig's History of the Song of Songs." *Jewish Studies Quarterly* 12 (2005): 194–212.

Myers, David. *Re-inventing the Jewish Past.* New York: Oxford University Press, 1995.

———. *Resisting History: Historicism and Its Discontents in German-Jewish Thought.* Princeton, N.J.: Princeton University Press, 2003.

Ofrat, Gideon. *Al ha-aretz: Ha-omanut ha-eretz-yisraelit; Pirkey 'avot* [On the Ground: Early Eretz-Israeli Art; Founding Fathers]. Jerusalem: Yaron Golan, 1993.

Oron, Michal. "Semalim u-motivim kabaliyim ba-sipur 'Edo ve-Enam' le-Shai Agnon" [Symbols and Kabbalistic Motifs in Agnon's "Edo and Enam"]. *Baseminar,* 1976, 160–72.

Oz, Amos. *The Silence of Heaven: Agnon's Fear of God.* Princeton, N.J.: Princeton University Press, 2000.

Ozick, Cynthia. "Agnon's Antagonisms." *Commentary* 86 (1988): 43–48.

Pardes, Ilana. *The Biography of Ancient Israel: National Narratives in the Bible.* Berkeley: University of California Press, 2000.

———. *Countertraditions in the Bible: A Feminist Approach.* Cambridge: Harvard University Press, 1992.

———. *Melville's Bibles.* Berkeley: University of California Press, 2008.

Paz, Yair. [The Botanical Garden and the Garden of the Prophets: Two Projects for the Establishment of Educational Gardens at the Hebrew University]. In *The History of the Hebrew University of Jerusalem: A Period of Consolidation and Growth,* edited by Hagit Lavsky, 2:443–72. Jerusalem: Magnes Press, 2005.

Pope, Marvin H. *Song of Songs.* The Anchor Bible. Garden City, N.Y.: Doubleday, 1977.

Ravitzky, Aviezer. *Messianism, Zionism, and Jewish Religious Radicalism.* Translated by Michael Swirsky and Jonathan Chipman. Chicago: University of Chicago Press, 1993.

Regev, Motti, and Edwin Seroussi. *Popular Music and National Culture in Israel.* Berkeley: University of California Press, 2004.

Rojtman, Betty. *Selihat ha-levana: 'Al ha-tragiyut ha-mikra'it* [The Forgiveness of the Moon: Essays on Biblical Tragedy]. Jerusalem: Carmel, 2008.

Rokem, Freddie. *Philosophers and Thespians: Thinking Performance*. Stanford, Calif.: Stanford University Press, 2010.

Rokem, Na'ama. *Prosaic Conditions: Heinrich Heine and the Spaces of Zionist Literature* Evanston, Ill.: Northwestern University Press, 2013.

Rolnik, Eran J. *Osey ha-nefashot: 'Im Freud le-Eretz Yisrael 1918–1948* [Freud in Zion: History of Psychoanalysis in Jewish Palestine/Israel, 1918–1948]. Tel Aviv: Am Oved, 2007.

Rosenzweig, Franz. *The Star of Redemption*. Translated by William W. Hallo. Boston: Beacon Press, 1964.

Sadan, Dov. *'Al Shai Agnon: Kerekh masot u-ma'amarim* [On S. Y. Agnon: Essays and Articles]. Tel Aviv: Hakibbutz Hameuchad, 1978.

Said, Edward. *Orientalism*. New York: Random House, 1978.

Schatz, Boris. *Yerushalyim habenuyah: Halom behakiz* [Rebuilt Jerusalem: A Daydream]. Jerusalem: Bezalel, 1924.

Schmidt, Christoph, and Eli Schonfeld, eds. *HaElohim lo ye'alem dom: Ha-moderna ha-yehudit ve-hate'ologia ha-politit* [God Will Not Stand Still: Jewish Modernity and Political Theology]. Jerusalem: Van Leer / Hakibbutz Hameuchad, 2009.

Scholem, Gershom. "Agnon in Germany: Recollections." Translated by Werner J. Dannhauser. In *On Jews and Judaism in Crisis: Selected Essays*, edited by Werner J. Dannhauser, 117–18. New York: Schocken Books, 1976.

———. "Gershom Scholem on Agnon." Interview by Dan Miron. Pts. 1 and 2. *Ariel—Israel Review of Arts and Letters* 52 (1982): 94–106; 53 (1983): 61–75.

———. *Kabbalah*. Jerusalem: Keter, 1974.

———. Letter to Franz Rosenzweig, December 26, 1926. In *Die Gabe: For Franz Rosenzweig on His 40th Birthday*, edited by Martin Goldner, 48–49. New York: Leo Baeck Institute, 1987.

———. *Magen-David: Toldotav shel semel* [The Star of David: History of a Symbol]. Edited by Galit Hasan-Rokem. Ein-Harod: Mishkan le-omanut, 2009.

———. *Major Trends in Jewish Mysticism*. New York: Schocken Books, 1961.

———. *On Jews and Judaism in Crisis: Selected Essays*. Edited by Werner J. Dannhauser. New York: Schocken Books, 1976.

———. *On Kabbalah and Its Symbolism*. New York: Schocken Books, 1969.

———. "Redemption through Sin." In *The Messianic Idea in Judaism, and Other Essays on Jewish Spirituality*, 78–141. New York: Schocken Books, 1971.

———. "Reflections on S. Y. Agnon." *Commentary*, December 1967, 59–66.

Schwartz, Yigal. *Ha-yada'ata 'et ha-eretz sham ha-limon poreah: Handasa enoshit ve-hashivat ha-merhav ba-sifrut ha-'ivrit* [Do You Know the Land Where the Lemon Blooms? Human Engineering and Landscape Conceptualization in Hebrew Literature]. Or Yehuda: Kinneret Zmora-Bitan, 2007.

Seroussi, Edwin. "Yesod ehad lahen: Giluy ha-mizrah ve-ahdutan shel mesorot ha-musika ha-yehudiyot be-mishnat Avram Zvi Idelsohn" [The Discovery of the East and the Affinity between Musical Traditions in the Writings of Abraham Zvi Idelsohn]. *Pe'amim* 100 (2004): 125–46.

Shahar, Galili. *She'erit ha-hitgalut: Ha-hok, ha-guf ve-she'elat ha-sifrut* [The Remnants of Revelation: The Law, the Body and Literature]. Jerusalem: Bialik Institute, 2011.

Shaked, Gershon. "Midrash and Narrative: Agnon's 'Agunot.'" In *Midrash and Literature*, edited by Geoffrey H. Hartman and Sanford Budick, 285–306. New Haven, Conn.: Yale University Press, 1986.

———. "Portrait of the Immigrant as a Young Neurotic." *Prooftexts* 7, no. 1 (1987): 441–52.

———. *Shmuel Yosef Agnon: A Revolutionary Traditionalist*. New York: New York University Press, 1989.

Shapira, Anita. "Ben-Gurion and the Bible: The Forging of a Historical Narrative?" *Middle Eastern Studies* 33, no. 4 (1997): 645–74.

———. "The Bible and Israeli Identity." *AJS Review* 28, no. 1 (2004): 11–42.

Sheehan, Jonathan. *The Enlightenment Bible: Translation, Scholarship, Culture*. Princeton, N.J.: Princeton University Press, 2005.

Shelem, Matityahu. "Al shir ha-shirim" [On the Song of Songs]. *Niv ha-kevutsa* 16 (1967): 136–43.

Simon, Uriel. "The Place of the Bible in Israeli Society: From National *Midrash* to Existential *Peshat*." *Modern Judaism* 19 (1999): 217–39.

Stephan, S. H. "Modern Palestinian Parallels to the Song of Songs." *JPOS* 2 (1922): 1–80.

Stern, David. "Ancient Jewish Interpretation of the Song of Songs in a Comparative Context." In *Jewish Biblical Interpretation and Cultural Exchange: Comparative Exegesis in Context*, edited by Natalie B. Dohrmann and David Stern, 87–107. Philadelphia: University of Pennsylvania Press, 2008.

Stern, Dina. *Ha-begidah ve-likcha: Shevu'at emunim me'et Shai Agnon* [Betrayal and Its Moral: S. Y. Agnon's *Betrothed*]. Jerusalem and Tel Aviv: Schocken, 1989.

Tochner, Meshulam. *Pesher Agnon* [Readings of Agnon]. Ramat Gan: Masada, 1968.

Tolidanu, Gila. *Sippura shel lehaka: Sara Levi-Tanai ve-te'atron ha-mahol Inbal* [A Story of a Company: Sara Levi-Tanai and the Inbal Dance Theater]. Tel Aviv: Resling, 2005.

Trible, Phyllis. *God and the Rhetoric of Sexuality*. Philadelphia: Fortress Press, 1978.

Virgil. *The Aeneid*. Translated by Robert Fitzgerald. New York: Vintage, 1983.

Wasserstrom, Steven M. *Between Muslim and Jew: The Problem of Symbiosis under Early Islam*. Princeton, N.J.: Princeton University Press, 1995.

———. *Religion after Religion: Gershom Scholem, Mircea Eliade, and Henry Corbin at Eranos*. Princeton, N.J.: Princeton University Press, 1999.

Weis, Hillel. *Agnon: Agunot, Edo ve-Enam; Mekorot, mivnim u-mashma'uyot*, vols. 2–3 [Agnon: "Agunot" and "Edo and Enam"; Sources, Structure, and Significance]. Tel Aviv: Open University Press, 1981.

Weiss, Tzachi. *Mot ha-Shekhinah bi-yetsirat Agnon: Kri'ah be-arba'ah sipurim* [Death of the Shekhinah: Readings in Four Agnon Stories and in Their Sources]. Ramat Gan: Bar-Ilan University Press, 2009.

———. "'Things That Are Better Concealed than Revealed': An Historical-Biographical Study of S. Y. Agnon's Attitude toward the Sabbatean Movement and the Traditional Jewish World." *AJS Review* 36, no. 1 (2012): 103–20.

Werses, Shmuel. "Agnon be-'olamo shel Bezalel" [Agnon in the World of Bezalel]. In *Shai Agnon ki-fshuto: Keri'a bi-khtavav* [S. Y. Agnon Literally: Studies of His Writings], 264–90. Jerusalem: Bialik Institute, 2000.

Wetzstein, J. G. "Die syrische Dreschtafel." *Zeitschrift für Ethnologie* 5 (1873): 270–301.

Wolfson, Elliot. *Through a Speculum That Shines: Vision and Imagination in Medieval Jewish Mysticism*. Princeton N.J.: Princeton University Press, 1994.

Zakovitch, Yair. *Shir ha-shirim: Mikra le-Yisrael* [The Song of Songs: Introduction and Commentary]. Jerusalem: Magnes Press; Tel Aviv: Am Oved, 1992.

Zemach, Adi. "Al ha-tefisa ha-historiosofit bi-shnayim mi-sipurav ha-me'uharim shel Agnon" [On the Historical Conception in Two of Agnon's Stories]. *Ha-Sifrut* 1, no. 2 (1968): 378–85.

Zerubavel, Yael. "Ha-Tanakh akhshav." *Mirkamim le-Galit Hasan-Rokem, Mehkarei Yerushalayim be-sifrut ivrit* 2 (2013): 755–74.

———. *Recovered Roots*. Chicago: University of Chicago Press, 1995.

Zohary, Michael. *Plants of the Bible*. Cambridge: Cambridge University Press, 1982.

Zuker, Shlomo. "Mekorot be-'itsuv ha-merhav ve-hadmuyot be-Edo ve-Enam le-Shai Agnon" [Sources for the Fashioning of Space and Characters in Agnon's "Edo and Enam"]. *Mehkarey Yerushalayim be-sifrut ivrit* 3 (1982): 28–66.

Zur, Muki, and Yuval Danieli. *Yots'im be-hodesh ha-aviv: Pesasch Eretz—Yisraeli be-hagadot min ha-kibbutz* [The Kibbutz Haggadah: Israeli Pesach in the Kibbutz]. Jerusalem: Yad Ben-Zvi, Makhon Ben-Gurion, Yad Tabenkin, and Yad Ya'ari, 2004.

Index

Note: page numbers in *italics* refer to figures; those followed by "n" indicate endnotes.

C

D

E

H

S

T

U

V

W

Y

Z